Empire Builders Series: Masterclasses in Business and Law

Mark Your Territory

ALSO BY AUTHORSDOOR GROUP

Empire Builders Series: Masterclasses in Business and Law

Mark Your Territory

Navigating Trademarks in the Modern Marketplace

L. A. MOESZINGER

AuthorsDoor Group
an imprint of The Ridge Publishing Group

Disclaimer: Any internet addresses, phone numbers, or company or product information printed in this book are offered as a resource and are not intended in any way to be or to imply an endorsement by AuthorsDoor Leadership, nor does AuthorsDoor Leadership vouch for the existence, content, or services of these sites, phone numbers, companies, or products beyond the life of this book.

Credit: This book was reviewed for grammatical accuracy with the assistance of ChatGPT, an Artificial Intelligence tool developed by OpenAI. We utilized ChatGPT to ensure clarity and correctness throughout the text, enhancing the reading experience while preserving the author's original voice. The integration of this advanced technology played a crucial role in maintaining the linguistic precision of each chapter.

Library of Congress Control Number: 2024920982

Mark Your Territory: Navigating Trademarks in the Modern Marketplace / by L. A. Moeszinger

ISBN 978-1-956905-30-4 (e-book)
ISBN 978-1-956905-29-8 (softcover)

1. Law / Intellectual Property / Trademark. 2. Business & Economics / Intellectual Property / General. 3. Business & Economics / Industries / Media & Communications. 4. Law / Intellectual Property / General. 5. Business & Economics / Marketing / General. I. Title. II. Series

Printed in the United States of America

To all the entrepreneurs forging their unique paths: may this guide help you protect what you create and claim your space in the marketplace.

AuthorsDoor Group
Coeur d'Alene, Idaho

INTRODUCTION TO THE
AUTHORSDOOR LEADERSHIP PROGRAM

The AuthorsDoor Leadership Program, separate from the Builders Empire Series, is a new initiative designed to empower authors and publishers with the skills to effectively sell books. It features three tailored series: (1) AuthorsDoor Series: *Publisher & Her World*, (2) AuthorsDoor Advanced Series: *Publisher & Her World*, and (3) AuthorsDoor Masterclass Series: *Publisher & Her World*; each series is meticulously structured to guide participants from foundational concepts to advanced strategies in selling books, book by book, in a chronological format. The courses, offered for free on our YouTube channels—Publisher & Her World at Ridge Publishing Group, AuthorsDoor Group: Publisher & Her World, and Authors Red Door #Shorts—complement the books and workbooks, each providing unique and valuable teachings.

Explore additional resources to enhance your journey:

- Follow our blog at AuthorsRedDoor.com.
- Subscribe to our Newsletters at AuthorsDoor.com.
- Join our AuthorsDoor Strategy Forum Facebook Group.
- Connect with our Facebook Page at AuthorsDoor Group.
- Become a fan on our social media channels @AuthorsDoor1.

For feedback or questions, contact us at info@authorsdoor.com. We are here to support your journey from writing to successfully selling your books.

Warm regards,

L. A. Moeszinger #PubHerWorld

Contents

PART 4: TRADEMARK TOOLKIT

Introduction

Charting the Course Through the Trademark Terrain

Welcome to the wild, wild world of trademarks—where the clever thrive, the cautious survive, and the uninformed are left to wander in the wilderness. "Mark Your Territory: Navigating Trademarks in the Modern Marketplace" is your seasoned guide through the thicket of legalese, the quick sands of infringement, and the lush meadows of brand identity. Ready your intellectual machetes, dear readers, and prepare to carve out a space in the competitive marketplace that is distinctly, indelibly yours.

Why bother with trademarks, you ask? Imagine stepping into the marketplace without one—it's like arriving at a masquerade ball without a mask. You're vulnerable, unnoticed, and, frankly, missing out on all the fun. Trademarks are not just legal tools; they are your brand's battle armor and beauty queen sash rolled into one, proclaiming your brand's identity while protecting it from poachers.

But fear not! This book is designed to transform even the greenest novices into savvy marksmen (and women) of trademark strategy. We'll start with the basics—

what a trademark really is (hint: it's more than just a snazzy logo) and why it's critical to your entrepreneurial conquests. From the adrenaline rush of crafting your first mark to the strategic maneuvers of global brand protection, we'll navigate every turn with precision and a pinch of panache.

As we delve deeper into the jungle, you'll learn how to wield the tools of the trade: robust searches, cunning applications, and the art of the timely renewal. And because the wilderness of commerce is both vast and teeming with competitors, we'll equip you with the skills to monitor your territory vigilantly and defend it fiercely against would-be infringers.

But what's an adventure without a glimpse into the future? Our bonus chapter will catapult you into the world of AI in trademark management—where algorithms predict trends and bots monitor markets, all while you sip coffee and plot your next big move.

This book is more than just a manual; it's a manifesto for marking your territory in the marketplace. So, button up your safari jackets and adjust your pith helmets. With wit as our companion and wisdom as our map, let's set forth into the bustling bazaar of trademarks. Ready, set, mark!

Historical Context

Embark on a journey through the riveting saga of trademark law, a narrative that stretches from ancient civilizations to today's digital marketplaces. Trademarks, once ancient artisans' seals, have evolved into modern symbols of commerce and identity, standing as potent sentinels throughout history. This section delves into the evolution of trademark law, exploring its impact on business practices and consumer protection across the ages.

The Dawn of Trademarks

The concept of trademarks dates back to ancient times when artisans from Egypt, Rome, and China marked their goods with symbols to signify source and quality, similar to today's branding practices. These early marks served not only as claims of craftsmanship but also as the first mechanisms of consumer protection, helping buyers identify goods from reputable makers. During the Middle Ages, European guilds regulated the use of marks to control the quality and origin of products such as pottery and silver, setting the stage for modern trademark registration systems.

The Legal Framework Emerges
The journey of trademark law into formal legal recognition began with the Statute of Monopolies in 1624 in Britain, which curbed the monarch's power to grant monopolies except for novel inventions. This was followed by the landmark Basset Case in 1603, recognized as the first known instance of trademark litigation, where the court protected a clothier's distinctive mark under common law, highlighting the role of trademarks in ensuring fair trade practices.

Modern Trademark Laws
The industrial revolution brought about significant changes, necessitating clearer, more structured trademark laws. The UK's Merchandise Marks Act of 1862 and the U.S. Trademark Act of 1870 were among the first laws to formally codify trademark protections, offering registration and exclusive rights to use distinctive marks. The late 19th and early 20th centuries introduced the first international agreements to protect intellectual property across borders, such as the Paris Convention and Madrid Agreement, acknowledging the increasingly global nature of trade.

Trademarks in the Digital Age
The internet era has transformed trademark law, introducing new challenges such as domain squatting and online counterfeiting. Legal systems worldwide have adapted to protect trademarks effectively in the digital realm. As globalization continues, international treaties like the Agreement on Trade-Related Aspects of Intellectual Property Rights (TRIPS) have sought to harmonize trademark laws to ensure consistent protection across countries.

Conclusion: A Legacy of Protection
From artisanal signatures in ancient markets to digital logos in global marketplaces, trademarks have consistently served as guardians of identity, quality, and reputation. Understanding this historical context enriches our appreciation of trademarks not merely as legal tools but as essential elements of commerce that have stood the test of time, adapting to protect and promote fair and competitive markets throughout human history.

Global Perspective

In today's interconnected economy, understanding the global landscape of trademark law is crucial for businesses aiming to expand beyond their national borders. Part One delves into the intricacies of international trademark management, illustrating how trademarks must be navigated and protected across different legal systems to maintain a cohesive global brand identity.

The Challenge of Diverse Legal Systems

Each country has its own set of rules and regulations governing trademarks, which can vary widely in terms of application processes, protection standards, and enforcement mechanisms. For instance, the United States uses a use-based trademark system, where rights are derived from actual use of the mark in commerce. In contrast, many other countries operate under a first-to-file system, where the first to register a trademark holds the rights to it, regardless of actual use. Navigating these differences requires a strategic approach tailored to each jurisdiction to ensure comprehensive protection of trademark rights.

Harmonization Efforts in Trademark Law

To address these challenges, several international treaties and agreements have been established to create a more harmonized approach to trademark registration and enforcement. The Madrid Protocol allows for the international registration of trademarks by filing a single application that can cover more than 120 countries. Similarly, the European Union offers a Unitary Trademark system, where a single registration provides trademark protection across all EU member states. These systems simplify the process for businesses to secure widespread trademark protection while reducing the complexity and cost of maintaining multiple registrations.

Strategic Considerations for Global Expansion

When expanding into new markets, businesses must consider not only legal factors but also cultural, linguistic, and commercial aspects. A trademark that works well in one cultural context might have negative connotations or be difficult to pronounce in another. Moreover, global brand consistency must be balanced with local market relevance. Companies often adapt their brands in subtle ways to better resonate with local consumers while maintaining the overarching identity.

Case Studies of Global Trademark Strategies

1. **A Major Tech Company**:
   o A global technology company faced challenges when expanding into Asian markets due to local competitors using similar trademarks. By utilizing the Madrid Protocol, the company was able to streamline enforcement efforts across multiple regions, successfully reclaiming its brand identity in critical markets.

2. **Consumer Goods Brand**:
   o A well-known consumer goods company adapted its trademarked brand names and logos to suit local languages and cultural nuances in various countries. This strategy not only ensured legal compliance but also increased brand affinity and market penetration.

Conclusion: Mastering Global Trademark Management

Mastering the art of global trademark management is essential for businesses looking to thrive in the international arena. By understanding and leveraging international treaties, respecting local legal and cultural differences, and strategically managing global brand identity, companies can protect their intellectual property and build a strong, recognizable brand on a global scale. The journey through international trademark law is complex, but with careful planning and strategic execution, it can lead to significant competitive advantages and long-term success.

The Role of Technology

In the fast-paced world of trademark management, technology plays a pivotal role in transforming practices, enhancing efficiency, and offering new ways to protect and manage trademarks. Part One also explores the various technological advancements that have reshaped the landscape of trademark law and how businesses can leverage these tools to stay ahead in the game.

Digitalization of Trademark Filings and Databases

The transition to digital platforms has revolutionized how trademarks are filed, searched, and maintained. Online databases and electronic filing systems have made the process more accessible, faster, and often less costly. For instance, the United States Patent and Trademark Office (USPTO) and the European Union Intellectual Property Office (EUIPO) provide comprehensive online portals where businesses can conduct trademark searches, file applications, and manage registrations without the need for physical paperwork.

AI and Machine Learning

Artificial Intelligence (AI) and machine learning are at the forefront of technological advancements in trademark management. AI systems can perform complex searches across global databases to identify potential conflicts and suggest the likelihood of registration success. Moreover, AI-driven analytics can predict trends and emerging threats, allowing businesses to proactively manage their trademark portfolios.

1. **Predictive Analytics**: AI algorithms analyze historical data and current market trends to forecast future trademark conflicts or identify opportunities for brand expansion. This predictive capability enables businesses to strategize more effectively and anticipate potential challenges.

2. **Automated Monitoring**: AI tools continuously monitor the internet, including e-commerce platforms and social media, for unauthorized use of trademarks. This real-time monitoring ensures that infringements are quickly identified and addressed, significantly reducing the potential damage to a brand.

Blockchain Technology

Blockchain offers a unique approach to trademark registration and protection. By creating a decentralized and immutable ledger of trademark registrations, blockchain technology can provide a transparent and tamper-proof system for recording and verifying trademark information.

1. **Enhanced Security**: The cryptographic nature of blockchain ensures that trademark data is secure from unauthorized access and alterations, making it an ideal platform for maintaining the integrity of trademark records.

2. **Global Accessibility**: A blockchain-based trademark system could facilitate easier access to trademark information across jurisdictions, simplifying the process for international registrations and enforcement.

Integrating Technology with Traditional Practices

While technology offers numerous advantages, it is most effective when integrated thoughtfully with traditional trademark management practices. Legal professionals must understand both the capabilities and the limitations of these technologies to use them effectively.

1. **Training and Adaptation**: Ensuring that legal teams and trademark professionals are well-trained in the latest technological tools is crucial. Regular training sessions and updates can help integrate these tools seamlessly into existing practices.

2. **Ethical Considerations**: As with any technology, ethical considerations must be addressed, particularly concerning data privacy and the potential for over-reliance on automated systems. Establishing clear guidelines and maintaining human oversight are essential to ensure that technology enhances, rather than replaces, human expertise.

Conclusion: Embracing Technological Advancements

The integration of technology into trademark management is not just a trend; it is a transformation that is reshaping the field. By embracing these technological advancements, businesses can enhance their trademark strategies, protect their intellectual property more effectively, and navigate the complexities of the global market with greater agility. The future of trademark management is here, and it is powered by innovation and technology.

Real-World Examples

In the intricate dance of trademark management, real-world examples offer a tangible glimpse into the strategies and challenges that businesses face. Part Two delves into case studies from various industries, showcasing how companies have successfully navigated trademark issues and sometimes stumbled along the way. These stories not only illustrate the practical application of the principles discussed earlier but also provide valuable lessons for businesses looking to strengthen their trademark strategies.

Case Study 1: The Battle of the Tech Titans

Background: Two leading technology companies found themselves embroiled in a high-stakes trademark dispute over similarly named consumer electronics. The conflict escalated to multiple international jurisdictions, reflecting the complexities of managing global trademarks.

Strategy and Outcome:

- **Preemptive Actions**: Both companies engaged in thorough trademark searches and monitoring systems, which should have prevented the overlap. However, differences in trademark laws across countries led to simultaneous approvals.

- **Resolution**: The dispute was settled through negotiation, with one company agreeing to a rebranding that distinguished its product more clearly, accompanied by a licensing agreement that allowed both companies to coexist in the market without further confusion.

Case Study 2: A Small Business Faces a Giant

Background: A small coffee shop in a European city received a cease-and-desist letter from a multinational corporation claiming that the shop's name infringed upon its trademarked brand name.

Strategy and Outcome:

- **Legal Defense**: The small business decided to fight the claim, arguing that there was no likelihood of confusion due to the vastly different scale and geographical focus of their operations.

- **Public Support**: The case garnered public support for the small business, leading to a PR crisis for the multinational. Eventually, the corporation withdrew its claim, and the coffee shop continued to operate under its original name.

Case Study 3: Fashion Forward - Protecting Design Trademarks

Background: A famous fashion designer introduced a distinctive pattern that quickly became synonymous with the brand. As the pattern grew in popularity, it was increasingly copied by competitors and counterfeiters.

Strategy and Outcome:

- **Trademark Registration**: The designer proactively registered the pattern as a trademark in key markets, ensuring legal grounds for enforcement.

- **Vigilant Enforcement**: Through constant monitoring and legal action, the fashion brand successfully sued multiple infringers, which deterred further unauthorized use and solidified the pattern as a key asset of the brand's identity.

Case Study 4: Reviving a Legacy

Background: An iconic beverage company decided to revive a discontinued product line that had once been popular several decades ago.

Strategy and Outcome:

- **Trademark Renewal**: The company had maintained the trademark registration despite the product being off the market, which simplified the relaunch process.

- **Marketing Strategy**: Leveraging the nostalgic value of the trademark, the company implemented a marketing campaign that emphasized the product's historical significance, resulting in successful re-entry into the market.

Conclusion: Lessons from the Trenches

These real-world examples underscore the significance of strategic trademark management across various scenarios. They highlight the importance of proactive measures such as thorough trademark searches and registrations, the benefits of vigilant monitoring and enforcement, and the power of public perception in legal disputes. By learning from these examples, businesses can better navigate the potential pitfalls and opportunities in trademark management, ensuring that their brands are not only protected but also positioned for success in the competitive marketplace.

Interactive Elements

In the dynamic field of trademark management, theoretical knowledge is only one piece of the puzzle. Practical, interactive elements that readers can engage with are crucial for deepening understanding and enhancing the applicability of the concepts discussed. Part Three introduces the various interactive tools and resources included in this book, designed to help readers apply the principles of trademark law effectively in real-world scenarios.

Trademark Registration Simulations

1. **Purpose and Design**:

    o   Simulations provide step-by-step scenarios that guide readers through the process of filing a trademark application. These interactive simulations include decision points where readers must choose how to proceed based on the information provided, mirroring real-life decisions.

    o   This tool helps demystify the registration process and prepares readers for the kinds of questions and challenges they might face when dealing with actual filings.

2. **Learning Outcomes**:

    o   Readers will gain hands-on experience in identifying the requirements for a strong trademark application, including how to articulate the basis for filing and how to describe goods and services accurately.

- o The simulations reinforce the importance of precision and foresight in trademark registration, emphasizing the potential pitfalls of inadequate preparation.

Interactive Checklists and Templates

1. **Comprehensive Checklists**:

   - o These checklists cover various aspects of trademark management, including pre-registration research, application checklists, renewal timelines, and enforcement protocols.

   - o Each checklist serves as a practical tool to ensure that all necessary steps are completed and nothing is overlooked in the management of trademarks.

2. **Downloadable Templates**:

   - o Templates for common documents such as cease-and-desist letters, licensing agreements, and monitoring reports are included. These templates provide a solid starting point that readers can customize for their specific needs.

   - o By using these templates, readers can save time and reduce errors, ensuring that their communications are professional and legally sound.

Interactive Webinars and Q&A Sessions

1. **Scheduled Webinars**:

   - o The book includes access to scheduled webinars featuring trademark experts who discuss complex topics and recent developments in trademark law.

   - o During these sessions, readers can interact directly with experts, ask questions, and discuss real-world cases, providing a deeper understanding of the nuances in trademark management.

2. **Live Q&A Sessions**:

   o   These sessions allow readers to submit their trademark queries and receive advice tailored to their particular situations. It's an opportunity for interactive learning and sharing experiences with peers.

   o   The live format encourages active participation and engagement, helping to clarify doubts and strengthen community learning.

Conclusion: Making Theory Practical

The interactive elements included in this book are designed to bridge the gap between theoretical knowledge and practical application. By engaging with these tools, readers not only learn about trademark law but also how to apply it effectively in their business or legal practice. These resources empower readers to take proactive steps in protecting their intellectual property, equipped with a clearer understanding and hands-on experience that simulates real-world trademark management challenges.

Expert Insights

Navigating the complex world of trademark law requires not just a solid understanding of the legal framework but also insights from those who have been in the trenches—experts who have shaped and witnessed the evolution of trademark practices. Part Four showcases perspectives from seasoned attorneys, branding experts, and industry leaders, providing readers with a comprehensive view of both the challenges and strategies in effective trademark management.

Interviews with Trademark Attorneys

1. **Purpose and Scope**:

   o   Conducted interviews with experienced trademark attorneys offer a window into the nuanced legal strategies employed in high-stakes trademark cases. These interviews cover topics such as navigating international trademark laws, dealing with infringement disputes, and the impact of new technologies on trademark practices.

2. **Key Takeaways**:

   o   Attorneys emphasize the importance of a proactive approach in trademark registration and vigilant monitoring to prevent infringement.

   o   Insights into the subtleties of legal negotiations and the defense of intellectual property in different jurisdictions provide practical advice for readers dealing with complex trademark issues.

Panels with Branding Professionals

1. **Roundtable Discussions**:

   o   Roundtable discussions with branding professionals delve into the creative aspects of developing and maintaining a strong trademark. These experts discuss the interplay between brand identity and trademark choice, the challenges of maintaining brand consistency across global markets, and strategies for rebranding.

2. **Strategic Recommendations**:

   o   Branding experts highlight the significance of understanding consumer psychology and market trends when choosing trademarks.

   o   Recommendations often include leveraging data analytics for brand development and the importance of aligning trademark strategies with overall marketing goals.

Insights from Industry Leaders

1. **Case Studies and Success Stories**:

   o   This book features detailed case studies from industry leaders who have successfully navigated the trademark landscape to build and protect powerful brands. These case studies provide real-world examples of how strategic trademark management can lead to market dominance and brand longevity.

2. **Lessons Learned**:

   o Industry leaders share the lessons they've learned from both successes and setbacks in trademark management, offering invaluable insights into risk management, crisis handling, and innovative trademark uses.

   o These narratives underscore the importance of adaptability and foresight in the rapidly changing world of trademark protection.

Interactive Expert Forums

1. **Live Expert Forums**:

   o The book includes access to live forums where readers can engage directly with experts in a dynamic exchange of ideas. These forums allow readers to discuss current issues in trademark law, get feedback on specific challenges, and explore new developments in real-time.

2. **Collaborative Learning**:

   o These forums foster a collaborative learning environment where readers can not only receive guidance but also share their experiences and strategies, enriching the learning experience for all participants.

Conclusion: A Mosaic of Perspectives

The expert insights provided in this book enrich the reader's understanding of trademark management by offering a mosaic of perspectives that span legal, creative, and strategic domains. By integrating these expert views, the book equips readers with a multidimensional understanding of how trademarks can be effectively managed and protected in various scenarios. This depth of knowledge ensures that readers are well-prepared to handle the complexities of trademark law with confidence and strategic acumen.

Future Forecasting

The landscape of trademark law is continuously evolving, shaped by technological advancements, shifts in consumer behavior, and changes in the global economy. The Bonus Chapter delves into the trends and innovations that are likely to influence trademark strategies in the coming years, providing readers with foresight to navigate the future effectively.

Technological Innovations

1. **AI and Machine Learning**:

   o The continued integration of AI into trademark management is set to transform how trademarks are searched, monitored, and enforced. As AI systems become more sophisticated, they will provide even more precise analytics, predictive capabilities, and automated processes, reducing human error and increasing efficiency.

2. **Blockchain for Trademarks**:

   o Blockchain technology is poised to significantly impact how trademarks are registered and verified across borders. Its ability to provide a secure, transparent, and immutable ledger will facilitate easier verification of trademark ownership and history, potentially reducing disputes and streamlining international transactions.

Regulatory and Legal Changes

1. **Global Intellectual Property Environment**:

   o As businesses continue to expand globally, international cooperation on intellectual property rights will become more critical. Future legal frameworks may need to adapt to the increasing interconnectivity of markets, leading to more standardized global trademark laws.

2. **Privacy Regulations**:

   o With the rise of data-driven marketing and online business operations, trademark strategies will increasingly intersect with privacy regulations. Future trademark practices will need to navigate these regulations carefully, particularly as consumer data plays a more significant role in branding and marketing.

Consumer Trends and Market Dynamics

1. **Shifts in Consumer Behavior**:

   o The digital transformation of the marketplace is changing how consumers interact with brands. Trademarks will need to evolve to protect not just traditional logos and names but also digital assets like domain names, social media handles, and even virtual goods in digital environments.

2. **Sustainability and Ethical Branding**:

   o Consumer demand for sustainability and ethical business practices is growing. Trademarks that signify eco-friendliness or ethical sourcing are becoming valuable assets, requiring new strategies for protection and exploitation.

Case Studies and Predictive Scenarios

1. **Emerging Markets**:

   o Case studies from emerging markets, where brand expansion is rapid and intellectual property laws are developing, will offer insights into managing trademarks in varied legal landscapes.

2. **Predictive Scenarios**:

   o Scenario planning exercises will help readers understand potential future environments for trademark law, including the impact of major geopolitical shifts or global economic events.

Conclusion: Preparing for Tomorrow

Understanding potential future developments in trademark law and market trends is essential for businesses looking to protect and leverage their trademarks long-term. By staying informed about upcoming technological, legal, and consumer-driven changes, trademark professionals and business leaders can ensure their trademark strategies remain robust and adaptive. This forward-thinking approach will not only safeguard intellectual property but also position brands to capitalize on new opportunities in a dynamic global marketplace.

Call to Action

As we conclude "Mark Your Territory: Navigating Trademarks in the Modern Marketplace," we understand that navigating the complex landscape of trademarks is crucial for businesses looking to establish and protect their brand identities. This book has equipped you with the necessary tools, insights, and strategies. Now, it's time to translate this knowledge into action.

Implement What You've Learned
Take this opportunity to review and revise your current trademark strategies in light of the insights and techniques discussed. Assess areas for improvement, whether it's enhancing your monitoring processes or updating your registration details. Embrace the technological advancements presented, from AI-driven search and monitoring systems to blockchain for secure registration processes, which can significantly enhance the efficiency and effectiveness of your trademark management.

Educate and Advocate
Spread the knowledge you have gained within your team, colleagues, and professional network. Organizing training sessions or workshops can help disseminate best practices and ensure that your organization recognizes the importance of effective trademark management. Additionally, advocate for robust trademark strategies within your industry by participating in forums, writing articles, or speaking at conferences to promote the significance of trademarks in protecting intellectual property and fostering fair competition.

Stay Informed and Adapt
Commit to continual learning as the field of trademark law is always evolving. Stay informed about the latest legal developments, technological innovations, and market trends by subscribing to industry publications, attending legal seminars,

and joining professional associations. Anticipate future challenges and opportunities using the forecasting insights provided and develop strategies that not only address current needs but also position your brand advantageously for future developments.

Engage with Experts

Build relationships with experienced trademark attorneys and consultants who can offer specialized knowledge and guidance tailored to your specific needs. Regular consultations can help navigate complex legal landscapes and make informed decisions. Engage with the community of readers and experts who have embarked on this journey; participate in interactive forums and webinars offered as part of this book's learning environment to share experiences and solutions.

Final Thoughts

Your trademarks are more than just legal protections; they embody your brand's identity and foundational value in the marketplace. With the knowledge and strategies from this book, you are well-prepared to mark your territory effectively. Embrace the challenges, harness the opportunities, and watch as your trademarks transform from mere marks of protection into symbols of innovation and success. Let us move forward, marking wisely, defending vigorously, and innovating continuously.

PART ONE

Trademark Essentials

Welcome to Part One: Trademark Essentials, your frontline guide to marking and defending your commercial territory. Think of this section as your intellectual property bootcamp, where we turn the esoteric world of trademarks into your strategic arsenal. Here, you'll learn to not just understand but wield trademarks with the precision of a seasoned legal marksman. From choosing distinctive marks that shout your brand's identity across the marketplace to navigating the labyrinthine paths of registration and protection, this is where you gear up. We'll decode the legalese and transform it into actionable insights that secure your brand's future. Buckle up—it's time to trademark your way to the top of your industry!

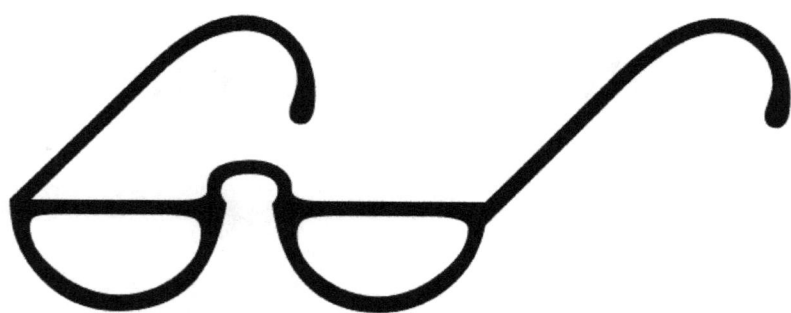

Decoding Trademarks: An Introduction

"A trademark does not just protect an asset, it projects your business's identity to the world, making it a cornerstone of your success."— RICHARD BRANSON, FOUNDER OF VIRGIN GROUP

Welcome to Chapter One: Decoding Trademarks—An Introduction. Here, we delve into the fundamental elements of trademarks, those powerful symbols, words, and sounds that declare the identity of your brand to the world. This isn't just an overview; it's your first step into a realm where the mundane transforms into a fortress of intellectual property.

Trademarks aren't merely about protecting a name or logo; they are the vanguard of your brand's reputation, the first line of defense against the competition's encroachments. In this chapter, we uncover the intricate dance between choosing a mark that is both unique and defensible. You'll learn why a trademark is more than just a legal shield; it's a critical component of your marketing arsenal, imbuing your brand with an invisible yet palpable force that engages customers and deters rivals.

We'll break down the legal intricacies, simplifying the complex interplay of laws and regulations into practical strategies that you can apply directly to your business. From the initial spark of creativity that inspires a trademark to the rigorous processes of registration and enforcement, this chapter prepares you to navigate the trademark terrain with confidence and savvy.

By the end of this chapter, you'll have a robust understanding of how to effectively leverage trademarks not just to safeguard your intellectual property, but to enhance your market position. Get ready to transform every element of your branding from commonplace to a cornerstone of your business strategy, ensuring that every aspect of your market presence is distinctly yours. With this knowledge, you're not just following the paths of commercial giants—you're carving your own.

The Essence of Trademarks

Trademarks are not just identifiers; they are the soul of a brand's recognition and differentiation in the marketplace. As the first touchpoint for consumers, trademarks play a pivotal role in the visual and perceptual connection with the customer. This section introduces the nature and purpose of trademarks, emphasizing their critical role in securing a brand's identity and competitive edge in the global market.

Defining Trademarks

At its core, a trademark is any distinctive sign or indicator used by a business to identify that its products or services originate from a unique source and to distinguish them from those of other entities. Trademarks are usually composed of names, words, phrases, symbols, designs, or a combination of these elements. They are used across various platforms and products, becoming synonymous with the brand's reputation and quality.

Types of Trademarks

Trademarks come in various forms, each serving a unique function in brand strategy:

- **Word Marks:** These are textual and include company names or product names (e.g., "Coca-Cola" or "Google").

- **Logos/Symbols:** Often stylized forms, such as Apple's apple or McDonald's golden arches.

- **Figure Marks:** Involving characters or mascots, like the Michelin Man or KFC's Colonel Sanders.

- **Sound Marks:** These include a unique sound associated with a brand, such as the MGM lion's roar or the Intel bong.

- **Color Marks:** Single colors or specific color combinations recognized in relation to a brand, like UPS's Pullman Brown or Tiffany's blue.

- **Shape Marks:** The distinctive shape of a product or packaging, like the Coca-Cola bottle.

- **Pattern Marks:** A specific pattern used as a trademark, which could be seen on Louis Vuitton's bags.

- **Position Marks:** Placement of the mark in a specific position on a product, which consistently appears in promotional materials.

- **Motion Marks:** A moving logo or an animated character that conveys branding, like the Google Doodle animations.

The Importance of Trademarks in Business

Trademarks are essential for multiple reasons:

- **Brand Identity:** They are a quick visual representation of your brand, which helps to build identity and differentiate it from competitors.

- **Communication Tool:** A trademark encapsulates the brand's promise, values, and reputation, communicating these elements effectively and efficiently to the consumer.

- **Legal Protection:** Owning a registered trademark provides legal clarity and exclusivity, granting the owner the rights to prevent others from using a similar identity for comparable products or services.

- **Asset Value:** Trademarks can become valuable assets over time. As the brand grows, the value of the trademark can increase, becoming a critical component of the company's equity.

- **Marketing and Advertising Leverage:** Trademarks are integral to marketing and advertising strategies, making brands recognizable across different media and reinforcing brand presence.

Understanding the essence of trademarks is foundational to recognizing their power as more than just legal tools—they are integral to the strategic development and recognition of a brand. They serve as the face of the company, fostering customer loyalty and serving as a vehicle for safeguarding the intellectual creativity at the heart of commercial success. As we delve deeper into the complexities of trademark selection, registration, and enforcement in the subsequent sections, remember that a well-chosen and protected trademark is a cornerstone of any enduring brand strategy.

Legal Framework and Registration

Trademark law is designed to protect the unique elements that distinguish one business's goods and services from another's, ensuring that consumers can clearly identify the source of the products they purchase. This section explores the legal underpinnings of trademarks, guiding you through the processes of trademark registration, which not only fortifies legal protections but also enhances the brand's market presence.

Understanding the Legal Basis of Trademarks
Trademark rights arise from either actual use in commerce or by registering the trademark with a national or regional trademark office. In the United States, trademarks are protected under the Lanham Act, which provides a national system for trademark registration and offers protection against infringement. Similar frameworks exist globally, governed by local laws and international agreements

such as the Madrid Protocol, which facilitates the registration of trademarks in multiple countries through one application.

The Registration Process

1. **Trademark Search**: Before filing for registration, it is crucial to conduct a thorough search to ensure that the proposed mark is not already in use. This includes checking the national trademark database and, if applicable, international databases to avoid potential conflicts and rejections.

2. **Application Filing**: The application should clearly describe the mark, the goods or services it will be associated with, and, if already in use, the date of first use. Applications can be made online through the respective trademark office's website.

3. **Examination**: After submission, the trademark office examines the application to ensure it meets all legal requirements. This includes checking for distinctiveness, potential confusion with existing marks, and any other statutory prohibitions.

4. **Publication for Opposition**: If the mark passes the examination phase, it is published in an official journal. This gives third parties an opportunity to oppose the registration if they believe it infringes on their rights.

5. **Registration**: If no oppositions are raised or if an opposition is successfully overcome, the trademark is registered, granting the registrant exclusive rights to use the mark in relation to the goods or services listed in the registration.

Legal Benefits of Registration

Registering a trademark provides several legal benefits:

- **Exclusive Rights**: The owner gains exclusive rights to use the trademark in commerce in connection with the goods or services listed. This prevents others from using a similar mark in a way that could cause confusion.

- **Legal Presumption**: Registration provides a legal presumption of the registrant's ownership of the mark and their exclusive right to use it nationwide.

- **Basis for International Registration**: A registered trademark can serve as a basis for applying for registration in other countries, facilitating global brand protection.

- **Ability to Use Federal Courts**: Trademark registration allows the owner to bring lawsuits concerning the trademark in federal court.

- **Record of Use**: Registration serves as an official record of the use of the mark, which can be vital in disputes or infringement cases.

The legal framework surrounding trademarks is intricate but navigable with the right knowledge and resources. Understanding and utilizing the registration process effectively can provide significant advantages, safeguarding a business's branding efforts and its competitive position in the market. In the next section, we will delve into strategies for selecting a robust and defensible trademark, which is critical for maximizing the benefits of registration and legal protection.

Strategic Selection of Trademarks

Choosing the right trademark is not just a creative endeavor but a strategic one. This section outlines the considerations and tactics involved in selecting a trademark that not only captures the essence of the brand but is also legally defensible and capable of achieving strong market recognition.

Criteria for Choosing an Effective Trademark

1. **Distinctiveness**: The more distinctive the mark, the easier it is to protect and enforce legally. Trademarks are categorized into five levels of distinctiveness:

   o **Fanciful or Coined**: These are made-up words with no inherent meaning (e.g., "Kodak").

   o **Arbitrary**: Real words used in a way that does not relate to their normal meaning (e.g., "Apple" for electronics).

- o **Suggestive**: Marks that hint at the nature of the product without describing it directly (e.g., "Greyhound" for bus services).

- o **Descriptive**: Words that describe the goods or services, which are not inherently distinctive and are protectable only if they acquire secondary meaning (e.g., "Sharp" for televisions).

- o **Generic**: Terms that are the common name of the product and cannot be trademarked (e.g., "Bicycle").

2. **Avoidance of Confusion**: The chosen mark should not be confusingly similar to existing trademarks, especially within the same industry. This involves considering visual, phonetic, and conceptual similarities to avoid potential infringement issues.

3. **Marketability and Branding**: The trademark should align with the brand's messaging and appeal to the target audience. It should be easy to pronounce, memorable, and capable of capturing the brand's essence.

Steps in the Strategic Selection Process

1. **Brainstorming**: Start with a creative process that involves all key stakeholders to generate a list of potential trademarks. Consider the brand's core values, target market, and the emotional impact you want the mark to convey.

2. **Preliminary Screening**: Conduct initial checks for direct conflicts with existing trademarks. This can be done via online searches and by checking with the relevant trademark office's database.

3. **Comprehensive Search**: Once you have a shortlist, a more thorough search should be conducted, ideally by a professional firm or an attorney who can interpret the results and assess risks of potential conflicts.

4. **Market Testing**: If feasible, market testing of the proposed trademark among consumers can provide valuable insights into its effectiveness and acceptance.

5. **Final Selection and Review**: Choose the mark that best meets the criteria of distinctiveness, legality, and marketability. Have trademark

counsel review the choice to ensure it has a high probability of registration and can be defended legally.

Selecting the right trademark is a critical decision that affects both the legal protection and the marketing success of a brand. It requires a balance between creative expression and strategic planning. With a carefully chosen trademark, a brand can build a strong identity that stands out in the marketplace and is capable of achieving lasting legal protection. In the following section, we will explore how to protect and enforce your trademark rights, ensuring your brand remains secure against potential infringements.

Protection and Enforcement

Cue the dramatic music and close-up: what if I told you that managing your time is actually the same as managing your life? That's right, it's the plot twist no one saw coming—not even the seasoned binge-watchers. If life were a movie, time management would be the twist in the tale that turns the struggling protagonist into a hero.

Once a trademark is selected and registered, the next crucial step is to protect and enforce it. This section explains how to maintain the strength and exclusivity of your trademark, ensuring it continues to represent your brand effectively and securely.

Maintaining Trademark Strength

1. **Consistent Use**: Use your trademark consistently in the form it was registered. Inconsistencies can weaken your legal protections and cause consumer confusion.

2. **Monitoring**: Regularly monitor the market for any unauthorized use of your trademark or similar marks. This can be done through online searches, hiring watch services, or setting up alerts.

3. **Renewals**: Ensure that your trademark registrations are renewed on time. In many jurisdictions, trademarks need to be renewed every 10 years, with declarations of continued use.

Legal Tools for Enforcement

1. **Cease and Desist Letters**: These are often the first step in taking action against infringement. A well-drafted letter can compel the infringing party to stop their unauthorized use without resorting to court action.

2. **Negotiation and Settlement**: Sometimes, it's possible to resolve trademark disputes through negotiation, which can be quicker and less costly than litigation.

3. **Litigation**: If infringement continues or a significant threat is posed to your brand, filing a lawsuit may be necessary. Trademark litigation can enforce your rights and seek damages for unauthorized use.

Strategies for Effective Enforcement

1. **Proactive Protection Plan**: Develop a strategy for regularly reviewing the use of your trademark in the marketplace and taking action against infringements. This includes training your team to recognize potential infringements and knowing when to seek legal advice.

2. **International Protection**: If your brand operates globally, consider securing trademark protection in key markets worldwide. Use international systems like the Madrid Protocol for broader enforcement capabilities.

3. **Online Vigilance**: With the rise of digital marketing and e-commerce, protect your trademark in digital realms by monitoring online platforms and taking action against unauthorized listings or counterfeit goods.

Collaborative Efforts

1. **Industry Cooperation**: Work with industry groups or trade associations, which can provide resources and support for trademark protection efforts.

2. **Governmental Assistance**: In cases of counterfeiting or massive infringement, collaborating with local and international law enforcement agencies can be effective.

Protecting and enforcing your trademark is an ongoing process that requires vigilance, consistency, and sometimes, legal action. By understanding and utilizing the tools and strategies available for trademark protection, you can safeguard your brand's identity and its competitive edge in the market. The robust defense of your trademark not only secures your intellectual property rights but also reinforces the overall value and perception of your brand. In the next section, we will delve into leveraging trademarks within your broader business and marketing strategy to maximize their impact and utility.

Leveraging Trademarks in Business Strategy

Trademarks are not merely defensive legal tools but are powerful assets in branding and business strategy. This section explores how to integrate trademarks into your broader business practices to enhance brand visibility, customer loyalty, and overall market competitiveness.

Enhancing Brand Identity with Trademarks

1. **Brand Storytelling**: Use your trademark as a central element in your brand's narrative. A distinctive trademark can embody your brand's values, heritage, and promises, making your story more memorable and relatable to consumers.

2. **Brand Extension**: Trademarks can facilitate brand extension by enabling the introduction of new products under the same trusted mark, thus reducing the market entry barriers and leveraging existing brand equity.

3. **Co-branding and Licensing**: Enter into co-branding or licensing agreements to expand your brand's reach and relevance. This can open up new markets and demographics by associating with other brands that have complementary strengths and audiences.

Driving Marketing Initiatives

1. **Marketing Campaigns**: Center your marketing campaigns around your trademark. Well-executed campaigns that highlight your trademark can reinforce brand recognition and deepen consumer engagement.

2. **Digital Marketing**: Optimize your online presence by ensuring that your trademark is prominently featured across digital platforms, including websites, social media, and online advertising. This consistency helps to strengthen your digital brand identity and improves search engine visibility.

3. **Merchandising**: Develop branded merchandise that features your trademark prominently. This not only serves as additional revenue streams but also enhances brand visibility and loyalty.

Legal Protection as a Business Advantage

1. **Consumer Trust**: A registered trademark assures customers of the authenticity and quality of your products or services, building trust and loyalty.

2. **Barrier to Entry**: By securing a trademark, you can prevent competitors from entering the market with similar brand identities, which can dilute your brand's strength and market share.

3. **Asset Appreciation**: Over time, as your business grows, your trademark can increase in value, becoming a significant intangible asset that can be leveraged in various financial transactions, such as securing loans or in business acquisitions.

Maximizing Global Reach

1. **International Trademark Strategy**: Develop a global trademark strategy that considers key markets and the potential for brand expansion. Registering your trademark in significant foreign markets ensures that you have exclusive rights to your brand worldwide.

2. **Cultural Adaptation**: Understand and adapt your trademarks to fit cultural nuances in different markets. This can include tweaking your brand name or logo to resonate better with local consumers while maintaining the core elements of your trademark.

Leveraging your trademark effectively within your business strategy is essential for building a strong, recognizable, and respected brand. It is not just about legal protection but about creating and maintaining a competitive edge in the marketplace. As your business grows, your trademark should evolve strategically to continue driving brand recognition, fostering consumer loyalty, and ultimately contributing to business success. With a well-integrated approach, your trademark becomes not just a symbol of your business but a key driver of its growth and profitability.

Quick Tips and Recap

- **Understand the Basics**: Recognize that trademarks are more than just symbols; they are crucial for distinguishing your brand and its products in the marketplace.

- **Distinctiveness is Key**: Choose a trademark that is unique and distinctive to ensure strong legal protection and brand recognition.

- **Conduct Thorough Searches**: Always conduct a comprehensive search before selecting a trademark to avoid potential conflicts and ensure the mark is defensible.

- **Leverage Legal Protections**: Register your trademark to gain exclusive rights and legal advantages, such as the ability to enforce your rights through federal courts.

- **Maintain Consistency**: Use your trademark consistently in the form it was registered to maintain its strength and legal protection.

- **Monitor the Market**: Regularly monitor for any unauthorized use of your trademark and take swift action against infringements.

- **Plan for Renewals**: Keep track of renewal deadlines to ensure your trademark protection remains in force without interruption.

- **Integrate Trademarks into Marketing**: Use your trademark strategically in marketing campaigns to enhance brand visibility and consumer recognition.

- **Expand Thoughtfully**: Consider international registrations if your business operates or plans to expand globally.

- **Stay Informed**: Keep updated on changes in trademark laws and practices to ensure ongoing compliance and protection.

- **Use Trademarks Strategically**: Incorporate trademarks into your business strategy to strengthen brand identity, enable brand extension, and increase market competitiveness.

- **Seek Professional Advice**: Consult with trademark attorneys for strategic advice and to navigate complex legal situations effectively.

The Trademark Legal Landscape: Understanding the Rules

"Understanding trademark law isn't just about protecting what's yours;
it's about staking a claim in the marketplace that no one can
challenge."— JEFF BEZOS, FOUNDER OF AMAZON

Welcome to Chapter Two: The Trademark Legal Landscape—
Understanding the Rules. Here, we'll dive headfirst into the byzantine
world of trademark law, where the sharp edges of legal statutes meet the fluid
dynamics of market creativity. Think of this chapter as your legal GPS, designed
to navigate the complex highways and byways of trademark regulations without
getting lost in the legalese.

Trademark law isn't just a set of dry rules; it's the playbook for brand protection,
crafted over centuries of commerce and conflict. You'll learn how these laws

shape your strategy, from the spark of brand conception to the full blaze of market presence. We'll decode everything from the basics of trademark eligibility to the nuances of federal and state laws that could impact your branding decisions.

But it's not all serious—expect a journey through some of the most intriguing, even absurd, trademark battles that have shaped the legal landscape. You'll see how businesses big and small have wielded trademark law not just as a shield, but as a strategic weapon in their arsenals.

By the end of this chapter, you'll be equipped to make informed decisions that align with legal requirements while pushing the boundaries of brand innovation. Armed with this knowledge, you're ready to turn the rule book into a secret weapon for your branding endeavors. Let's demystify the legalese and discover how understanding the rules can set you free to innovate!

Foundations of Trademark Law

Trademark law has evolved as a crucial component of commerce, providing businesses with the tools necessary to protect their brand identity and ensure consumer confidence. This section explores the historical evolution and foundational principles of trademark law, setting the stage for understanding how trademarks function within the legal and business worlds.

Historical Overview
The concept of trademarks dates back to ancient times when artisans would mark their goods to indicate origin and quality. Over the centuries, as trade expanded and markets became more sophisticated, the need for more structured trademark systems emerged. By the 19th century, many countries began to formalize trademark laws to protect businesses and consumers from deception. Today, trademarks are governed by a combination of national and international laws designed to foster fair competition and clear market communication.

Fundamental Principles of Trademark Law
1. **Distinctiveness**: A trademark must be distinctive enough to be recognized as a source identifier for goods or services. The

distinctiveness can be inherent or can be acquired through extensive use in the marketplace.

2. **Priority**: Trademark rights are generally awarded to the first to use a particular mark in commerce in a specific geographic area, not necessarily the first to register the mark. This principle supports the premise that trademark law not only protects the trademark owner but also protects the public from being misled about the origins of goods or services.

3. **Secondary Meaning**: Some marks are not inherently distinctive and must acquire a secondary meaning. Secondary meaning occurs when consumers come to recognize a mark as a source identifier over time due to extensive and exclusive use.

4. **Non-Functionality**: A trademark must not be functional; that is, the feature that makes up the mark must not be essential to the use or purpose of the product. This ensures that trademark law does not grant a monopoly on useful product features.

Legal Frameworks Governing Trademarks

- **National Laws**: Each country has its own trademark laws, which typically include provisions for the registration, protection, and enforcement of trademarks. In the United States, the primary statute is the Lanham Act, which governs federal trademark registration and protection.

- **International Treaties**: Several international treaties influence how trademarks are handled globally. The Paris Convention for the Protection of Industrial Property and the Agreement on Trade-Related Aspects of Intellectual Property Rights (TRIPS) are key frameworks that facilitate international trademark protection.

Registration and its Benefits

Registering a trademark provides several advantages:

- **Legal Presumption of Ownership**: Registration with the national trademark office provides a legal presumption of ownership and exclusive rights to use the trademark nationwide.

- **Basis for International Registration**: Registered trademarks can serve as a basis for applying for trademark protection in other countries.

- **Enhanced Remedies**: Registration allows access to greater legal remedies, including the possibility of obtaining statutory damages for infringement.

Understanding the foundations of trademark law is essential for any business seeking to protect its brand identity effectively. These principles form the basis for all aspects of trademark selection, registration, and enforcement. As we delve deeper into the specific rules and processes in the following sections, keep in mind these foundational elements that make trademarks a critical part of business strategy and consumer protection.

Trademark Eligibility and Registration

A trademark serves as a key identifier for businesses, distinguishing their goods or services from those of competitors. Before a business can effectively protect its brand identity with a trademark, it is crucial to understand what constitutes a trademark and the specific criteria that determine its eligibility for legal protection. This knowledge ensures that the marks you select will not only resonate with consumers but also withstand legal scrutiny.

Detailed Criteria for Trademark Eligibility

1. **Distinctiveness**: The primary criterion for a trademark is its distinctiveness—the mark's ability to be recognized by consumers as a source identifier for certain goods or services. Distinctiveness is often the most critical factor in the eligibility and protection level of a trademark, categorized as follows:

- **Fanciful or Arbitrary**: These are inherently distinctive and provide the strongest protection. Fanciful marks are invented words with no prior meaning (e.g., "Exxon" for oil products), while arbitrary marks involve common words applied in an unrelated context (e.g., "Apple" for computers).

- **Suggestive**: Suggestive marks hint at an attribute or characteristic of the goods or services but require some imagination to make the connection (e.g., "Blu-ray" for disc technology).

- **Descriptive**: These marks directly describe the product or an attribute thereof and must acquire a secondary meaning to be protected. Secondary meaning occurs when the public primarily associates the descriptive term with a particular commercial source (e.g., "British Airways" for airline services).

- **Generic**: These are terms that are the common names for products or services and cannot be trademarked (e.g., "Tablet" for tablet computers). Generic terms are public domain and provide no proprietary rights.

2. **Non-functionality**: The mark must be non-functional; it should not provide a utilitarian advantage or relate to the product's cost or quality. Trademark law is designed to protect branding elements, not functional features of products, which are better suited for patent protection.

The Comprehensive Registration Process

The process of registering a trademark is multifaceted, involving several critical steps that require careful attention to detail:

1. **Preliminary Search**: Conduct a thorough search in relevant trademark databases to ascertain whether the proposed mark or similar marks are already in use within the same category of goods or services. This initial step prevents potential conflicts and legal challenges post-registration.

2. **Application Preparation and Filing**: Prepare a detailed application that includes:

   o A graphical representation of the mark.

   o A precise listing of the goods or services to be covered, categorized according to the international classification.

   o A statement regarding the current use of the mark in commerce or an intent-to-use declaration for future applications.

   o The application is typically submitted online via the website of the national trademark office.

3. **Examination Process**: After submission, the trademark office reviews the application for compliance with trademark laws. An examiner assesses the distinctiveness, potential conflicts with existing trademarks, and any other legal barriers to registration.

4. **Public Publication and Opposition Period**: Successful applications are published in an official trademark journal or gazette. This publication allows third parties to view the pending trademark and file opposition if they believe the registration would infringe on their rights or cause confusion.

5. **Final Registration**: If no opposition is filed or if the applicant successfully overcomes any challenges, the trademark is formally registered. This registration confers exclusive rights to use the trademark in commerce in relation to the goods or services listed.

Navigating the criteria for trademark eligibility and understanding the registration process are foundational to protecting a brand legally and effectively. As brands grow and evolve, ensuring that trademarks are properly registered and maintained becomes a pivotal element of strategic brand management. With a clear understanding of these processes, businesses can secure their branding efforts and safeguard their market position. In the next section, we'll explore the nuances of federal and state trademark laws and how they interplay with these principles to impact your branding decisions.

Federal vs. State Trademark Laws

Trademark law in the United States is governed at both the federal and state levels, offering layers of protection that can be tailored to the needs of businesses depending on their operational scope and strategic goals. This dual system allows companies to secure legal rights over their trademarks in ways that best suit their market presence and future expansion plans.

Federal Trademark Protection: The Lanham Act

The Lanham Act is the federal statute that governs trademark law in the U.S. It offers comprehensive protections and several significant advantages for trademarks used in interstate and international commerce:

1. **Nationwide Protection**: Federal registration provides an exclusive right to use the trademark across the entire United States, superseding any state law claims within its jurisdiction. This is particularly valuable for businesses that operate across state lines or online.

2. **Constructive Notice**: A federal trademark registration puts the public on notice nationwide of the registrant's claim of ownership of the mark, thereby a crucial defensive tool against claims of innocent infringement.

3. **Legal Presumption**: Federal registration grants a legal presumption of the validity of the trademark and the registrant's exclusive right to use the trademark in connection with the goods or services listed in the registration.

4. **International Registration Benefits**: Federal trademarks can serve as a basis for applying to register the mark in other countries through international treaties such as the Madrid Protocol, facilitating global brand protection.

5. **Enhanced Remedial Measures**: Owners of federally registered trademarks can sue for infringement in federal courts and potentially recover statutory damages, attorney's fees, and even triple damages for willful infringement, providing strong legal recourse against unauthorized use.

State Trademark Laws

State trademark registrations, while more limited in geographic scope, offer strategic benefits for certain businesses:

1. **Local Domain Protection**: State trademark registration protects a trademark within the state's boundaries. This level of protection is suitable for businesses whose commercial activities are confined to a single state or who wish to secure additional protection in a state not covered adequately by their federal registration.

2. **Accessibility and Cost Efficiency**: Obtaining a state trademark registration is generally less expensive and involves a simpler process than federal registration. It is an accessible option for small businesses or startups managing budget constraints.

3. **Supplementary Protection**: For businesses with both local and national presence, state registration can supplement a federal trademark by strengthening the local claim to the mark and offering evidence of long-standing use in potential disputes.

Deciding Between Federal and State Registration

The decision to pursue federal registration, state registration, or both should be informed by several factors:

1. **Business Reach and Strategy**: Evaluate the geographic reach of your business activities. If your business crosses state borders or operates online, federal protection is essential. If your activities are confined to one state, consider starting with state registration.

2. **Legal Protection Needs**: Assess the level of legal protection needed based on your market exposure and risk of infringement. Federal registration offers robust legal tools and broader enforcement options.

3. **Budget and Resources**: Consider your budget for trademark registration and ongoing enforcement. Federal registration, while more costly, provides significant long-term benefits for businesses planning to expand.

Navigating between federal and state trademark registrations involves a strategic assessment of your business's current needs and future ambitions. Understanding the nuances of each jurisdiction enables businesses to effectively plan their trademark protection, ensuring robust defense and support for their brand's growth. In the next section, we delve into the complexities of protecting your trademark on the international stage, a critical consideration for businesses looking to expand beyond U.S. borders.

Navigating International Trademark Laws

As businesses increasingly operate on a global scale thanks to the internet and global supply chains, understanding how to protect trademarks internationally becomes essential. This section explores the complexities and strategies involved in securing trademark rights across different countries, helping you navigate the varied legal landscapes and cultural nuances.

Key International Treaties and Agreements

1. **The Madrid Protocol**: This is an international treaty that allows for the registration of a trademark in multiple member countries through a single application filed with the World Intellectual Property Organization (WIPO). It simplifies the process of obtaining and managing trademark protections in up to 124 countries (as of the last update).

2. **The Paris Convention**: This convention allows for the national treatment of foreigners seeking to register trademarks and the right of priority, which means that an applicant from a signatory country has a priority period of six months to file in other signatory countries and receive the same filing date as their original application.

3. **The Agreement on Trade-Related Aspects of Intellectual Property Rights (TRIPS)**: Administered by the World Trade Organization (WTO), TRIPS sets minimum standards for many forms of intellectual property regulation as applied to nationals of other WTO Members. It includes detailed provisions on how trademarks should be protected.

Strategies for International Trademark Registration

1. **Research and Understand Local Laws**: Before entering a new market, it is crucial to understand the local trademark laws, which can vary significantly from country to country. What may be registrable in one country might not be in another due to different criteria for distinctiveness or because the trademark contains culturally sensitive imagery or language.

2. **Use of International Systems**: Leverage international systems like the Madrid Protocol to streamline the application process across multiple countries. This not only reduces administrative burdens but also helps in managing renewal dates and any legal challenges through a centralized system.

3. **Engage Local Experts**: It's advisable to work with local trademark attorneys who can provide valuable insights into the specific nuances of trademark law in their jurisdiction. They can help navigate the application process, opposition proceedings, and any enforcement issues that arise.

4. **Regular Monitoring and Enforcement**: Protecting a trademark doesn't end with registration. Regular monitoring of markets is essential to detect and address infringements promptly. International monitoring services can help identify unauthorized use of trademarks and counterfeit products, enabling timely legal action.

5. **Adaptation and Flexibility**: Be prepared to adapt your trademarks if necessary. In some markets, cultural differences and local consumer behavior might require adjustments to your branding strategies to ensure relevance and respectfulness, which can influence trademark registration and enforcement.

Protecting trademarks internationally requires careful planning and strategic thinking. Understanding the complexities of international trademark laws, leveraging global treaties, and working with local experts are all crucial for effectively managing trademark portfolios across borders. As global commerce continues to evolve, so too must the strategies businesses use to protect their intellectual property. In the next section, we will explore intriguing case studies that highlight the challenges and strategies of international trademark protection in action.

Case Studies: Landmark Trademark Battles

Trademark law is not just theoretical; its application in high-stakes legal battles across various industries highlights its importance and complexity. These landmark cases serve as invaluable lessons for businesses on the potential risks and strategies involved in trademark protection. This section delves into several pivotal trademark disputes that have left a significant mark on legal practices and business strategies worldwide.

Case Study 1: Apple Inc. vs. Apple Corps

One of the most famous trademark disputes involves Apple Inc., the tech giant, and Apple Corps, the music company founded by The Beatles. The contention started in 1978 and spanned several decades, centering on the use of the "Apple" name and logo. Both companies operated in distinct domains until Apple Inc. ventured into music with iTunes, which led to renewed disputes. The resolution came in 2007 when Apple Inc. agreed to pay Apple Corps $500 million for the ownership of all Apple-related trademarks and subsequently licensed certain trademarks back to Apple Corps.

Lesson: This saga underscores the necessity for precise trademark agreements and proactive management of potential industry overlaps as businesses evolve. It also illustrates how settlement can sometimes be more strategic than prolonged litigation.

Case Study 2: Adidas vs. Payless

In a battle to protect its iconic three-stripe design, Adidas took action against Payless Shoesource, accusing it of selling knockoffs that infringed on its trademarked three-stripe design. After a protracted legal fight, in 2008, a court awarded Adidas $305 million, citing clear trademark infringement, although this amount was later reduced to $65 million on appeal.

Lesson: This case highlights the importance of defending trademark rights against similar or imitative products. It demonstrates the power of distinctive design trademarks in the market and the severe financial implications for those found guilty of infringement.

Case Study 3: McDonald's and the "Mc" Prefix Disputes

McDonald's has vigorously defended its trademark, especially its iconic "Mc" prefix, in various global markets. A notable case involved McCurry, a Malaysian restaurant, where McDonald's initially succeeded in litigation but lost on appeal. The Malaysian Supreme Court ruled that "Mc" could not exclusively belong to McDonald's, especially when used in non-competing food categories.

Lesson: This case exemplifies the limits of trademark protection and the importance of understanding cultural and legal nuances in international markets. It also stresses that trademark rights might be interpreted differently across jurisdictions, affecting global branding strategies.

Case Study 4: Google vs. American Blind & Wallpaper Factory

This dispute revolved around Google's practice of selling AdWords ads based on keywords that were also trademarks of other companies. American Blind & Wallpaper Factory claimed that Google's actions allowed competitors to bid on keywords like "American blinds," which they argued infringed on their trademarks. The lawsuit, filed in 2003, settled in 2011, with Google making minor changes to its policies but largely continuing its keyword advertisement practices.

Lesson: The resolution of this case sheds light on the complexities of trademark law in the context of digital advertising and search engine practices. It emphasizes the need for brands to adapt to the evolving digital landscape and consider new forms of consumer interaction and brand exposure.

These case studies from the trademark litigation field offer crucial insights into the dynamics of trademark enforcement and defense. They reveal that while trademarks are powerful tools for brand protection, they also require careful and strategic legal management. For businesses, understanding these precedents is vital for crafting robust trademark strategies that are responsive not only to current legal frameworks but also to evolving market and technological landscapes. By studying these landmark battles, companies can better prepare to protect their brands and navigate the complexities of trademark law.

Quick Tips and Recap

- **Understand the Framework**: Familiarize yourself with key international treaties like the Madrid Protocol, the Paris Convention, and TRIPS to navigate global trademark protection effectively.

- **Research Local Laws**: Before entering a new market, thoroughly research and understand the specific trademark laws and cultural nuances of that country to avoid potential legal pitfalls.

- **Utilize International Systems**: Leverage international systems like the Madrid Protocol for streamlined trademark registration across multiple countries, reducing complexity and managing costs effectively.

- **Engage Local Experts**: Collaborate with local trademark attorneys who specialize in the trademark laws of their respective countries. Their expertise can provide crucial insights and facilitate smoother registration processes and dispute resolution.

- **Monitor and Enforce**: Implement regular monitoring of your trademarks globally to detect any misuse or infringement quickly. Swift action can prevent market confusion and protect your brand integrity.

- **Adapt and Be Flexible**: Be prepared to adapt your trademark strategy based on local market responses and legal feedback. Flexibility can help overcome challenges related to cultural differences and local consumer behavior.

- **Understand Enforcement Limits**: Recognize that trademark enforcement can vary significantly between countries. A strong trademark in one country might not be enforceable in another due to different legal interpretations or standards.

- **Plan for Disputes**: Develop a proactive strategy for handling potential trademark disputes. Understanding historical cases can offer valuable lessons in both what to do and what to avoid.

- **Keep Learning**: Stay updated on changes and developments in international trademark laws, as these can directly impact your global trademark strategy and enforcement options.

CHAPTER THREE

Choosing Your Mark: Strategy and Insight

"Selecting your brand's mark isn't just about aesthetics; it's a strategic decision that encapsulates your mission, vision, and the unique promise you deliver to your customers." — PHILIP KOTLER, MARKETING AUTHOR AND PROFESSOR

Chapter Three, "Choosing Your Mark: Strategy and Insight," is where your trademark journey gets personal. Think of it as the dating scene of the branding world, where first impressions are everything and commitment is not to be taken lightly. Choosing a trademark isn't just about snagging a catchy name; it's about finding the one—the mark that resonates with your audience, distinguishes you from the pack, and sticks in the minds of consumers like a catchy chorus in a summer hit song.

This chapter will guide you through the flirtatious beginnings of brainstorming sessions to the serious relationships of market research. You'll learn how to court public opinion with the finesse of a seasoned suitor and avoid the common pitfalls that lead to legal heartbreak. We'll discuss how to align your business vision with a mark that communicates your message and values at a glance.

But it's not all serious business. Get ready for tales of trademark triumphs and the missteps of well-intentioned blunders that teach valuable lessons. With strategy as your wingman and insight as your compass, you're set to navigate the crowded dance floor of the marketplace and spot the mark that will have everyone talking.

By the end of this chapter, you'll be equipped to select a trademark that not only captures the essence of your brand but also positions it for long-term success in the ever-evolving marketplace. So sharpen your pencils and your wits—it's time to mark your territory in the world of commerce!

Brainstorming Your Trademark

The journey of selecting a trademark begins with brainstorming—a vibrant and imaginative process that serves as the bedrock of your brand's identity. This critical stage combines creativity with strategic insight, aiming to generate a list of potential trademarks that embody your brand's essence, appeal to your audience, and ensure distinctiveness in the market.

Preparing for a Productive Brainstorming Session

1. **Deep Understanding of Your Brand**: Start by thoroughly analyzing your brand's mission, vision, core values, and target audience. Understanding these elements is essential for generating trademark ideas that truly reflect what your brand stands for and how it wishes to be perceived.

2. **Assembling the Right Team**: Bring together a diverse group from across your organization, including members from marketing, product development, and even finance. Each participant brings a unique perspective that can contribute to a more comprehensive set of ideas.

3. **Creating the Right Environment**: Choose a setting that encourages creativity and open communication. Whether it's a quiet room decorated with inspiring imagery or a more informal space that breaks the

traditional office mold, the environment should foster free thinking and comfort.

Effective Brainstorming Techniques

1. **Mind Mapping**: Begin with the central theme of your brand and expand outwards with related words, images, and concepts. This visual approach can spark creativity and lead to innovative ideas that might not surface in a conventional discussion.

2. **Word Association**: This classic creative exercise involves saying or hearing a word and responding with the first word that comes to mind. This can lead to surprising and creative connections that resonate with your brand's identity.

3. **Analyzing Competitors**: Examine the trademarks of competitors to identify gaps and opportunities in the market. Understanding what's already out there can help you pinpoint directions that are both unique and strategic.

4. **Leveraging Foreign Languages**: Sometimes, words from other languages can capture a brand's essence with a flair that English cannot match. Ensure any foreign terms are appropriate and resonate well with your primary audience, checking for any negative or unintended meanings.

5. **SCAMPER Technique**: This creative thinking technique involves Substituting, Combining, Adapting, Modifying, Putting to another use, Eliminating, and Reversing existing ideas. SCAMPER can transform a basic concept into a distinctive and viable trademark.

Filtering and Refining Ideas

1. **Relevance Check**: Evaluate how well each idea aligns with your brand's core attributes. Discard any that fail to encapsulate the brand's essence or could potentially dilute its identity.

2. **Memorability and Simplicity**: Consider whether the potential trademarks are easy to remember and pronounce. A good trademark should be catchy, making a lasting impression on consumers.

3. **Preliminary Trademark Screening**: Use online trademark databases to conduct a preliminary check for existing trademarks that are similar or identical to your ideas. This step can save time and resources by eliminating options that are already in use.

4. **Scalability and Longevity**: Think about how the trademarks might grow along with your brand and adapt to future market changes. Choose marks that are versatile and scalable across different products or services.

Brainstorming for trademarks is an exhilarating phase that sets the foundation for your brand's identity. By utilizing diverse brainstorming techniques and meticulously filtering the outcomes, you can ensure that the selected trademark not only captures the essence and uniqueness of your brand but also positions it for enduring success in the marketplace. Next, we will explore how to evaluate the strength and viability of these brainstormed trademarks, ensuring they are legally defensible and capable of achieving your business objectives.

Evaluating Trademark Strength and Viability

After the creative outburst of brainstorming, the next critical step in the trademark selection process is evaluation. This phase involves assessing the strength and viability of the generated ideas to ensure that they not only resonate with your brand identity but also meet legal standards for protection and are practical for market implementation.

Assessing Trademark Strength

1. **Legal Protectability**: The strength of a trademark is heavily influenced by its ability to be legally protected. Trademarks are categorized based on their inherent strength:

   o **Fanciful or Coined**: These are the strongest types of trademarks because they are invented words with no prior meaning (e.g., "Kodak" or "Xerox").

   o **Arbitrary**: These involve common words used in an unrelated context (e.g., "Apple" for computers), providing strong protection due to their distinctiveness.

33

- o **Suggestive**: These require imagination to connect the mark with the product (e.g., "Netflix"), offering good protection without the need for secondary meaning.

- o **Descriptive**: These directly describe the product or an attribute and can only be protected if they acquire a secondary meaning through extensive and exclusive use.

- o **Generic**: Terms that have become the common name for products or services cannot be protected because they are too common.

2. **Market Differentiation**: Evaluate how well the proposed trademarks distinguish your products from those of competitors. A strong trademark should clearly differentiate your offerings, helping to avoid market confusion and strengthening your brand's positioning.

Viability Assessment

1. **Market Resonance**: Analyze how the proposed trademarks resonate with your target market. This involves consumer perception studies or market testing to gather feedback on how the trademarks are perceived, ensuring they align with consumer expectations and the brand persona.

2. **Cultural Considerations**: Consider the cultural implications of your trademarks, especially if you plan to market your products internationally. Ensure that the trademark does not have negative connotations or inappropriate meanings in other languages and cultures.

3. **Domain Availability**: Check the availability of domain names corresponding to your trademarks. In today's digital marketplace, having a matching or related domain name is crucial for online branding and marketing.

Practical Considerations for Trademark Selection

1. **Longevity and Adaptability**: Consider whether the trademarks can grow and evolve with your brand. Choose trademarks that are flexible enough to encompass future expansions or variations in your product lines.

2. **Visual and Phonetic Appeal**: Evaluate the visual and phonetic appeal of the trademarks. They should be easy to pronounce, spell, and remember. A visually appealing trademark can significantly enhance brand recognition and recall.

3. **Cost Implications**: Consider the costs associated with registering and defending the trademarks. Some trademarks might require more substantial investment in legal protection, especially if they border on the descriptive or are already popular in related fields.

Evaluating the strength and viability of potential trademarks is a multifaceted process that blends legal scrutiny with market strategy. This evaluation not only ensures that the trademarks you choose are legally defensible but also that they are potent tools for market engagement and brand growth. By rigorously assessing each potential trademark against these criteria, you can select a mark that not only captures the essence of your brand but also stands the test of time and competition. In the next section, we will delve deeper into conducting effective market research to further refine your choice of trademark.

Conducting Market Research

Choosing the right trademark is not only a matter of creativity and legal vetting but also requires a deep understanding of market dynamics and consumer preferences. Market research plays a critical role in this process, providing valuable insights into how potential trademarks resonate with target audiences and perform in competitive environments. This section explores the methods and benefits of conducting thorough market research to refine your trademark selection.

Designing Effective Market Research Studies

1. **Define Objectives**: Clearly outline what you aim to learn from the market research. Are you testing the appeal of the trademark, its memorability, or how well it communicates your brand values?

2. **Select Appropriate Research Methods**: Choose the methods that best suit your objectives:

- o **Surveys and Questionnaires**: Collect quantitative data on consumer reactions to proposed trademarks.

- o **Focus Groups**: Gather qualitative insights through guided discussions among target demographic groups.

- o **A/B Testing**: Compare responses to different trademarks in controlled groups to see which performs better in terms of recognition and preference.

3. **Crafting the Research Tools**: Develop research instruments that effectively measure consumer response to your trademarks. Ensure questions are unbiased and structured to elicit clear, actionable insights.

Analyzing Consumer Feedback

1. **Initial Impressions**: Gauge first reactions to the trademark to understand immediate associations and impressions. Initial reactions can be telling about the potential impact of the trademark in the marketplace.

2. **Brand Alignment**: Assess how well each trademark conveys the intended brand message and values. Does the trademark reinforce the brand persona you aim to project?

3. **Memorability and Pronunciation**: Test how easily consumers can recall and pronounce the trademarks. Memorable and easy-to-pronounce trademarks are more likely to stick in consumers' minds.

4. **Cultural Relevance**: Ensure the trademark is appropriate and resonant across all intended markets, paying close attention to cultural nuances and potential misunderstandings.

Utilizing Market Research Data

1. **Data Interpretation**: Analyze the data gathered to discern clear patterns and preferences. Look for statistically significant trends that indicate a strong candidate.

2. **Refinement**: Use the insights gained to refine your trademark choices. This might involve tweaking a trademark based on feedback or even discarding options that did not perform well.

3. **Decision Making**: Integrate the market research findings with legal and creative evaluations to make an informed decision about the best trademark for your brand.

Market research is an indispensable component of the trademark selection process. It ensures that the chosen mark will not only be legally defensible and creatively distinctive but also appealing and relevant to your target market. By methodically collecting and analyzing consumer feedback, you can enhance the likelihood that your trademark will successfully represent and grow your brand in the competitive marketplace. Armed with these insights, you're better prepared to make a strategic decision that aligns with both your brand identity and market opportunities. In the next section, we'll discuss the crucial legal considerations to further ensure that your chosen trademark can thrive without legal impediments.

Navigating Legal Considerations

Selecting a trademark that is both impactful and legally secure is a critical component of brand strategy. This section delves into the legal landscape surrounding trademarks, providing insights into how to navigate these waters effectively. Understanding legal constraints and opportunities can safeguard your brand from potential disputes and strengthen its position in the marketplace.

Comprehensive Trademark Searches

1. **Purpose of Trademark Searches**: Conducting a thorough trademark search is crucial to ensure that your chosen mark is not only unique but also free from potential legal conflicts. These searches can identify existing trademarks that might be similar or identical, potentially leading to legal challenges and market confusion.

2. **Scope of Searches**:

   o **Direct Hits**: Look for exact matches in the relevant trademark databases, including national and international registries.

   o **Similar Marks**: Search for phonetically similar names, visual similarities in logos, and conceptual parallels that could confuse consumers.

o **Industry-Specific Searches**: Focus on your industry to check for marks that, while not identical, could be considered similar enough to cause confusion among your target audience.

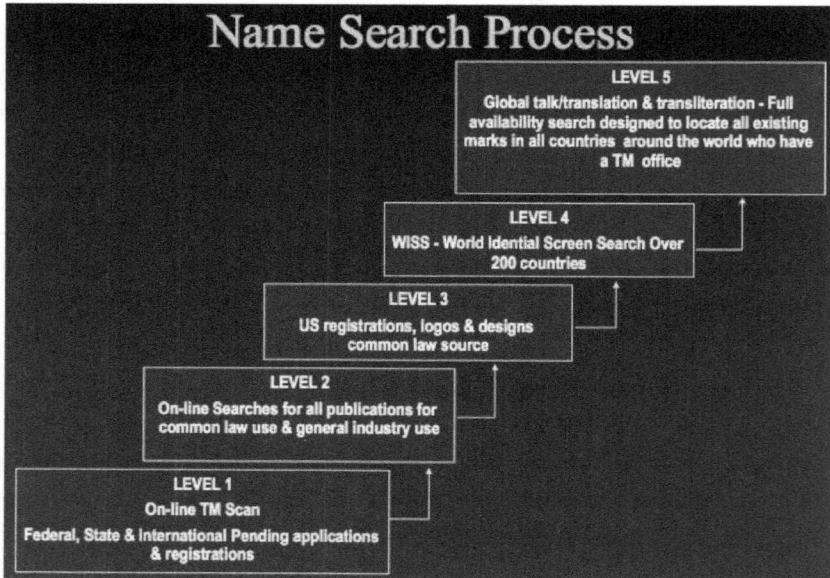

Name Search Process

LEVEL 5
Global talk/translation & transliteration - Full availability search designed to locate all existing marks in all countries around the world who have a TM office

LEVEL 4
WISS - World Idential Screen Search Over 200 countries

LEVEL 3
US registrations, logos & designs common law source

LEVEL 2
On-line Searches for all publications for common law use & general industry use

LEVEL 1
On-line TM Scan
Federal, State & International Pending applications & registrations

Figure 1: Name Search Process

Evaluating Search Results

1. **Risk Assessment**: Assess the risk level of proceeding with a mark that has potential conflicts. Consider factors like geographic reach, industry overlap, and the strength of existing marks.

2. **Legal Opinion**: It is advisable to obtain a legal opinion from a trademark attorney who can interpret search results and provide guidance on the likelihood of registration success and potential infringement risks.

Understanding Trademark Classes and Registration

1. **Classification of Goods and Services**: Trademarks are registered under specific classes that correspond to different types of goods and services.

Understanding which class your goods or services fall into is essential for ensuring comprehensive protection.

2. **Multi-class Registration**: In cases where your brand spans multiple categories, consider registering the trademark in multiple classes to ensure broad protection across different sectors.

Managing Oppositions and Objections

1. **Opposition Proceedings**: Be prepared for potential oppositions to your trademark application. This can occur during the publication phase, where third parties can object to the registration of your mark.

2. **Strategies for Overcoming Oppositions**: Develop strategies to address and negotiate oppositions, which might include altering the mark, negotiating coexistence agreements, or defending the uniqueness and distinctiveness of your mark through legal arguments.

Securing International Trademark Protection

1. **Global Strategy**: If your business operates internationally, consider securing trademark protection in key markets abroad. Utilize international agreements such as the Madrid Protocol for streamlined multinational registration.

2. **Local Legal Nuances**: Each country has its trademark laws and registration processes. Understanding these nuances is crucial for effective international protection and enforcement.

Navigating the legal considerations for trademarks is a complex but necessary process to ensure that your brand is protected against legal challenges. By conducting thorough searches, understanding classification systems, and preparing for potential oppositions, you can secure a trademark that not only resonates with your audience but is also legally robust. With these legal strategies in place, your brand is well-positioned to thrive in competitive markets, both domestic and international. In the next section, we will explore real-world examples of trademark successes and failures, providing valuable lessons and actionable insights.

Use of Trademarks By Others

1. **Trademark Licensing**: Companies may allow business partners to use their trademarks under specific legal conditions:

    o **Validity Acknowledgment**: Partners must acknowledge the validity of trademarks.

    o **Avoid Similar Marks**: Partners agree not to use marks that closely resemble the company's.

    o **Guideline Adherence**: Partners must follow strict usage guidelines.

    o **Quality Control**: Companies retain control over product quality linked to their trademarks to maintain brand standards.

2. **Quality Risks**: Inferior quality products can negatively impact customer perception of the brand.

3. **Exceptions to Approval**:

    o **Incidental Uses**: One-off uses in third-party media are typically not opposed but must adhere to trademark usage rules, including correct symbol use and ownership attribution.

4. **Employee Responsibility**:

    o **Monitor Misuse**: Employees should watch for misuse or similar trademarks that could confuse.

    o **Reporting**: Employees should report unauthorized trademark use to the legal department for necessary action.

In conclusion, the effective management of trademarks is essential for maintaining the integrity and value of a brand. By setting clear legal standards for the use of trademarks, companies ensure that their brand identity is not only recognized but also respected in the marketplace. This involves a strategic approach that includes thorough vetting, strict guidelines, and vigilant monitoring of how trademarks are used by both the company and its partners. Additionally, employee awareness and proactive legal practices play crucial roles in safeguarding against potential infringements that could undermine the brand. By adhering to these practices, companies can protect their trademarks, thereby securing their business identity and promoting long-term success.

▶ A Trade Name License Agreement can be found in the **Appendix**. If you are interested in receiving an electronic copy of this document, please email us at documents@AuthorsDoor.com with the subject line "Request for Trade Name License Agreement." Upon receiving your email, we will promptly send you a Microsoft Word copy of the document. **Disclaimer:** Please note that all agreements are provided for informational purposes only and should not be construed as legal advice. We recommend consulting with a qualified attorney to ensure that any legal documents or decisions are tailored to your specific circumstances.

Learning from Past Trademark Tales

Trademark selection and protection can be a high-stakes endeavor, with significant implications for brand identity and business success. This section delves into historical examples of both successful and problematic trademarks. By examining these real-world cases, you can glean valuable insights into effective trademark strategies and learn critical lessons from others' experiences.

Analyzing Trademark Successes

1. **Nike's Swoosh**: The Nike Swoosh is one of the most recognized symbols worldwide, exemplifying a highly effective trademark strategy. Created in 1971, the Swoosh represents motion and speed, aligning perfectly with Nike's athletic products. Nike's consistent enforcement and marketing around the Swoosh have reinforced its strong association with the brand, making it an emblem of athletic excellence and dynamic performance.

2. **Amazon's Smiling Arrow**: Amazon's logo, featuring a smiling arrow from A to Z, reflects the brand's aim to deliver a wide range of items from A to Z with a customer-friendly approach. This logo not only enhances brand recognition but also communicates the brand's commitment to customer satisfaction, illustrating how a trademark can convey a company's business philosophy and objectives effectively.

3. **Apple's Apple Logo**: Apple's bitten apple logo is universally recognized and has become a symbol of innovation and high-quality electronics. The simplicity of the design and its consistent application across all Apple products help maintain a strong brand presence that is immediately identifiable, demonstrating the power of visual simplicity in trademark design.

Lessons from Trademark Challenges

1. **Kleenex**: Similar to Xerox, Kleenex became a victim of its own success when its brand name started being used generically for any facial tissue. The company had to undertake significant efforts to educate consumers and preserve its trademark, highlighting the risks of a trademark becoming too generic through common usage.

2. **Budweiser**: The Budweiser name has been the subject of one of the longest-running legal battles in trademark history, primarily due to disputes between an American and a Czech brewery. This case illustrates the complexities of trademark disputes in a global market and emphasizes the importance of understanding and navigating international trademark laws.

3. **McDonald's and McCafé**: McDonald's successfully trademarked the "Mc" prefix for its various products, creating a recognizable branding pattern that strengthens its brand identity. However, its attempt to trademark "McCafé" faced opposition from McCafe, a coffee shop in Ireland, showcasing challenges in trademarking names that can be seen as descriptive or non-distinctive.

Extracting Key Lessons

1. **The Importance of Distinctiveness**: Choosing a distinctive and unique trademark is crucial for strong legal protection and brand differentiation. Trademarks should be memorable and not easily confused with existing marks.

2. **The Risk of Genericide**: Brands like Kleenex and Xerox demonstrate the risk of trademarks becoming generic terms. Vigilant marketing and

legal strategies are necessary to maintain the proprietary status of a trademark.

3. **Global Strategy and Local Nuances**: Trademarks must be carefully chosen and protected not just in domestic markets but also internationally. Understanding cultural and linguistic implications can prevent conflicts and enhance brand perception across global markets.

The tales of trademark triumphs and tribulations provide a rich source of knowledge for any brand considering the development and protection of a trademark. These stories underscore the need for a strategic approach to trademark selection, the importance of ongoing protection efforts, and the value of understanding the broader cultural and legal landscape. By learning from these precedents, your brand can navigate the complex waters of trademark registration and protection with greater confidence and strategic acumen.

Quick Tips and Recap

- **Emphasize Distinctiveness**: Always strive for a unique and distinctive trademark that stands out in the marketplace and is eligible for strong legal protection.

- **Conduct Thorough Research**: Perform comprehensive trademark searches to ensure your chosen mark doesn't infringe on existing trademarks and is legally defensible.

- **Understand Your Audience**: Use market research to gauge how your target audience perceives potential trademarks, ensuring alignment with consumer expectations and brand identity.

- **Consider Cultural Implications**: Be aware of cultural sensitivities and linguistic meanings of your trademark, especially if you plan to market your products globally.

- **Monitor Market Trends**: Stay informed about industry trends to ensure your trademark remains relevant and effective in attracting consumer attention.

- **Seek Legal Advice**: Consult with trademark attorneys to navigate the registration process, handle legal complexities, and protect against potential infringements.

- **Prepare for Opposition**: Anticipate and prepare for possible opposition to your trademark registration, and have a strategy in place to address challenges.

- **Evaluate Long-Term Viability**: Choose a trademark that can grow with your company and remain relevant as your market evolves.

- **Learn from Others**: Study successful and unsuccessful trademarks to understand effective strategies and common pitfalls in trademark selection and protection.

- **Secure Matching Domains**: When possible, secure domain names that match or closely relate to your chosen trademark to strengthen your online presence.

By following these tips, you can effectively navigate the complexities of choosing and protecting a trademark, ensuring it supports your brand's growth and market success.

Navigating the Trademark Registration Process

"Registering a trademark is like planting a flag in your market space—
it declares your presence and protects your territory."
— SATYA NADELLA, CEO OF MICROSOFT

Chapter Four, "Navigating the Trademark Registration Process," is essentially the obstacle course of the trademark world—fraught with hurdles, paperwork sprints, and the occasional legal pitfall. This isn't just a stroll through bureaucratic red tape; it's an adventure, a strategic game where knowledge and precision are your best tools.

Here, we'll turn the complex maze of trademark registration into a guided tour with flags marking the critical checkpoints. From filling out your initial application to tackling the nuances of classifying your goods and services, this chapter treats the trademark process as a treasure map, leading you to the X that marks your brand's protection.

Expect to dive deep into the intricacies of the registration process with anecdotes that highlight both triumphs and cautionary tales. We'll explore how to artfully dodge common missteps that could delay your registration or weaken your legal stance. Each section is designed to equip you with insider tips to streamline your journey, making the convoluted seem concise.

By the end of this chapter, you'll not only understand the 'whats' and 'hows' of registering your trademark but also appreciate the 'whys' behind each step. So grab your gear and prepare to navigate the twists and turns of trademark registration—it's time to secure your brand's identity with the finesse of a seasoned explorer!

Preparing for Trademark Registration

Before embarking on the trademark registration journey, meticulous preparation is essential. This foundational step not only streamlines the subsequent application process but also significantly enhances the likelihood of securing your trademark rights effectively. This section outlines the critical preparatory steps that are vital to ensure a robust application, thereby protecting your brand's identity and legal standing.

Importance of Comprehensive Trademark Search

1. **Purpose of Trademark Searches**: Conducting a detailed trademark search is crucial in identifying any existing trademarks that may conflict with yours. This step is instrumental in avoiding potential legal disputes and ensuring that your proposed trademark is unique and registrable.

2. **Scope of Searches**:

   o **Direct Hit Search**: This involves checking for exact matches in the trademark databases, including national and international registers.

   o **Similarity Search**: Beyond exact matches, this search looks for trademarks that are phonetically similar or conceptually related to your proposed mark, which could be grounds for rejection.

o **Industry-Specific Search**: Focusing searches within your industry is vital as it provides insight into prevalent naming conventions and potential conflicts within your direct competitive landscape.

3. **Professional Search Services**: While basic searches can be conducted using online trademark databases, engaging with a professional, such as a trademark attorney or a specialized search firm, can provide a deeper analysis and identify potential legal obstacles that might not be apparent from a preliminary search.

Identifying Your Market and Classifying Your Goods/Services

1. **Market Definition**: Define the geographical and demographic characteristics of your market. Understanding where your brand will operate and who your customers are helps tailor your trademark for maximum protection and relevance.

2. **Classification of Goods and Services**: Trademarks need to be registered under specific classes that correspond to different types of goods and services. Proper classification is crucial as it directly impacts the scope of trademark protection:

   o **Single Class Applications**: Suitable for brands with a narrow product line or service offering.

   o **Multi-Class Applications**: Necessary for businesses with diverse products or services, ensuring comprehensive protection across different categories.

Gathering Required Documentation

1. **Owner Information**: Detailed information about the trademark owner is necessary, whether it's an individual entrepreneur or a corporate entity. This includes identification details and legal status.

2. **Mark Representation**: How you represent your trademark in the application affects how you can legally enforce your trademark rights:

- o **Standard Character Mark**: For text-only trademarks without claim to any particular font, style, or color.

- o **Stylized/Design Mark**: Involves specific graphic elements or stylization.

- o **Sound Mark**: Includes audio elements that need to be represented in a specific format.

3. **Description of Goods/Services**: Providing a precise and comprehensive description of the goods or services to be associated with the trademark is critical. This description must conform to the accepted nomenclature of the registering authority.

4. **Specimen of Use**: If the trademark is already in use, you must submit a specimen showing how the mark is used in commerce. This could include photographs of the product, screenshots of websites, or marketing materials where the trademark is prominently displayed.

Thorough preparation is the cornerstone of a successful trademark registration process. By conducting an extensive trademark search, correctly identifying your market and product classifications, and gathering all requisite documentation, you can significantly enhance the efficacy and speed of the trademark registration process. Well-prepared applicants are more likely to navigate the process without substantial legal hurdles, securing their brand's identity effectively. Next, we will delve into the specifics of filing your trademark application, ensuring every detail is meticulously covered to protect your intellectual property rights.

Internal Trademark Application Form

Once a suitable "candidate" trademark is selected, the next step in the trademark acquisition process is to fill out an internal trademark application form. This form should be designed to collect all necessary information to support the rationale for adopting the new trademark, aiming to streamline the review and approval process by management. It should detail the proposed use, potential markets, and any anticipated challenges, ensuring that all legal and strategic aspects are considered.

This comprehensive approach facilitates quicker and more informed management decisions regarding the trademark's adoption.

INTERNAL NEW TRADEMARK APPLICATION FORM AND INSTRUCTIONS

New Trademark Application Form

Application number

Date

1. Trademark requested: _____

2. Alternative trademarks, if any: _____
   (If a logo and/or distinctive print style are described, please illustrate on separate piece of paper and attached.)

3. Name of requestor: _____
   Title: _____   Department: _____
   Telephone: _____   Mail stop: _____

4. Reason for requesting this trademark: _____

5. Goods or services with which trademark will be used: _____

6. Date of anticipated first use of trademark: _____

7. Countries of intended trademark use: United States: ☐ Yes   ☐ No
   Others: _____

8. Other comments or relevant information: _____

9. Trademark illustration (from part 1.)

Figure 2: Internal Trademark Application Form

10. Signatures		
Signature of requestor	Date	
Signature of Vice President	Date	

Trademark Committee:	Trademark Search	☐ Yes	☐ No
	U.S. Registration	☐ Yes	☐ No
	Foreign Registration	☐ Yes	☐ No

Instructions for Completing the Company Trademark Application Form

1. Carefully type or print the trademark being requested and list any alternate trademarks in exactly the style, form and spelling desired. Please pay special attention to the use of capital letters, spaces, hyphens, slashes, etc. If a logo and/or distinctive script are desired, an accurate pictorial representation should be made either on the space provided in the application form or on a separate blank sheet of paper which should be attached to the Application Form.

2. Fill in all the requestor contact information.

3. Briefly state the reasons for requesting this new trademark: such as, "to support marketing efforts for new product."

4. Identify the specific products or services with which the proposed trademark will be used. Also, give the anticipated date of first sale of the products or services (including date of first "beta site" shipments). This date will be important in deciding whether or not to register the mark under the federal "intent to use" trademark registration provisions.

5. Indicate the countries into which the products or services will be marketed and/or sold in volume.

6. Provide any additional information concerning the new trademark that you feel is relevant, such as specifically recommending certain foreign registrations or pointing out a need for urgent action due to anticipated use of the mark by others.

7. Please sign and date the Application Form on its reverse side and have it approved and signed by your reporting Vice President.

8. Please submit the completed Application Form to your legal counsel. If you should have any questions concerning the completion of this form (or its status after submission) please call the intellectual property counsel for assistance.

Figure 3: Internal Trademark Application Form

The application form should be completed with precision and detail as it is typically reviewed by a trademark committee for formal approval. Given the potential delays before final authorization—particularly if a trademark search or federal "intent to use" registration is involved—it is prudent to submit the application at least sixty days before the planned introduction of a new product. If a "candidate" trademark is deemed unregistrable due to prior use or rejected for other reasons, additional time must be allowed to complete another trademark approval cycle before launching the product.

To streamline the approval process for a product or service-related trademark, applicants should consider listing one or two alternative marks on the application form. The unpredictability of trademark searches and the vast number of existing federal and common law trademarks mean that the initial choice may not be available.

This same application form should also be utilized when naming subsidiary businesses of the company. While not exactly the same, corporate name trademarks face many similar legal and business considerations as product trademarks. Furthermore, the form should be employed for seeking foreign registrations or expanding U.S. registrations of existing company trademarks. It is also useful for formally discontinuing or abandoning marks that are no longer in use by the company.

Filing Your Trademark Application

Filing a trademark application is a pivotal stage in securing legal protection for your brand identity. This step demands careful attention to detail and adherence to specific procedural requirements to ensure a smooth process and successful outcome. This section provides a comprehensive guide on how to navigate the filing process effectively, highlighting key considerations and common pitfalls to avoid.

Understanding the Application Process

1. **Choosing the Right Form**: It's essential to select the appropriate application form based on your trademark usage:

- o **Use-Based Application**: Choose this if your trademark is already in commercial use. You will need to provide evidence of use, such as dates and examples of the mark as used in commerce.

- o **Intent-to-Use Application**: Select this option if you intend to use the trademark in the future. This allows you to reserve the mark before it is actually used, which is critical in securing your rights ahead of actual deployment.

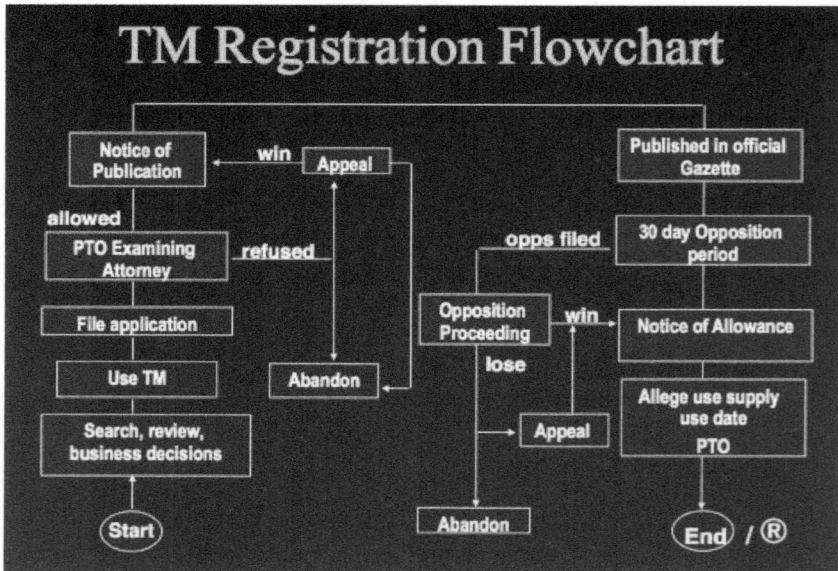

Figure 4: TM Registration Flowchart

2. **Completing the Application**: The application must be filled out meticulously. Key sections usually include:

- o **Owner Information**: This includes the name, address, and type of legal entity owning the trademark. Ensure accuracy as this information is crucial for future correspondence and legal proceedings.

- o **Mark Information**: Describe and depict the trademark exactly as it is used or intended to be used. If your trademark includes design elements, you may need to submit a professionally prepared drawing.

- o **Description of Goods/Services**: Enumerate the specific goods or services associated with the trademark, categorized according to the international classification of goods and services. Accuracy here is crucial for defining the scope of trademark protection.

- o **Declaration**: Most jurisdictions require a declaration affirming the truthfulness of the information and the applicant's belief in their right to use the trademark.

3. **Submitting the Application**: Online submissions are preferred for their ease and efficiency. Ensure that all supporting documents, such as images of the trademark and specimens showing usage, comply with the submission guidelines regarding format, size, and quality.

Navigating Common Mistakes

1. **Incorrect Classification**: One of the most common errors is misclassifying goods or services, which can delay processing or result in refusal. Verify that your classification aligns with the official trademark office guidelines.

2. **Vague Descriptions**: Ambiguity in describing your goods or services can lead to broad and unenforceable protection. Be precise and detailed to ensure the scope of protection is clear and enforceable.

3. **Inadequate Specimens**: The specimens provided must clearly depict the trademark as used in commerce. Inadequate specimens might not demonstrate the mark's use effectively, leading to challenges in proving the legitimacy of your claim.

Tips for Smooth Submission

1. **Double-Check Details**: Before submission, review all details meticulously to ensure there are no errors or omissions that could lead to delays or rejections.

2. **Monitor Submission Deadlines**: Keep track of any deadlines, especially if filing an intent-to-use application, as there are specific timelines for proving use of the trademark in commerce.

3. **Seek Professional Help**: While not mandatory, consulting with a trademark attorney can provide valuable insights, especially in navigating complex legal nuances or responding to office actions.

Filing your trademark application correctly is crucial for securing your brand's legal protection. This process, while complex, can be managed effectively with thorough preparation and attention to detail. By adhering to the guidelines and being proactive about potential pitfalls, you can enhance the likelihood of a successful trademark registration. In the following section, we will delve into how to address office actions and other formal communications from the trademark office, ensuring you are equipped to advance your registration to final approval.

Responding to Office Actions

After submitting your trademark application, it's not uncommon to receive an "office action" from the trademark office. This is an official communication that raises issues or requests additional information before the application can proceed. Understanding how to effectively respond to office actions is crucial for advancing your trademark registration towards approval.

Types of Office Actions

1. **Non-substantive (or Procedural) Office Actions**: These typically address minor errors or omissions in your application, such as unclear goods/services descriptions, improper specimen, or missing information. Non-substantive actions generally require straightforward corrections or clarifications.

2. **Substantive Office Actions**: More complex, these involve legal issues related to the trademark itself, such as likelihood of confusion with existing trademarks, descriptiveness, or issues concerning the distinctiveness of the mark. Addressing substantive office actions often requires a detailed legal argument and additional supporting evidence.

Preparing Effective Responses

1. **Understanding the Concerns**: Carefully review the office action to understand fully the concerns raised. Determine whether the action is procedural or substantive and tailor your response accordingly.

2. **Gathering Information and Evidence**: For non-substantive issues, gather the required information or correct the errors noted. For substantive issues, you may need to compile evidence such as market surveys, declarations of distinctiveness, or documentation of your mark's acquired secondary meaning.

3. **Drafting Your Response**: Your response should be clear, precise, and supported by legal precedents or trademark law where necessary. Address each issue raised by the trademark examiner point by point.

   o **For non-substantive responses**, ensure that all requested clarifications or corrections are included.

   o **For substantive responses**, construct a strong legal argument to overcome objections such as likelihood of confusion or descriptiveness. This might include evidence of your trademark's unique use in commerce or data showing consumer recognition and association of the mark with your goods or services.

4. **Consulting with a Trademark Attorney**: Particularly for substantive office actions, consider consulting with a trademark attorney who can provide legal expertise and help in crafting a persuasive response. An attorney can also help navigate complex legal arguments and ensure that your response maximizes the chances of overcoming the examiner's objections.

Timeliness and Follow-up

1. **Adhering to Deadlines**: Respond promptly to office actions. The U.S. Patent and Trademark Office (USPTO), for example, typically requires a response within six months from the mailing date of the office action. Failing to respond by the deadline can result in the abandonment of your trademark application.

2. **Continuous Monitoring**: After submitting your response, continue to monitor the status of your application through the trademark office's online system. This will inform you of any further actions, additional requirements, or the decision regarding your application.

Responding effectively to office actions is a critical component of the trademark registration process. Whether addressing simple procedural issues or engaging with more complex substantive matters, a well-prepared response can significantly influence the outcome of your application. By understanding the issues, crafting thorough and legally sound responses, and adhering to response deadlines, you can navigate this phase successfully and move closer to securing your trademark protection.

Monitoring and Managing Your Trademark Application

Once you've submitted your trademark application and responded to any office actions, the next crucial steps involve monitoring the progress of your application and managing it through to registration. This phase requires vigilance and strategic oversight to ensure that your application moves smoothly through the review process and that your trademark rights are secured effectively upon registration.

Monitoring Your Trademark Status

1. **Tracking Application Progress**: Regularly check the status of your trademark application using the trademark office's online system. This will help you stay informed of any updates, additional requirements, or decisions made regarding your application.

2. **Understanding Trademark Office Timelines**: Familiarize yourself with the typical timelines of the trademark registration process. Knowing what to expect in terms of review times can help you manage your expectations and prepare for subsequent steps.

Managing Publication and Opposition

1. **Publication for Opposition**: If your application is approved by the examiner, it will be published in an official trademark journal or gazette. This publication phase allows third parties to view your trademark and potentially file an opposition if they believe it infringes on their rights.

2. **Handling Oppositions**: Should your trademark face opposition, it's crucial to respond appropriately. This may involve negotiating with the opposing party or defending your trademark's registrability through legal arguments. Having a trademark attorney can be particularly valuable in navigating opposition proceedings.

Post-Registration Management

1. **Maintaining Trademark Rights**: After your trademark is registered, you must maintain the registration by fulfilling specific requirements. These include submitting periodic declarations of continued use and renewing the registration at intervals prescribed by the trademark office.

2. **Monitoring for Infringement**: Continuously monitor the market for any unauthorized use of your trademark. Early detection of infringement allows for timely legal action to enforce your rights and prevent dilution of your brand.

3. **Expanding Trademark Protection**: As your business grows, consider registering your trademark in additional classes or countries to expand your legal protection. Keeping your trademark portfolio updated is essential for comprehensive brand protection.

Utilizing Technology and Professional Services

1. **Leverage Technology**: Use trademark monitoring services that can alert you to new applications that might be similar to yours, publications for

opposition, and potential infringements. These services use algorithms to scan multiple databases, helping to simplify the monitoring process.

2. **Engaging with Professionals**: Maintaining a relationship with a trademark attorney can provide ongoing support for managing your trademark. Professionals can offer strategic advice on expansion, handle legal disputes, and assist with international registrations.

Monitoring and managing your trademark application is a dynamic and continuous process that extends beyond the initial registration. By actively overseeing your trademark's status, responding to legal challenges, and maintaining your registration, you ensure that your trademark remains a strong and enforceable asset for your brand. In the next section, we will delve deeper into strategies for dealing with oppositions and other legal challenges to safeguard your trademark rights effectively.

Dealing with Oppositions and Legal Challenges

The path to trademark registration can sometimes encounter legal challenges, including oppositions from third parties who believe your trademark infringes on their rights. Effectively managing these oppositions is crucial for securing your trademark registration and protecting your brand's integrity. This section provides a roadmap for navigating oppositions and other legal hurdles that may arise during the trademark process.

Understanding the Grounds for Opposition

1. **Likelihood of Confusion**: One of the most common grounds for opposition, where a party believes your trademark is too similar to theirs, potentially causing confusion among consumers.

2. **Descriptiveness or Genericness**: If your trademark is deemed too descriptive of the goods/services it represents, or if it falls into common use (generic), third parties may challenge its registrability.

3. **Prior Rights**: Opposers may claim that they have prior rights to the trademark, either through earlier use in commerce or previous registrations.

Preparing to Respond to an Opposition

1. **Review and Assess the Claim**: Thoroughly review the notice of opposition to understand the specific grounds cited. Evaluate the strength of the opposing party's claim and your potential responses.

2. **Gather Evidence**: Compile evidence that supports your case. This may include proof of your trademark's distinctiveness, the differences between your goods/services and those of the opposer, or documentation of your prior use of the trademark in commerce.

3. **Legal Representation**: Consider hiring a trademark attorney who specializes in opposition proceedings. An experienced lawyer can provide invaluable guidance, help prepare your response, and represent you in proceedings before the trademark office.

Strategies for Handling Oppositions

1. **Negotiation and Settlement**: Often, oppositions can be resolved through negotiation and settlement. This might involve agreeing to certain limitations on your trademark use, such as restricting the geographical area or product lines.

2. **Filing a Response**: If negotiation isn't feasible or desirable, you will need to file a formal response to the opposition. This response should address each point raised by the opposer and lay out your legal arguments and supporting evidence.

3. **Trial Proceedings**: If the opposition progresses to a trial phase, be prepared to present your case through written submissions and, potentially, oral arguments. The proceedings might involve testimony from witnesses, experts, and further submission of evidence.

Managing Legal Costs

1. **Budget for Legal Expenses**: Opposition proceedings can be costly. Budgeting for potential legal expenses from the outset of your trademark application can help manage financial risks.

2. **Consider Alternative Dispute Resolution**: In some cases, mediation or arbitration can be a cost-effective alternative to trial proceedings, leading to a faster resolution.

Dealing with oppositions and legal challenges is an integral part of the trademark registration process. Successfully navigating these challenges requires a clear understanding of trademark law, a strategic approach to dispute resolution, and effective legal representation. By adequately preparing and engaging in these battles wisely, you can secure and maintain the protection of your trademark, reinforcing the strength and value of your brand in the marketplace. In the upcoming sections, we will explore further aspects of trademark management, ensuring comprehensive brand protection.

Quick Tips and Recap

- **Conduct a Thorough Trademark Search**: Before filing, ensure a comprehensive search is done to avoid future legal complications and oppositions.

- **Understand the Forms and Requirements**: Familiarize yourself with the different forms and specific requirements for a use-based or intent-to-use application to ensure accurate submission.

- **Double-check Application Details**: Pay careful attention to every detail in your application, particularly the description of goods/services and the trademark representation.

- **Respond Promptly to Office Actions**: Address office actions thoroughly and within the given deadlines to avoid delays or rejections of your trademark application.

- **Prepare for Publication and Opposition Phases**: Be proactive and prepared to defend your trademark during the publication phase; consider strategies for negotiation or legal defense if faced with opposition.

- **Maintain and Monitor Your Trademark**: After registration, regularly monitor the use of your trademark in the marketplace and renew your registration as required to maintain its protection.

- **Utilize Professional Services**: Consider hiring a trademark attorney for guidance throughout the application process, especially when dealing with complex legal issues or oppositions.

- **Keep Documentation Organized**: Maintain all records and correspondence related to your trademark application and registration. This documentation can be vital in addressing future legal challenges.

- **Stay Informed on Trademark Laws**: Keep up-to-date with any changes in trademark law that could affect your registration or the protection of your trademark.

- **Plan Financially for Potential Disputes**: Budget for potential costs involved in opposition proceedings or other legal disputes to ensure you can defend and maintain your trademark rights effectively.

By following these tips, you can navigate the trademark registration process more confidently and efficiently, securing the protection needed to safeguard your brand's identity in the marketplace.

CHAPTER FIVE

Overcoming Obstacles in
Trademark Registration

"Securing a trademark is not merely a formality; it's a declaration of
your brand's uniqueness in the marketplace. Handle it with the same
attention to detail as you would any major business initiative."
— TIM COOK, CEO OF APPLE

A h, the thrilling world of trademark registration—where the brave venture to
stake their claims in the wilds of commerce and creativity. If you thought
the journey to branding nirvana was all smooth sailing, think again! Here, you'll
encounter more hurdles than a track meet in a rabbit warren. But fear not, for with
a dash of wit and a sprinkle of perseverance, you can navigate this bureaucratic
labyrinth.

First up, there's the "Name Game." It sounds fun, doesn't it? Almost like a party
game until you realize that every other entrepreneur has also been invited. Finding

a unique name that hasn't already been claimed is akin to finding a polite conversation at a political rally. You'll search high and low, brainstorm day and night, and just when you've nailed the perfect moniker—you guessed it—someone else owns it. Back to the drawing board!

Once you've successfully picked a name that's both catchy and legally available, welcome to the waiting room. Patience is not just a virtue here; it's a requirement. The waiting period for your trademark application to process is the perfect time to take up new hobbies, like knitting or perhaps a brief study of Latin. Yes, it can be that long.

Just when you thought you were in the clear, enter objections and oppositions. Think of it as the universe testing how much you really want your trademark. It's like telling your friends you're starting a diet, then having them offer you cake at every turn. You'll need to defend your claim, sharpen your arguments, and perhaps sweet-talk a bureaucrat or two.

And don't forget the fine print. Reading through the terms and conditions of trademark registration is like reading "War and Peace" on a smartphone screen. But within those endless pages lies the path to protection—skim at your peril. Every clause is a potential trap for the unwary, and ignorance is definitely not bliss.

But remember, with every challenge comes an opportunity. Each obstacle on your path to registering a trademark is just a stepping stone to building a brand that stands the test of time. Navigate these waters with your wits about you, and soon enough, you'll plant your flag on the peak of Brand Mountain—visible for all in the marketplace to see and respect!

The Challenge of Selecting a Unique Name

Choosing a unique and compelling trademark in today's crowded marketplace is akin to navigating a minefield filled with legal and competitive challenges. A distinctive trademark does more than just identify your business—it encapsulates your brand's essence, setting the tone for interactions in the marketplace and establishing a legal fortification against infringement. This section explores the complexities of finding a unique and legally sound trademark, providing you with strategies to surmount these initial hurdles effectively.

The Critical Need for Uniqueness in Trademarks

1. **Legal Imperatives**: A unique trademark is not merely preferable but essential for legal protection. Trademarks that closely resemble existing ones risk rejection by trademark offices and can lead to legal disputes if perceived as infringing on established rights.

2. **Brand Impact**: A distinctive trademark can significantly enhance your brand's visibility and memorability in the marketplace, fostering consumer loyalty and distinguishing your offerings from those of competitors.

Developing Creative Strategies for Brainstorming Unique Names

1. **Broad Conceptualization**: Initiate the brainstorming process with expansive thinking. Reflect on your brand's mission, vision, core values, and the emotions you wish to evoke in your audience. These elements are the seeds from which compelling trademark ideas can sprout.

2. **Creative Techniques to Spark Ideas**:

   o **Alliteration and Rhyme**: These linguistic tools enhance memorability (e.g., PayPal, Dunkin' Donuts).

   o **Metaphors and Symbolism**: Use powerful imagery or metaphors that resonate with your brand's ethos (e.g., Red Bull).

   o **Foreign Languages**: Incorporate non-English words to add intrigue and flair to your brand, ensuring they carry positive connotations and are pronounceable by your target audience.

3. **Utilizing Digital Tools**: Maximize online resources for inspiration and validation:

   o **Name Generators**: These tools can spark creative ideas that might not have been immediately obvious.

- o **Thesauruses and Dictionaries**: Expand your vocabulary and find synonyms that might offer a fresh take on standard industry terms.

- o **Domain and Social Media Availability Checks**: Ensure the potential trademark is available as a domain and on key social media platforms to maintain brand consistency online.

Conducting Comprehensive Trademark Searches

1. **Initial Online Searches**: Use free online tools from intellectual property offices to perform preliminary searches for direct hits and closely related trademarks.

2. **Engaging Professional Services**: For a deeper analysis, employ trademark attorneys or professional search firms who can conduct thorough searches and evaluate the likelihood of registration success based on current trademark law and similar active trademarks.

3. **Interpreting Search Results**:

   - o **Direct Matches**: These are usually disqualifying as they indicate a trademark is already in use.

   - o **Similar Marks**: Evaluate the risk of confusion, considering factors such as the relatedness of goods/services, visual and phonetic similarities, and market segments.

Adapting to Challenges

1. **Flexibility and Resilience**: Be prepared to pivot if your first-choice names encounter legal barriers. Maintaining flexibility throughout the naming process is key to overcoming challenges without significant setbacks.

2. **Iterative Naming Process**: View the naming process as iterative, where each round of feedback and search results refines and hones your trademark choice, enhancing its strength and marketability.

Navigating the complexities of selecting a unique trademark name requires a balanced approach of creativity, strategic thinking, and meticulous legal vetting.

By employing diverse brainstorming techniques, leveraging digital tools for preliminary checks, and understanding the nuances of trademark searches, you can craft a trademark that not only captivates your audience but also stands on solid legal ground. This foundational step paves the way for building a robust and distinctive brand identity in the competitive business landscape.

Navigating the Waiting Game

Patience is more than a virtue in the trademark registration process; it's a necessity. Once your application is filed, the waiting period begins, often stretching for months or even longer. This section explores the typical timeline you'll encounter after submitting your trademark application and offers strategic advice on using this time effectively.

Understanding the Timeline

1. **Initial Processing**: After submission, your application will undergo an initial review to ensure it meets basic filing requirements. This phase typically takes a few weeks but can vary depending on the workload of the trademark office.

2. **Examination Period**: If your application passes initial review, a trademark examiner will assess it for substantive issues, such as potential conflicts with existing trademarks or issues with the descriptiveness of the mark. This examination can take several months, during which the examiner may issue an office action requiring your response to specific concerns.

3. **Publication for Opposition**: If your trademark overcomes all hurdles in the examination phase, it will be published in an official trademark journal. This publication initiates a period (usually 30 days in the U.S.) during which third parties can oppose the registration of your trademark if they believe it infringes on their rights.

4. **Final Steps and Registration**: If no oppositions are filed, or if you successfully overcome any challenges, your trademark will proceed to

registration. This final approval can take a few weeks to a couple of months, culminating in the issuance of a registration certificate.

Making the Most of the Waiting Period

1. **Prepare Your Brand Strategy**: Use the waiting time to refine your marketing strategies and prepare for the launch or expansion of your brand. Developing marketing materials, planning promotional campaigns, and establishing distribution channels can be time-consuming tasks that fit well during this period.

2. **Monitor the Market**: Keep an eye on the marketplace for any new trademarks that might conflict with yours. Early detection of potential infringements can be crucial for taking timely action once your trademark is registered.

3. **Educate Yourself and Your Team**: This downtime is ideal for educating yourself and your staff about the importance of trademark protection and the proper use of your mark. Understanding how to correctly use the trademark symbols (™ for unregistered and ® for registered marks), and the implications of improper use can prevent costly mistakes.

4. **Legal Preparations**: If your trademark is likely to face opposition or if you anticipate needing to enforce your trademark rights, consult with your attorney to prepare your legal strategies in advance. This preparation can include gathering evidence to support the distinctiveness and prior use of your trademark.

While the waiting period in the trademark registration process can be lengthy, viewing this time as an opportunity rather than a setback can significantly benefit your brand. By actively preparing your market entry and legal strategies, you can ensure that once your trademark is registered, you are ready to maximize its value immediately. Additionally, staying proactive during this period can help mitigate potential challenges, ensuring a smoother path to securing your brand's identity.

Handling Objections and Oppositions

The trademark registration process often involves navigating through objections raised by the trademark office and oppositions filed by third parties. These hurdles can be critical tests of your trademark's viability and your preparedness to defend it. This section guides you through the strategies for addressing these challenges effectively, ensuring your application has the best chance of success.

Understanding Office Actions

1. **Identifying the Types of Office Actions**: Office actions can be either non-final or final. Non-final actions typically request additional information or clarification, while final actions may reject the trademark application based on more substantive grounds.

2. **Common Reasons for Office Actions**:

    o **Likelihood of Confusion**: The examiner may believe your trademark is too similar to an existing one, potentially confusing consumers.

    o **Descriptiveness and Lack of Distinctiveness**: If your mark directly describes your products or services or lacks distinctiveness, it may not qualify for trademark protection.

    o **Improper Specification of Goods/Services**: The description of goods or services may be too broad, unclear, or incorrectly classified.

Crafting Effective Responses

1. **Timeliness**: Respond promptly to office actions. Typically, you have six months to respond, but timely replies can keep your application process moving smoothly.

2. **Thoroughness and Precision**: Address each issue raised by the examiner meticulously. Provide clear, concise, and legally sound arguments and evidence to overcome the objections.

3. **Seek Professional Help**: Engaging a trademark attorney can significantly enhance the quality of your responses. Experienced legal

counsel can provide strategic advice, especially when crafting arguments against substantive legal challenges.

Managing Opposition Proceedings

1. **Understanding Opposition Grounds**: Oppositions can be based on various grounds, including prior rights, likelihood of confusion, or the claim that your trademark might dilute the distinctiveness of an existing mark.

2. **Navigating the Opposition Process**:

   o **Preparation**: Gather evidence supporting your trademark's distinctiveness and your right to use it. This may include data on consumer recognition, advertising expenditure, and sales volume.

   o **Negotiation and Mediation**: Before the conflict escalates to a formal proceeding, consider negotiating with the opposer. Mediation can be a cost-effective way to resolve disputes without lengthy litigation.

   o **Formal Response**: If negotiations fail, you will need to formally respond to the opposition. This involves submitting a defense detailing why your trademark should be registered despite the claims against it.

Post-Resolution Actions

1. **Continued Vigilance**: After overcoming an office action or opposition, continue to monitor for any further legal challenges and maintain the integrity and distinctiveness of your trademark.

2. **Implementing Learnings**: Use the experience to refine your trademark strategy. This might involve more proactive searches for potential conflicts before adopting new marks or adjusting how you describe your goods/services in future applications.

Handling objections and oppositions during the trademark registration process requires a strategic and informed approach. By understanding the reasons behind these challenges and preparing comprehensive responses, you can safeguard your application and strengthen your brand's legal protection. Moreover, navigating these hurdles successfully not only secures your trademark but also enhances your understanding of the legal landscape, better preparing you for future brand expansions.

Deciphering the Fine Print

Understanding the legal complexities of trademark registration is crucial for ensuring that your trademark rights are secure and enforceable. This section delves into the often overlooked but critically important fine print in trademark registration documentation. Deciphering these details can prevent future legal complications and strengthen your brand's protection.

Importance of Understanding Registration Terms

1. **Legally Binding Details**: The registration documents contain terms and conditions that are legally binding. Understanding every clause is crucial to avoid breaches that could invalidate your trademark or expose you to legal risks.

2. **Scope of Protection**: The fine print outlines the precise scope of protection afforded by your trademark, including any limitations. Knowing these limits is essential for enforcing your rights effectively.

Key Areas of Focus in Trademark Documentation

1. **Goods and Services Description**: Pay close attention to how your goods or services are described. Ambiguities or inaccuracies in this section can limit the effectiveness of your trademark protection or lead to disputes over the scope of your trademark rights.

2. **Geographical Limitations**: Some trademarks may have geographical restrictions. Understanding these limitations is vital for planning your market expansion and avoiding infringement in regions not covered by your registration.

3. **Renewal and Maintenance Clauses**: Be aware of the conditions and deadlines for renewing your trademark and maintaining its registration. Missing these deadlines can result in losing trademark protection.

4. **Use Requirements**: Some jurisdictions require you to actively use the trademark in commerce within a certain period and to continue using it to maintain the registration. Failure to meet these use requirements can lead to cancellation of the trademark.

Strategies for Managing Complex Legal Language

1. **Consultation with a Trademark Attorney**: Given the legal complexities, consulting with a trademark attorney is advisable. They can provide clarity on the legal jargon and implications of the terms in your trademark registration.

2. **Regular Review and Updates**: Trademark laws and regulations can evolve. Regularly reviewing your trademark documentation in light of new legal developments or changes in business operations is crucial to ensuring ongoing compliance and protection.

3. **Training and Knowledge Sharing**: Educate your team, especially those involved in brand management and development, about the critical elements of your trademark registration. This collective understanding can help prevent actions that might inadvertently compromise your trademark.

Deciphering the fine print in your trademark registration documents is not merely a bureaucratic exercise—it's a crucial strategy to protect and leverage your intellectual property effectively. Understanding every detail ensures that you are fully aware of your rights and responsibilities, helping you to avoid legal pitfalls and utilize your trademark to its fullest potential. This proactive approach to understanding trademark law nuances will empower you to navigate the complexities of intellectual property protection and support your brand's longevity and success in the marketplace.

Turning Challenges into Opportunities

In the journey of trademark registration, challenges are not merely obstacles; they are opportunities to enhance your brand's strength and market position. From legal hurdles to opposition from competitors, each challenge encountered can serve as a catalyst for strategic growth and innovation. This section explores how to transform potential setbacks in the trademark process into powerful opportunities for your brand.

Refining Your Approach Through Rejections

1. **Analyzing Feedback**: Every rejection or office action provides crucial feedback about the aspects of your trademark that may not align with registration standards or may infringe on existing trademarks. Carefully analyze this feedback to understand the underlying issues.

2. **Improving Trademark Design**: Use the insights gained from official feedback to refine your trademark. This might involve altering the design, changing the trademark's wording, or more clearly defining its application to better meet registration criteria. Each adjustment not only increases the likelihood of approval but also enhances the trademark's distinctiveness and marketability.

3. **Building Legal Expertise**: The process of addressing rejections and complying with trademark laws sharpens your legal understanding. This knowledge is invaluable, making your business more adept at navigating future intellectual property challenges and protecting your assets more effectively.

Harnessing Opposition for Market Insight

1. **Understanding Competitor Strategies**: Opposition to your trademark registration often reveals competitors' views and strategies regarding market entry and brand positioning. Analyzing the basis of their opposition can provide deep insights into competitive dynamics and potential market threats.

2. **Strategic Re-positioning**: Leverage the intelligence gathered from opposition proceedings to fine-tune your brand positioning. This might

involve targeting different market segments, adjusting marketing strategies, or even renegotiating brand identity elements to better carve out a unique space in the market.

3. **Fostering Industry Relationships**: Engage constructively with those who oppose your trademark. This engagement can lead to negotiations that may result in valuable partnerships or agreements that benefit both parties, such as co-branding opportunities or market-sharing agreements.

Capitalizing on Legal Challenges to Strengthen the Brand

1. **Boosting Public Visibility**: Publicizing your efforts to secure and defend your trademark can significantly enhance brand visibility. It demonstrates to your customer base and industry peers that your brand is a valuable asset worth protecting.

2. **Crafting a Compelling Narrative**: Share your journey through the trademark registration process, highlighting your commitment to overcoming challenges. This narrative can resonate with your audience, building an image of resilience and dedication that strengthens customer loyalty and brand affinity.

3. **Preparation for International Markets**: Successfully navigating domestic trademark challenges arms you with the experience and confidence to tackle international markets. This prepares you for global expansion, where understanding and navigating diverse trademark laws becomes crucial.

Challenges in trademark registration are veiled opportunities for strategic development and brand enhancement. By effectively leveraging the insights and experiences gained from each hurdle, your brand can achieve not only a stronger legal standing but also a more pronounced market presence. Embrace these challenges as opportunities to innovate, refine your brand, and prepare for broader success. This proactive and strategic approach will ensure that your brand not only survives but thrives in the competitive global marketplace.

Quick Tips and Recap

- **Embrace Rejections as Opportunities**: Use feedback from office actions to refine your trademark and enhance its distinctiveness and registrability.

- **Conduct Thorough Research**: Before filing, ensure a comprehensive trademark search to mitigate the risk of rejections and oppositions.

- **Utilize Professional Assistance**: Consider hiring a trademark attorney to navigate complex legal challenges and craft strategic responses to office actions and oppositions.

- **Stay Informed and Responsive**: Keep abreast of all communications from the trademark office and respond promptly to any issues or requests for additional information.

- **Negotiate and Mediate**: Where possible, seek to negotiate or mediate oppositions to find a mutually beneficial resolution and possibly forge new business relationships.

- **Document Everything**: Maintain detailed records of all applications, communications, and key decisions related to your trademark registration.

- **Prepare for Delays**: Anticipate and plan for potential delays in the trademark registration process; use this time to strengthen your brand strategy.

- **Monitor the Market**: Continuously monitor the market for potential infringements and emerging competitors that could affect your trademark.

- **Plan for the Long Term**: Consider future growth and international expansion in your trademark strategy, ensuring your trademark is scalable and adaptable.

By following these tips, you can effectively navigate the complexities of trademark registration, transforming potential setbacks into opportunities for branding success and legal robustness.

PART TWO

Mastering Trademark Strategy

Mastering the art of trademark strategy is akin to becoming a grandmaster in chess—every move is critical and can either set you up for a resounding success or leave you vulnerable to the cunning tactics of competitors. It's not just about claiming a piece of the intellectual property pie; it's about crafting a fortress around your brand that even the most determined rivals would hesitate to besiege. Dive deep into the intricacies of trademark law, wield your knowledge like a finely-tuned rapier, and watch as your adversaries retreat, overwhelmed by your strategic prowess and impeccable foresight.

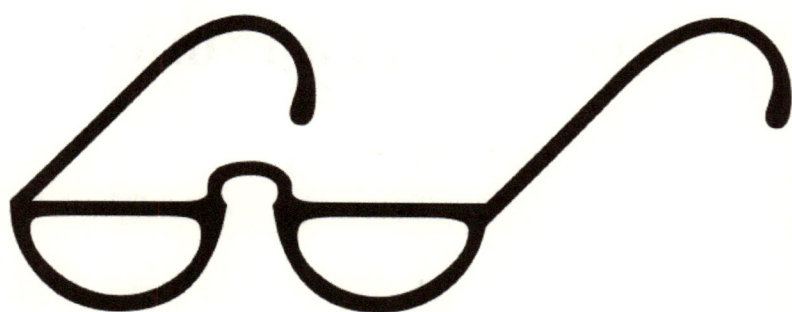

CHAPTER SIX

Keeping Your Trademarks Alive: Maintenance Essentials

"Maintaining a trademark requires the same attention and care as nurturing a leading brand. Regularly renew, monitor, and enforce your trademarks to ensure they remain a potent symbol of your company's quality and reputation."— MARY BARRA, CEO OF GENERAL MOTORS

Keeping your trademark alive isn't unlike tending to a high-maintenance houseplant: it needs constant attention, the right environment, and a touch of love now and then. Think of it as the pet goldfish of the business world—you can't just set it and forget it. Regular filings? Mandatory. Routine check-ups? Absolutely necessary. This is not the area to procrastinate or skimp on, lest you find your trademark, once a vibrant badge of honor, wilting under the harsh lights of legal challenges.

First things first, remember those renewal deadlines like you remember your wedding anniversary or the finale of your favorite TV series. Miss them and brace yourself for the kind of drama that would make even reality TV producers blush. Renewal isn't just a formality; it's a ritualistic reaffirmation of your claim to your brand's throne, warding off any pretenders to the crown.

Next up, stay vigilant against the barbarians at the gates: the infringers. These marauders can dilute your brand's power faster than a scandal can tank a politician's career. Regular monitoring of the marketplace is not just advisable; it's your brand's line of defense. When you spot a copycat, act swiftly—legal cease and desist letters should be as ready to go as fire extinguishers in a fireworks factory.

Lastly, don't let your trademark go stale. Keep it connected to your active products and services. A trademark that's left to gather dust like last year's hit toy is at risk of becoming generic. And in the trademark world, 'generic' is the kiss of death, the point of no return where your once mighty brand name becomes just another word for the product itself (think 'Escalator' or 'Aspirin').

In essence, your trademark is not just a symbol, but a living part of your business. Nurture it, protect it, and keep it active. Do this, and your trademark will not just survive—it will thrive, continuing to stand as a testament to your brand's authority and distinction in the marketplace.

Understanding Renewal Requirement

Like many critical assets, trademarks don't just sustain themselves indefinitely without some maintenance. One of the key components of maintaining a trademark's validity and enforceability is understanding and adhering to renewal requirements. This section explores the processes, timelines, and strategic considerations necessary to successfully renew your trademark and prevent lapses that could jeopardize your brand's protection.

The Basics of Trademark Renewal

1. **Renewal Intervals**: Trademarks are not granted perpetual protection upon registration; they require periodic renewals. For instance, in the

United States, the first renewal is due between the 5th and 6th year after registration, and subsequent renewals are required every 10 years. Each jurisdiction may have different rules and timelines, so it's essential to familiarize yourself with the specific requirements applicable to your trademark.

2. **Documentation and Fees**: Renewing a trademark typically involves filing specific documents with the trademark office, along with paying a renewal fee. These documents often require demonstrating continued use of the trademark in commerce, supported by examples of the trademark as it is currently used.

Preparing for Renewal

1. **Tracking Renewal Deadlines**: Set up a system to track renewal deadlines well in advance. Utilizing calendar reminders and dedicated trademark management software can help ensure that no renewal deadline is missed.

2. **Gathering Necessary Evidence of Use**: Prepare by regularly collecting and organizing evidence of your trademark's use in commerce, such as advertising materials, packaging, or screenshots of websites. This evidence will be crucial in demonstrating the active and continuous use of your trademark during the renewal process.

3. **Budgeting for Renewal Fees**: Anticipate and budget for the costs associated with trademark renewal. These fees can vary depending on the number of classes under which your trademark is registered and the specific requirements of the trademark office.

Common Pitfalls in Trademark Renewal

1. **Procrastination**: Waiting until the last minute to prepare for trademark renewal can lead to rushed submissions that may be incomplete or incorrect, risking refusal of the renewal.

2. **Failure to Demonstrate Use**: Not providing sufficient or appropriate evidence of use can lead to a trademark being considered abandoned or

non-renewable. Ensure that the evidence clearly depicts the trademark as used in connection to the goods or services listed in the registration.

3. **Overlooking Changes in Law**: Trademark laws can evolve, and renewal procedures and requirements can change. Staying informed about legal updates is essential to comply with current standards and avoid unintended non-compliance.

Understanding and managing trademark renewal requirements are critical to maintaining the legal protection and strength of your trademark. By proactively preparing for renewals, tracking deadlines, and staying informed about legal requirements, you can ensure that your trademark remains a viable and enforceable asset for your brand. This proactive approach not only protects your trademark but also reinforces the stability and longevity of your brand identity in the marketplace.

Monitoring for Infringement

Ensuring your trademark remains exclusive and unchallenged involves more than just handling renewals and paperwork; it requires vigilant monitoring of the market to detect any unauthorized use of your mark. Continuous trademark surveillance is crucial to maintaining the integrity and value of your brand. This section explores effective strategies for monitoring your trademark and identifying potential infringements.

Setting Up Monitoring Systems

1. **Online Monitoring Tools**: Use specialized online services that track trademark usage across various platforms and jurisdictions. These tools scan the internet, including e-commerce sites, social media, and domain registrations, to alert you to any potential unauthorized use of your trademark.

2. **Google Alerts and Similar Services**: Set up alerts using Google or similar services to notify you whenever your trademark is mentioned online. This can provide early warnings about possible infringements or misuse.

3. **Watching Competitor Activity**: Keep an eye on your competitors' activities, including new product launches and marketing campaigns, which can sometimes encroach on your trademark rights.

Responding to Potential Infringements

1. **Initial Assessment**: When potential infringement is detected, first assess the seriousness and impact of the infringement on your brand. Not every unauthorized use poses a significant threat; determine if the infringement is worth pursuing legally.

2. **Cease and Desist Letters**: For clear-cut cases of infringement, sending a cease and desist letter can be an effective first step. These letters warn infringers of their unauthorized use and demand immediate cessation, potentially resolving the issue without the need for litigation.

3. **Legal Action**: If a cease and desist letter does not resolve the infringement, or if the infringement is damaging enough, consider escalating to legal action. Consult with a trademark attorney to discuss the feasibility and implications of taking the matter to court.

Proactive Versus Reactive Monitoring

1. **Proactive Monitoring**: Implement a routine schedule for checking the use of your trademark. Regular reviews can help catch infringements early before they cause significant damage to your brand.

2. **Reactive Monitoring**: While proactive monitoring is ideal, be prepared to react quickly to unexpected cases of infringement. This might involve setting up rapid-response legal strategies or having a public relations plan in place to address any negative publicity.

Keeping Documentation

1. **Record of Monitoring Activities**: Maintain detailed records of your monitoring activities and any findings of unauthorized use. This documentation can be crucial in legal proceedings, demonstrating your diligence in protecting your trademark.

2. **Evidence of Infringement**: Collect and preserve evidence of any infringement as soon as it is discovered. This includes screenshots, purchase samples, and any correspondence with the infringer.

Vigilant monitoring for infringement is a critical component of trademark management. By actively overseeing how your trademark is used and swiftly addressing unauthorized use, you can protect your brand's reputation and legal standing. Implementing both proactive and reactive strategies will ensure that your trademark continues to serve as a unique identifier of your products and services, maintaining its strength and value in the marketplace.

Enforcing Your Trademark Rights

Successfully securing a trademark is just the beginning; vigorous enforcement is crucial to protect and maintain the value of your brand. Effective enforcement not only deters potential infringements but also ensures that your trademark continues to be uniquely associated with your products or services. This section delves into comprehensive strategies for enforcing your trademark rights, emphasizing the importance of consistency, and the use of legal measures to safeguard your brand's integrity.

Establishing a Robust Enforcement Strategy

1. **Formulating Enforcement Policies**: Develop clear, documented policies outlining how to approach and handle trademark infringements. These policies should detail the steps for initiating contact with infringers, the escalation procedures, and the criteria for pursuing legal action.

2. **Case Prioritization**: Due to resource constraints, it is crucial to prioritize enforcement actions. Focus on infringements that pose the greatest risk to your brand's reputation or have significant financial implications. High-priority cases often include infringements in key markets or those by direct competitors.

3. **Consistent Application of Policies**: Consistently applying your enforcement policies is essential. Inconsistent enforcement can

undermine your trademark's perceived value and can potentially weaken your legal standing in future disputes.

Tools and Techniques for Effective Enforcement

1. **Cease and Desist Letters**: Typically the first line of defense, a cease and desist letter should be tailored to the specific infringement and clearly outline the legal basis for your claims. These letters serve as a formal request for the infringer to stop unauthorized use of the trademark and can often resolve issues without resorting to court.

2. **Negotiation and Mediation**: When possible, resolving disputes through negotiation or mediation can be advantageous. These methods are generally less adversarial and can lead to quicker, cost-effective solutions. Outcomes might include licensing agreements or other compromises that respect your trademark rights while resolving the conflict.

3. **Litigation**: If informal resolution attempts fail, or if the infringement is causing significant harm to your brand, litigation may be necessary. Legal action should be considered carefully, weighing the costs against potential benefits. Successful litigation can not only stop the infringement but also potentially recover damages and reinforce the strength of your trademark protection.

Leveraging Legal Expertise and Resources

1. **Engaging Trademark Attorneys**: Partner with experienced trademark attorneys who can navigate the complexities of intellectual property litigation. Their expertise is invaluable in crafting a solid legal strategy and ensuring that your actions are legally sound and effective.

2. **International Considerations**: For brands with global reach, enforcing trademark rights across different jurisdictions can present additional challenges. International trademark laws vary, and having specialized legal counsel can help manage these complexities.

3. **Utilizing Government and Trade Resources**: In cases of widespread infringement or counterfeiting, collaborating with governmental bodies

or international trade organizations can enhance your enforcement efforts. These entities often have resources and legal frameworks in place to assist in larger-scale enforcement actions.

The enforcement of trademark rights is a dynamic aspect of brand management requiring a proactive approach and strategic foresight. By establishing clear enforcement policies, utilizing various tools and resources effectively, and engaging with legal professionals, you can protect your trademark from dilution and unauthorized use. Remember, the goal of enforcement is not just to challenge every infringement but to strategically protect and enhance the value of your brand. Through vigilant and consistent enforcement, your trademark can continue to serve as a key asset in your business's success and growth.

Keeping Your Trademark Relevant

Maintaining the relevance of your trademark is essential for continued legal protection and market presence. A trademark that becomes disconnected from the products or services it was intended to represent risks becoming generic or abandoned. This section explores effective strategies for ensuring that your trademark remains active and closely associated with your ongoing business activities.

Active Usage and Marketing

1. **Consistent Use in Commerce**: Regularly use your trademark in the course of conducting business. This includes using the trademark on products, packaging, marketing materials, and in digital content. Consistent use not only reinforces brand recognition but also strengthens legal claims by demonstrating ongoing usage.

2. **Adaptation to Market Changes**: Markets evolve, and so must your brand. Ensure that your trademark adapts to changing market conditions and consumer preferences. This might involve updating the trademark's visual elements or extending its use into new product categories to keep it relevant and modern.

3. **Strategic Marketing Campaigns**: Invest in marketing campaigns that highlight your trademark. Effective branding efforts not only boost sales but also reinforce the association between your trademark and the distinctive qualities of your goods or services.

Legal Strategies for Maintaining Relevance

1. **Monitoring Trademark Health**: Regularly review how your trademark is perceived in the marketplace. This can involve conducting consumer surveys to gauge brand recognition and perception. Such data can inform strategic decisions to revitalize a trademark that may be losing its distinctiveness.

2. **Filing for New Trademarks**: As your business grows and diversifies, consider filing new trademark applications for logos, slogans, or product names that could enhance your existing trademark portfolio. This proactive approach can prevent gaps in protection and support the overall brand strategy.

3. **Renewal and Documentation**: Stay diligent with renewal deadlines and maintain meticulous records of your trademark usage. Documentation should include examples of how the trademark is used in commerce, which is crucial for renewals and any potential legal disputes.

Avoiding Genericide

1. **Educating Consumers and Partners**: Actively educate consumers, distributors, and marketing partners on the proper use of your trademark. Incorrect usage by the public or even by partners can lead to a trademark becoming generic.

2. **Correct Branding Practices**: Use the trademark as an adjective, not a noun or verb, to maintain its status as a brand identifier. For example, emphasize "Kleenex tissues" instead of just "Kleenex" to avoid the brand name becoming synonymous with the product category.

3. **Vigilance Against Misuse**: Monitor and correct misuse of your trademark in all forms of media and communication. This includes

online content, third-party advertising, and even internal corporate communications.

Keeping your trademark relevant requires a multifaceted approach involving consistent use, strategic marketing, and legal vigilance. By actively engaging in these practices, you ensure that your trademark continues to function as a vital asset, safeguarding your brand's identity and legal integrity. A well-maintained trademark not only enhances brand recognition but also fortifies your competitive edge in the marketplace.

Legal and Strategic Updates

In the dynamic landscape of trademark law and market competition, staying informed and adaptable is crucial. Continuous legal and strategic updates are essential for maintaining the efficacy and relevance of your trademark protection. This section outlines how regular updates to your trademark strategy and staying abreast of legal changes can safeguard your intellectual property over the long term.

Keeping Up with Legal Developments

1. **Monitoring Legal Changes**: Trademark laws can evolve due to legislative changes, judicial rulings, or shifts in intellectual property policies both domestically and internationally. Regularly review legal updates from reliable sources, including intellectual property offices, legal publications, and industry news.

2. **Engaging with Legal Professionals**: Maintain a relationship with a trademark attorney who specializes in intellectual property law. Regular consultations can help you navigate changes and ensure that your trademark strategies are always aligned with current laws.

3. **Participating in Workshops and Seminars**: Attend workshops, seminars, and webinars focused on trademark law. These forums provide insights into industry trends, legal updates, and allow networking with other professionals who can offer different perspectives and strategies.

Adapting Your Trademark Strategy

1. **Revisiting Your Portfolio**: Periodically review your trademark portfolio to ensure it aligns with your current business goals and market realities. This might involve renewing certain trademarks, letting others lapse, or filing new applications as your business evolves into new products or markets.

2. **Strategic Enforcement**: As market conditions change, so too should your approach to enforcing your trademark rights. Adapt your enforcement strategies based on the current business environment, competitive landscape, and the specific challenges your brand faces.

3. **International Considerations**: If your business operates globally, stay informed about international trademark developments. Different countries may have varying requirements and protections, which can significantly impact your global branding strategy.

Utilizing Technology for Strategic Updates

1. **Trademark Management Software**: Utilize advanced trademark management software tools that offer features like deadline tracking, document storage, and alerts on legal updates relevant to your trademarks.

2. **Digital Monitoring Tools**: Leverage digital tools that monitor the internet for potential trademark infringements or misuse. These tools can provide real-time alerts and detailed reports, helping you respond swiftly to protect your rights.

3. **Analytics and Reporting**: Employ analytics tools to track the performance and strength of your trademark in the marketplace. Regular reports can help you make informed decisions about where to focus your protection efforts and when to adapt your strategies.

Staying proactive with legal and strategic updates is critical for the continued protection and effectiveness of your trademark. By regularly engaging with legal developments, revisiting and adapting your trademark strategy, and employing modern technology, you can ensure that your trademark remains a strong defender of your brand's identity and value. This approach not only prevents legal vulnerabilities but also enhances your brand's resilience and adaptability in a constantly changing market.

Quick Tips and Recap

- **Set Reminder Systems for Renewals**: Never miss a renewal deadline by setting up automated reminders well in advance.

- **Regularly Monitor the Market**: Use online tools to continuously monitor the marketplace for unauthorized uses of your trademark to act quickly against potential infringements.

- **Respond Swiftly to Infringements**: Address infringements decisively with cease and desist letters or legal action when necessary to protect your brand integrity.

- **Keep Your Trademark Active**: Ensure your trademark is actively used in commerce to avoid risks of it becoming generic or abandoned.

- **Stay Informed on Legal Changes**: Regularly update yourself on changes in trademark law that could affect your rights and strategy.

- **Consult with IP Professionals**: Maintain a relationship with intellectual property attorneys to get expert advice and stay ahead of complex legal issues.

- **Adapt Your Strategy to Market Changes**: Periodically review and adjust your trademark strategy based on new market entries, product expansions, or shifts in consumer behavior.

- **Utilize Technology**: Implement trademark management software and digital monitoring tools to streamline tracking, management, and enforcement of your trademarks.

- **Educate Your Team**: Make sure your marketing and legal teams are aware of the proper use of trademarks to prevent misuse that could weaken your rights.

- **Document All Usage and Enforcement Actions**: Keep thorough records of how and where your trademark is used, as well as any enforcement actions taken, to support your claims of active use and protection in any legal proceedings.

By following these tips, you can effectively maintain your trademark's vitality and legal protection, ensuring it continues to support your brand's success and market presence.

CHAPTER SEVEN

Vigilance and Valor: Monitoring and Enforcing Your Trademarks

"Maintaining vigilance over your trademarks is akin to guarding the crown jewels; it's essential for ensuring your brand's legacy and authority in the marketplace remain intact."
— ANNE WOJCICKI, CEO OF 23ANDME

Welcome to the frontline of trademark defense, where vigilance meets valor, and every skirmish over intellectual property could make or break your brand's stronghold. Monitoring and enforcing trademarks is less like a quiet game of chess and more like a high-octane round of laser tag—where the lasers are legal documents and the targets are infringing competitors.

Think of trademark monitoring as your brand's security system, constantly scanning the horizon for potential threats. It's like having a guard dog that barks at the slightest whiff of trouble—except this dog is equipped with legal briefs and a keen sense of corporate identity. You'll want to keep your eyes peeled and your lawyers on speed dial, ready to spring into action the moment you spot a copycat trying to sneak past your defenses.

Enforcing your trademark is where the valor comes in. It's not for the faint of heart. Once you've identified a rogue trader or a misguided mimic, it's time to don your armor and enter the fray. This may involve firing off a cease-and-desist letter sharp enough to make a pirate walk the plank. Or, if things escalate, girding yourself for a courtroom battle that's as strategically demanding as a game of three-dimensional chess played during a hurricane.

Remember, the goal here isn't just to swing your legal sword at every shadow. It's about knowing when to fight and when diplomacy might be the better valor. Strategic enforcement enhances your brand's value and deters would-be infringers without turning your legal department into the corporate equivalent of a war zone.

In the grand saga of your business, think of trademark vigilance as the epic quest to protect your kingdom. It's about watching over your realm with the eagle eyes of a hawk and the brave heart of a lion. Do it well, and your brand's legacy will live on as a beacon of integrity and valor in the marketplace.

Setting Up a Trademark Monitoring System

In the realm of trademark protection, vigilance is key. Establishing a robust trademark monitoring system is akin to setting up a sophisticated security system for your brand. This system's purpose is to detect potential infringements early, allowing you to respond proactively and protect your intellectual property rights effectively. This section provides a step-by-step guide on how to set up an effective trademark monitoring system that acts as your first line of defense against potential infringers.

Choosing the Right Tools

1. **Digital Monitoring Tools**: Leverage advanced software solutions that scan the internet for unauthorized uses of your trademark. These tools can monitor various platforms including e-commerce sites, social media,

and even domain name registrations. They provide alerts whenever they detect usage that matches or closely resembles your trademark.

2. **Manual Searches**: While digital tools are useful, they are not infallible. Supplement them with periodic manual searches. This can include checking major online marketplaces, industry-specific forums, and new website launches to ensure comprehensive coverage.

3. **Custom Alerts**: Set up custom alerts using search engines and specialized services like Google Alerts. Input your trademark terms to receive notifications of any mentions across the web, which could indicate unauthorized usage.

Integrating Monitoring into Daily Operations

1. **Routine Checks**: Integrate monitoring activities into your daily business operations. Assign responsibilities to specific team members to conduct regular checks and review alerts from monitoring tools. This ensures that surveillance is continuous and that potential infringements are spotted quickly.

2. **Stakeholder Training**: Educate your team about the importance of trademark monitoring. Ensure that they understand what constitutes infringement and how to report potential violations they might come across in their regular work activities.

3. **Legal Team Involvement**: Keep your legal team or external trademark attorney informed about your monitoring setup. They can provide insights on the legal thresholds for infringement and help refine your monitoring strategies.

Responding to Alerts

1. **Initial Assessment**: Once an alert is received, conduct an initial assessment to determine the legitimacy and severity of the potential infringement. Not every alert will warrant further action; deciding which cases to pursue is crucial for efficient resource allocation.

2. **Documentation and Evidence Collection**: For alerts that do warrant further action, begin collecting evidence immediately. This includes

screenshots, product listings, dates, and any other relevant information that can support a potential legal claim.

3. **Prioritization of Cases**: Prioritize which cases to address based on factors such as the infringement's clearness, the potential damage to your brand, and the infringer's reach and impact in the market.

Setting up an effective trademark monitoring system is an essential component of proactive trademark management. By choosing the right tools, integrating monitoring into your daily operations, and responding swiftly to alerts, you can protect your brand from infringement and maintain its integrity and value in the marketplace. This proactive approach not only prevents legal issues but also strengthens your brand's position and reputation over the long term.

Identifying Infringement

Effectively identifying trademark infringement is essential for maintaining the integrity and value of your brand. It involves understanding the subtle and often complex nuances of trademark law and recognizing when unauthorized use of your trademark by third parties crosses legal boundaries. This section provides detailed guidance on identifying various types of trademark infringements and evaluating their impact on your brand.

Types of Trademark Infringement

1. **Direct Infringement**: Occurs when another entity uses a mark that is identical or confusingly similar to your registered trademark on related goods or services, leading to potential consumer confusion. This is the most straightforward type of infringement to identify.

2. **Counterfeiting**: Represents a severe and deliberate infringement, involving the production or distribution of goods under a forged trademark that is identical to a registered mark. Counterfeiting not only misleads consumers but also directly damages your brand's reputation and can have legal ramifications.

3. **Dilution**: Affects well-known or famous trademarks. Dilution can occur in two forms:

- o **Blurring**: Where the unique significance of the trademark is weakened by its association with dissimilar products.

- o **Tarnishment**: Where the trademark's reputation is harmed through association with inferior or inappropriate products.

4. **Indirect Infringement**: Includes contributory and vicarious liability where third parties facilitate or benefit from the infringement without directly infringing themselves. This can be more challenging to detect and prove.

Strategies for Spotting Infringement

1. **Visual and Phonetic Examination**: Carefully analyze the visual and phonetic similarities between your trademark and the alleged infringer's mark. Even minor alterations that do not significantly alter the overall impression of the mark might constitute infringement.

2. **Contextual Use Analysis**: Evaluate how and where the mark is used. Infringement can occur across various platforms — from product labels to digital advertisements and even domain names. The context in which the mark is used can significantly affect the interpretation of infringement.

3. **Assessing Market Overlap**: Determine whether the alleged infringer operates in the same or overlapping market channels and targets similar consumer demographics. Overlapping markets increase the likelihood of confusion and strengthen the case for infringement.

Documenting and Prioritizing Infringements

1. **Systematic Documentation**: Establish a systematic approach to documenting potential infringements. This should include collecting visual evidence, recording the date and location of the infringement, and any other supporting documentation that can establish a pattern or single instance of infringement.

2. **Impact Evaluation**: Assess the potential impact of the infringement on your brand, considering factors like the scale of the infringement, the reach of the infringing products, and the potential for reputation damage.

3. **Setting Enforcement Priorities**: Given limited resources, prioritize enforcing against infringements based on their potential impact. High-priority targets typically include cases with a significant threat to your market position or those that pose a direct financial loss.

Identifying trademark infringement requires a vigilant approach and a thorough understanding of your brand's legal protections. By utilizing strategic monitoring, detailed documentation, and careful assessment of potential impacts, you can effectively identify and prioritize actions against infringements. Protecting your trademark through proactive identification and enforcement preserves your brand's reputation and ensures its long-term viability in a competitive market landscape.

Strategies for Initial Contact and Negotiation

The initial steps in addressing a trademark infringement are critical, as they set the tone for potential resolutions and can significantly influence the outcome of the dispute. Effective initial contact and subsequent negotiations require a balanced approach, combining assertiveness with tact and understanding. This section delves into crafting precise initial communications and outlines strategies for negotiating resolutions that uphold your trademark rights while fostering a cooperative atmosphere.

Developing Effective Initial Contact

1. **Cease and Desist Letters**: This is often the primary method for addressing infringement formally. A well-crafted cease and desist letter should clearly outline your trademark rights, detail the specific instances of infringement, and state your demands, such as the immediate cessation of the infringing activities. The letter should strike a balance between firmness to convey the seriousness of the infringement and professionalism to maintain a potential for amicable resolution.

2. **Tailored Communication Strategies**: Adjust the tone and content of your communications based on the infringer's background and the severity of the infringement. For unintentional infringers, such as small businesses or individuals who might not be aware of the infringement, a

more educational and friendly approach may be effective. In cases of willful infringement, a more stringent tone may be necessary.

3. **Clarity and Directness**: Communicate your points clearly and directly, avoiding complex legal jargon that could confuse or escalate tensions. Clearly outline the necessary actions they must take to remedy the situation and provide a precise deadline for compliance.

Effective Negotiation Tactics

1. **Understanding the Infringer's Perspective**: Begin with an attempt to understand why the infringement occurred. Was it a mistake, ignorance, or deliberate? Knowing the infringer's side can help you tailor your negotiation tactics effectively.

2. **Maintaining Open Communication**: Foster an open dialogue. Encourage the infringer to discuss their perspective and possibly contest your claims. This open line can lead to more comprehensive solutions and demonstrate goodwill that could facilitate a quicker resolution.

3. **Proposing Constructive Solutions**: Offer solutions that mitigate the infringement while potentially preserving the infringer's ability to operate. For instance, propose licensing agreements, adjustments in their brand design, or a reasonable timeline for phasing out the infringing products. These solutions can help resolve the conflict without a complete loss on either side.

Navigating Legal Nuances During Negotiation

1. **Documentation of All Exchanges**: Keep detailed records of all communications, agreements, and negotiations. This documentation is vital if the dispute escalates to legal proceedings, providing evidence of your efforts to resolve the issue amicably.

2. **Involvement of Legal Experts**: Engage your legal team in reviewing all outward communications to ensure they are legally accurate and do not inadvertently compromise your position. Legal experts can also provide strategic advice tailored to the nuances of trademark law.

3. **Knowing When to Escalate**: Recognize when negotiations are failing and when it is necessary to escalate the matter to formal legal action. If negotiations do not yield a satisfactory resolution, or if the infringer continues their activities despite agreements, moving forward with litigation may be the appropriate course of action.

Effective initial contact and negotiation are key to managing trademark infringements efficiently. By strategically engaging with infringers, you can often resolve disputes without resorting to costly and time-consuming legal battles. These engagements not only protect your intellectual property but also maintain the integrity and reputation of your brand by demonstrating a responsible and assertive approach to trademark enforcement.

Legal Actions and Litigation

When negotiations fail or infringement persists, escalating to legal action becomes necessary to protect your trademark rights effectively. Litigation can be a complex and demanding process, but it is sometimes the only way to stop infringement and recover damages. This section outlines the steps involved in preparing for and engaging in trademark litigation, providing a roadmap for navigating these legal waters with confidence.

Preparing for Litigation

1. **Evaluating the Case**: Before proceeding with litigation, conduct a thorough evaluation of the case. Assess the strength of your trademark claim, the evidence of infringement, and the potential financial and reputational impacts on your business. This evaluation will help determine if litigation is the most prudent course of action.

2. **Gathering Evidence**: Compile all necessary evidence to support your case. This includes documentation of your trademark registration, proof of the infringing activities, any communication with the infringer, and evidence of consumer confusion or damage to your brand caused by the infringement.

3. **Legal Team Assembly**: Assemble a skilled legal team specialized in intellectual property law. Your legal team will play a crucial role in developing your case strategy, handling court procedures, and negotiating possible settlements.

Navigating the Litigation Process

1. **Filing the Lawsuit**: Initiate the lawsuit by filing a complaint in the appropriate court. The complaint should clearly outline your legal claims against the defendant, the facts supporting those claims, and the relief you are seeking, such as an injunction to stop further infringement and monetary damages.

2. **Discovery Phase**: Engage in the discovery process, where both sides exchange relevant information and evidence. This phase can include depositions, interrogatories, and requests for documents. Discovery is crucial for uncovering additional evidence and understanding the defendant's arguments.

3. **Pre-Trial Motions**: Participate in pre-trial motions, which can set the boundaries for the trial or potentially resolve the case without going to trial. For instance, motions for summary judgment can be filed if the facts are undisputed and the law clearly favors one side.

Conducting the Trial

1. **Presenting Your Case**: During the trial, present your case effectively through arguments, witness testimony, and exhibits. Your goal is to demonstrate convincingly that infringement has occurred and that it has caused your brand harm.

2. **Responding to Defense**: Be prepared to counter the defendant's arguments and defenses, such as claims that there is no likelihood of confusion or that their use is protected under fair use doctrines.

3. **Seeking Remedies**: Advocate for the appropriate remedies if the case is decided in your favor. Remedies can include permanent injunctions, monetary compensation for damages, and possibly the recovery of attorney's fees if applicable under the law.

Engaging in trademark litigation requires careful preparation, a strong legal strategy, and effective presentation in court. Although litigation can be resource-intensive, it is sometimes necessary to protect the integrity of your brand and prevent further infringement. By understanding the steps involved and assembling the right legal team, you can navigate the complexities of trademark litigation to uphold your rights and achieve a favorable outcome.

Maintaining Trademark Vigor Through Strategic Enforcement

The protection of your trademark does not end with registration or even a successful litigation—it requires ongoing, strategic enforcement to maintain its strength and relevance in the market. Vigorous enforcement not only deters potential infringers but also reinforces the association of your trademark with your brand and products. This section explores strategies for maintaining the vitality of your trademark through proactive and thoughtful enforcement actions.

Developing a Strategic Enforcement Plan

1. **Assessment of Enforcement Landscape**: Regularly assess the enforcement landscape by monitoring how your trademark is used within the industry and by competitors. Understand the common threats and challenges in your sector to tailor your enforcement strategies effectively.

2. **Prioritization of Enforcement Efforts**: Not every instance of potential infringement requires full-scale legal action. Prioritize your enforcement efforts based on the threat level to your brand, potential for consumer confusion, and the economic impact of the infringement. Focus resources on the most damaging violations to ensure optimal use of your enforcement budget.

3. **Consistency in Enforcement**: Apply your trademark policies consistently across all platforms and jurisdictions. Inconsistent enforcement can weaken your legal position and dilute the strength of

your trademark. Establish clear guidelines for when and how to enforce your trademark rights, and stick to them.

Leveraging Technology for Efficient Enforcement

1. **Automated Monitoring Tools**: Utilize advanced software and online tools that continuously scan the internet and marketplaces for unauthorized use of your trademark. These tools can provide real-time alerts, allowing for swift action against infringements.

2. **Data Analytics**: Use data analytics to understand patterns of infringement and to measure the effectiveness of your enforcement actions. Analytics can provide insights into which strategies are working, where vulnerabilities may lie, and how enforcement efforts can be improved.

Engaging Stakeholders in Trademark Protection

1. **Internal Training**: Educate your employees about the importance of trademark protection and how they can help enforce it. Regular training sessions can help staff identify potential infringements and understand the correct usage of the trademark in various contexts.

2. **Collaboration with Partners**: Work with distributors, licensees, and other business partners to ensure they understand and comply with your trademark usage guidelines. Strong partnerships can extend the reach of your enforcement efforts and provide additional layers of monitoring and protection.

3. **Public Awareness Campaigns**: Raise awareness about your trademark by engaging with consumers directly through marketing and public relations campaigns. Educated consumers are often the first to spot and report counterfeits or misuse, acting as additional eyes and ears for your brand.

Maintaining the vigor of your trademark requires more than reactive measures; it demands a proactive and strategic approach to enforcement. By assessing risks, prioritizing efforts based on potential impact, leveraging technology, and engaging with stakeholders, you can ensure that your trademark continues to serve as a strong and enforceable asset. This comprehensive approach not only protects your intellectual property but also enhances the overall value and longevity of your brand in the competitive market landscape.

Quick Tips and Recap

- **Establish Robust Monitoring Systems**: Set up comprehensive monitoring systems using digital tools to detect potential infringements promptly.

- **Document All Infringements**: Keep detailed records of any suspected infringements, including screenshots, URLs, and descriptions, to support any future legal actions.

- **Prioritize Enforcement Actions**: Focus your resources on the most harmful infringements that pose a significant risk to your brand's reputation and market position.

- **Use Cease and Desist Letters Effectively**: Employ cease and desist letters as a first step to address infringement, tailoring the tone and content based on the severity and nature of the infringement.

- **Engage in Negotiations Prudently**: When possible, engage in negotiations to resolve disputes amicably, saving time and resources while maintaining business relationships.

- **Prepare for Litigation**: Assemble a skilled legal team and prepare thoroughly if litigation becomes necessary to ensure that you are well-positioned to defend your trademark rights.

- **Apply Enforcement Consistently**: Enforce your trademark rights consistently across all cases to maintain the strength and integrity of your trademark.

- **Leverage Technology**: Utilize technology not only for monitoring but also for managing and documenting enforcement actions.

- **Educate Your Team and Partners**: Regularly educate your employees and business partners about the importance of trademark protection and how they can help enforce it.

- **Stay Informed on Legal Developments**: Keep up to date with the latest changes in trademark law and enforcement practices to ensure your actions are always compliant and effective.

By following these tips, you can ensure a proactive approach to trademark enforcement, safeguarding your intellectual property rights and supporting the long-term success of your brand.

CHAPTER EIGHT

Trademarks in the Digital Realm: Online Strategies

"In the digital age, vigilance in protecting your trademark is not optional—it's critical. Treat your online brand presence as you would your most valuable asset, because in many ways, it is."— SUNDAR PICHAI, CEO OF GOOGLE

Ah, the digital realm—a place where trademarks roam as freely as cat videos and memes. But don't let the casual vibes fool you; this is the modern battleground for brand protection. Navigating trademark strategy online is like playing a video game on expert mode: it's fast-paced, ever-changing, and one wrong move can send you back to the start screen.

First, let's talk about domain names. Securing your trademark as a domain is like claiming your own piece of digital real estate. It's essential, yes, but it's just the start. Imagine you've built a fortress to showcase your brand; now you must ensure no one builds a deceptive shack next door. Watching over your domain names and swiftly dealing with cybersquatters who try to profit off your good name is a task for the swift and savvy.

Social media is another arena where your trademarks need to shine—and be shielded. Every platform, from Twitter to TikTok, is a potential minefield of misuse. It's like hosting a party where anyone can put on your brand's costume and play the part. Monitoring these spaces isn't just about keeping an eye out; it's about engaging actively. Register your trademarks, handle, and hashtag across all relevant platforms. Then, set alerts to keep track of how your brand is being mentioned or misused.

And let's not forget about online marketplaces—eCommerce's bustling bazaars. Here, your trademark isn't just your identity; it's your shield. Counterfeit goods can pop up like whack-a-moles, and your job is to wield the legal mallet with precision and authority. Work closely with platforms like Amazon and eBay that have processes in place to help trademark owners fight counterfeit listings. It's a bit like having a neighborhood watch, but for your products.

In the digital age, trademark strategy requires a combination of tech-savvy, legal know-how, and a pinch of old-fashioned gumption. Stay vigilant, engage actively, and remember, in the vast wilderness of the internet, your trademark is both your banner and your barrier.

Securing and Managing Domain Names

In the digital marketplace, domain names represent not just your brand's online address but its identity and credibility. A domain name that aligns with your trademarks is an invaluable asset, acting as a beacon for your customers in the digital chaos. Securing and managing these domain names effectively is crucial for maintaining control over your brand's narrative and preventing cybersquatting or other detrimental activities. This section delves into strategies for acquiring the right domain names and managing them to maximize your brand's online presence and security.

Strategic Acquisition of Domain Names

1. **Alignment with Brand Identity**: Prioritize securing domain names that match or closely resemble your registered trademarks. This strategy enhances brand consistency across platforms and fortifies your brand's online identity, making it easier for customers to find and recognize your official sites.

2. **Proactive Registration**: Adopt a proactive approach by securing your main domain across key top-level domains (TLDs) like .com, .net, and .org, as well as considering newer TLDs relevant to your business (.tech, .store, .app). Additionally, protect your brand in global markets by registering country-specific TLDs (.co.uk, .de, .jp) that cater to particular regions.

3. **Defensive Domain Registration**: To safeguard against cybersquatting, register common misspellings, phonetic variations, and other potential iterations of your brand name. By controlling these domains, you prevent malicious entities from exploiting them to divert traffic or tarnish your brand's reputation.

Comprehensive Management of Domain Portfolios

1. **Centralized Control**: Utilize a centralized domain management platform to maintain an organized inventory of all your domain registrations. Such systems help track renewal dates, manage domain settings, and ensure consistent administrative handling across your portfolio.

2. **Automated Renewal Systems**: Implement automatic renewals to maintain ownership of critical domains. For domains where automatic renewal is not available or practical, maintain a rigorous schedule of reminders well ahead of expiration dates to prevent lapses in registration.

3. **Enhancing Domain Security**: Protect your domain privacy by opting into WHOIS privacy services where available, which keep your personal

information hidden from the public database. Strengthen security protocols by enabling features like two-factor authentication, registrar lock, and DNSSEC (Domain Name System Security Extensions) to defend against unauthorized transfers and DNS-related attacks.

Addressing Domain Disputes and Infringement

1. **Vigilance Against Infringement**: Regularly monitor the web for unauthorized domain registrations that mimic your trademarks or could be mistaken for your official domain. Services that scan domain registrations for similar names can be instrumental in catching infringements early.

2. **Legal Frameworks and Dispute Resolution**: Familiarize yourself with mechanisms like the Uniform Domain-Name Dispute-Resolution Policy (UDRP) for challenging bad-faith domain registrations. Understanding these procedures ensures you are prepared to act decisively to reclaim domains that infringe on your trademarks.

3. **Negotiation and Legal Action**: Attempt to resolve disputes through direct negotiation as a first step. If this fails, be prepared to pursue formal dispute resolution or litigation to recover domains or seek damages for trademark infringement.

Effective management and strategic foresight in handling domain names are crucial for protecting your brand in the online world. By securing domain names aligned with your trademarks, proactively managing your domain portfolio, and being prepared to address disputes legally and decisively, you can ensure your brand's digital presence remains robust and secure. This proactive approach not only protects your intellectual property but also strengthens your brand's reputation and customer trust in an increasingly digital marketplace.

Trademark Protection on Social Media

Social media has transformed from a digital meeting place into a vibrant marketplace and a crucial battleground for trademark protection. As brands navigate this dynamic environment, the strategic management of trademarks becomes essential to maintaining brand integrity and consumer trust. This section outlines comprehensive strategies for protecting trademarks on social media, ensuring they contribute positively to your brand's identity and reputation.

Proactive Steps for Trademark Registration and Management on Social Media

1. **Securing Brand Handles and Names**: Prioritize securing your trademark as your username or handle across all relevant social media platforms. This prevents others from registering your brand name and helps maintain consistency in your digital presence.

2. **Seeking Account Verification**: Work to get your social media profiles verified. Verification badges are critical as they signal to users the authenticity of the account, reducing the risk of brand impersonation. This is especially important on platforms where brand impersonation is common.

3. **Uniform Brand Presentation**: Ensure that your use of logos, taglines, and overall visual branding is consistent across all social media channels. This not only reinforces trademark claims but also aids in creating a seamless and recognizable brand experience for users across different platforms.

Monitoring and Addressing Infringements on Social Media

1. **Implementing Monitoring Solutions**: Use specialized monitoring tools that scan social media for unauthorized uses of your trademark. These tools can detect instances of your trademark being used in user handles, profiles, posts, or even as hashtags without permission.

2. **Strategic Response to Infringements**: When an infringement is detected, assess its nature and impact. For minor misuses, a direct message to the infringer requesting the removal or modification of the content may suffice. For more severe or damaging cases, use the social media platform's reporting system to address the violation formally.

3. **Escalating Legal Action When Necessary**: In cases of persistent or high-impact infringement, consider escalating to legal action. This

should involve consultation with legal professionals specializing in intellectual property rights to discuss options such as sending cease and desist letters or pursuing further legal recourse.

Collaborative Efforts with Social Media Platforms

1. **Leveraging Platform Policies**: Become well-versed with the intellectual property policies of each social media platform. Understanding these policies will help you navigate their systems more effectively and enforce your trademark rights when violations occur.

2. **Establishing Contact with Platform Representatives**: Develop relationships with point contacts within social media companies. These relationships can be crucial for resolving complex issues that are not adequately addressed through standard reporting mechanisms.

3. **Using Platform-Specific Tools**: Engage with and utilize proprietary tools provided by platforms designed to help protect and manage digital content. For example, Facebook's Rights Manager tool allows creators to upload and protect their copyrighted content at scale.

Effective trademark protection on social media is not only about defense but also about proactive management and strategic enforcement. By securing your digital assets, actively monitoring for misuse, and engaging with social media platforms, you can protect your trademark and enhance your brand's standing in the digital marketplace. Through vigilant management and strategic engagement, your trademark can serve as both a defender of your brand's integrity and an enhancer of its digital presence.

Combating Counterfeiting on Online Marketplaces

Online marketplaces have revolutionized the way we shop but have also made it easier for counterfeit goods to reach consumers. These platforms, while offering immense opportunities for legitimate businesses, also pose significant risks as they can be exploited by those seeking to profit from the unauthorized use of registered trademarks. Protecting your brand against counterfeits in this complex digital ecosystem is critical to maintaining your reputation and ensuring customer trust. This section outlines effective strategies for combating counterfeiting and safeguarding your trademarks on online marketplaces.

Developing a Comprehensive Anti-Counterfeiting Strategy

1. **Registration and Brand Gating**: Ensure your trademarks are registered with each major online marketplace. Many platforms, like Amazon's Brand Registry, offer programs that provide enhanced tools for monitoring and controlling your brand. These programs often allow for brand gating, which restricts who can sell goods under your brand name.

2. **Proactive Monitoring Tools**: Utilize advanced monitoring tools provided by online marketplaces or third-party services to detect and report counterfeit listings. These tools can scan product listings across various platforms to identify unauthorized use of your trademarks or sale of counterfeit items.

3. **Educating Consumers**: Actively educate your customers about how to identify authentic products and the dangers of counterfeit goods. Use your website, social media, and product packaging to communicate the key features of genuine products and where customers should shop to ensure they receive authentic goods.

Collaborating with Online Marketplaces

1. **Utilizing Reporting Tools**: Familiarize yourself with the reporting processes of each online marketplace. Platforms like eBay, Amazon, and Alibaba have specific procedures for reporting counterfeit listings, which can lead to their removal and the enforcement of selling privileges against repeat infringers.

2. **Building Relationships with Marketplace Authorities**: Develop direct relationships with the intellectual property (IP) enforcement teams at major marketplaces. These relationships can facilitate faster action on reported infringements and provide insight into new tools and policies designed to protect brand owners.

3. **Legal Enforcement Actions**: In cases where reporting through standard marketplace channels is ineffective, consider legal actions such as cease

and desist letters to infringers, or, if necessary, litigation. Marketplaces often respond more promptly and take stronger action when legal steps are initiated.

Leveraging Data and Analytics

1. **Data-Driven Decisions**: Use data analytics to understand the scope and impact of counterfeiting on your brand. Analytics can help identify trends in counterfeit activity, high-risk products, and regions, enabling targeted enforcement efforts.

2. **Performance Metrics**: Track the effectiveness of your anti-counterfeiting measures by setting and monitoring key performance indicators (KPIs) such as the number of counterfeit listings removed, reduction in customer complaints related to counterfeit goods, and recovery of revenues from prevented counterfeit sales.

Combating counterfeiting on online marketplaces requires a multi-faceted approach that includes securing your brand's presence, monitoring and enforcement, consumer education, and collaboration with marketplace platforms. By implementing a comprehensive strategy that leverages both technology and legal tools, you can effectively protect your trademark and maintain the integrity of your brand in the digital marketplace. This proactive stance not only deters counterfeiters but also reinforces your commitment to quality and consumer trust, strengthening your brand's reputation and competitive edge.

Utilizing Content Monitoring Tools

In the expansive digital landscape, keeping track of how and where your trademark is used can be daunting. Content monitoring tools are essential for automating the surveillance of your brand's presence online, enabling you to respond swiftly to unauthorized uses or infringements. This section explores the various types of content monitoring tools available and how to effectively integrate them into your trademark protection strategy.

Types of Content Monitoring Tools

1. **Automated Search Tools**: These tools continuously scan the internet for specified keywords, phrases, or images associated with your trademark. They can monitor a broad range of digital spaces including websites, e-commerce platforms, blogs, and forums. Automated alerts notify you of potential infringements as they happen, allowing for timely intervention.

2. **Social Media Monitoring Tools**: Specialized software is available to monitor social media platforms where your trademark might be mentioned or misused. These tools can track posts, hashtags, and even images across platforms like Facebook, Twitter, Instagram, and LinkedIn, providing comprehensive oversight of your brand's portrayal in social media spaces.

3. **Domain Name Watch Services**: These services keep an eye on domain registrations that could be confusingly similar to your trademark. They alert you to new registrations that may infringe on your trademark or could be used for cybersquatting, enabling you to take preventive action.

Implementing Monitoring Tools Effectively

1. **Setting Clear Objectives**: Define what you need to monitor and why. Whether it's keeping an eye on new product launches, safeguarding against counterfeit goods, or protecting against brand dilution, your monitoring tools should be configured to meet specific objectives that align with your overall brand protection strategy.

2. **Choosing the Right Tools**: Select monitoring tools that best suit your needs based on the breadth and depth of coverage required. Consider factors such as ease of use, integration capabilities with other management systems, and the specificity of the alerts provided.

3. **Regular Review and Adjustment**: Periodically review the performance of your monitoring tools to ensure they are effectively capturing relevant data without overwhelming you with false positives. Adjust parameters and filters as your brand evolves and new threats emerge.

Leveraging Data for Strategic Decisions

1. **Analyzing Data for Insights**: Use the data collected from monitoring tools to gain insights into potential vulnerabilities and trends in trademark use or abuse. This information can inform strategic decisions such as entering new markets, launching new product lines, or intensifying enforcement in certain regions.

2. **Integrating Data into Overall IP Strategy**: Combine data from content monitoring tools with other intellectual property management systems. This integrated approach provides a holistic view of your trademark's status and can help in making informed decisions about registrations, renewals, and enforcement priorities.

Content monitoring tools are invaluable for maintaining the integrity and value of your trademarks in the digital realm. By utilizing these tools strategically, you can ensure continuous vigilance over your brand's online presence, enabling proactive responses to threats and informed decision-making. As digital landscapes evolve, so should your monitoring strategies, adapting to new challenges and leveraging technological advancements to safeguard your trademarks effectively.

Legal Strategies for Online Trademark Enforcement

In the realm of online commerce and communication, trademark infringement can spread rapidly, making swift and effective legal response crucial. To protect your brand's integrity and the value of your trademarks in the digital space, it is essential to develop and implement robust legal strategies. This section outlines the legal avenues available for enforcing trademark rights online and provides guidance on when and how to deploy these strategies effectively.

Preparing for Legal Enforcement

1. **Understanding Digital Jurisdiction Issues**: Online infringement cases often involve complex jurisdictional issues, as infringers can operate from anywhere in the world. Understanding the legal frameworks and jurisdictional boundaries is crucial before initiating legal action.

2. **Documenting Infringement Evidence**: Maintain comprehensive records of all instances of infringement, including screenshots, URLs, and timestamps. This documentation will be critical in legal proceedings to prove the infringement and demonstrate its impact on your brand.

3. **Cease and Desist Notices**: Often the first step in legal enforcement, a cease and desist letter can be an effective tool. Tailor these notices to each specific case, clearly stating your legal rights and the actions required by the infringer. The tone should be firm but professional, aiming to resolve the issue without escalating to litigation.

Legal Remedies and Actions

1. **Digital Millennium Copyright Act (DMCA) Takedowns**: For copyright-related infringements that involve your trademarked content, utilize DMCA takedown notices. These can compel hosting services and websites to remove infringing content swiftly.

2. **Uniform Domain-Name Dispute-Resolution Policy (UDRP)**: If the infringement involves domain names, the UDRP provides a mechanism to challenge and potentially transfer domain ownership. This process is quicker and less costly than traditional litigation and is handled through arbitration.

3. **Litigation**: When other methods fail, litigation may be necessary. This involves filing a lawsuit in a relevant jurisdiction, which can be costly and time-consuming but might be essential for stopping egregious or persistent infringement.

Collaborating with Online Platforms

1. **Utilizing Platform Enforcement Policies**: Most major online platforms, including social media sites and eCommerce platforms, have policies and tools in place for intellectual property enforcement. Familiarize yourself with these policies and use the provided tools to report and resolve infringements.

2. **Building Relationships with Platform Legal Teams**: Establish contacts within the legal or IP enforcement teams of major platforms.

These relationships can facilitate faster and more effective responses to infringement notifications.

Strategic Considerations for Online Enforcement

1. **Choosing Battles Wisely**: Given the vastness of the internet and the potential for widespread infringement, prioritize cases based on their impact on your brand and business. Focus resources on significant threats rather than pursuing every minor infringement.

2. **Public Relations Considerations**: Be mindful of the public relations aspect of legal enforcement. Aggressive legal actions can sometimes lead to negative publicity, especially if perceived as overreach. Balance legal actions with public relations strategies to maintain a positive brand image.

Effective online trademark enforcement requires a combination of legal acumen, strategic planning, and proactive digital monitoring. By employing a range of legal strategies tailored to the nature of the infringement and the specifics of the digital environment, you can protect your brand effectively while minimizing potential damage to your brand's reputation. Legal enforcement should always be considered as part of a broader intellectual property strategy that aligns with your business goals and brand values.

Quick Tips and Recap

- **Secure Domains Early**: Prioritize registering domain names that align with your trademarks to prevent cybersquatting and ensure brand consistency online.

- **Utilize Verification on Social Media**: Seek verification for your brand's profiles on social media platforms to establish authenticity and deter impersonators.

- **Implement Comprehensive Monitoring**: Deploy content monitoring tools to continuously scan for trademark misuse across websites, social media, and online marketplaces.

- **Act Swiftly on Infringements**: Use cease and desist letters and platform reporting tools to address infringements quickly and prevent further misuse.

- **Leverage Legal Frameworks**: Familiarize yourself with legal mechanisms like the DMCA for copyright infringement and UDRP for domain disputes to effectively take down infringing content or recover domains.

- **Engage with Platform Enforcement Teams**: Establish relationships with IP enforcement teams on major platforms to facilitate quicker resolutions to infringement issues.

- **Educate Your Consumers**: Run campaigns to educate your consumers on how to identify genuine products and the importance of purchasing from authorized channels.

- **Monitor and Adapt Strategies**: Regularly review the effectiveness of your trademark protection strategies and adapt them in response to new trends in infringement and changes in technology.

- **Prioritize Significant Threats**: Focus your legal and enforcement efforts on infringements that pose the most significant risk to your brand's integrity and customer trust.

- **Balance Enforcement with PR**: Consider the public relations impact of your enforcement actions to ensure that your brand maintains a positive image while protecting its intellectual property.

By following these tips, you can ensure robust protection of your trademarks in the digital realm, safeguarding your brand against infringement and maintaining its reputation among consumers.

CHAPTER NINE

Borderless Brands: Crafting an International Trademark Strategy

"Building a brand that crosses international borders isn't just about visibility, it's about strategic adaptation. You must tailor your trademarks to resonate globally while respecting local nuances."
— HOWARD SCHULTZ, FORMER CEO OF STARBUCKS

Welcome to the global village, where your brand can travel faster than a jet plane—no passport required. But before you take off, let's chat about crafting an international trademark strategy that ensures your brand isn't just visiting foreign markets but thriving in them. Navigating the world of international trademarks is like playing a game of Risk: every move is strategic, every territory valuable, and every opponent ready to challenge your claim.

First things first: not all trademark laws are created equal—think of them as local cuisines. What's savory in one country can be sour in another. Your trademark might be a champion in the U.S., but in another country, it could be just another face in the crowd. Before you go stamping your brand on products overseas, do your homework. Research local trademark laws as thoroughly as a tourist would their travel itinerary. Know the nuances, and prepare for surprises—like finding out your brand name means something embarrassing in another language!

Next, consider the Madrid Protocol, not just a fancy treaty but your international trademark butler. It can handle the paperwork in multiple countries through a single application. It's like having a golden key that unlocks several doors at once, but remember, it's not infallible. Each country still has the right to refuse your mark based on their local laws, so don't put all your eggs in one basket—or one filing, in this case.

And let's talk about enforcement. Protecting your trademark internationally isn't just about filing the right papers; it's about keeping a vigilant eye in every market you enter. Set up a global monitoring system, because infringement can come from any corner of the world. Think of it as setting up a worldwide web (and not the internet kind) to catch any copycats. When you do catch them, act decisively. You'll need a network of local experts—legal ninjas, if you will—to help you navigate the complexities of each country's legal landscape.

Remember, a borderless brand needs a robust international strategy. It's about being as culturally savvy as you are legally astute. With the right preparation and protection, your brand can become a global citizen—respected and recognized from Timbuktu to Tokyo. Keep your strategy sharp, your eyes open, and your brand might just become the world's next big thing.

Understanding Global Trademark Laws

As brands expand beyond their domestic borders, understanding the complexities of global trademark laws becomes crucial. Trademark protection is not universal; it varies significantly from one country to another. This section will explore the diversity of international trademark laws and highlight the importance of thorough research and local expertise in developing an effective global trademark strategy.

Variability of Trademark Laws Across Countries

1. **National Differences**: Trademark laws are primarily national, meaning each country has its own set of rules and regulations governing trademark registration and enforcement. What is protected in one country may not be protected in another. For instance, some countries require 'use' of the trademark in commerce for registration, while others allow registration based solely on 'intent to use'.

2. **First-to-File vs. First-to-Use**: Understanding whether a country operates under a first-to-file or first-to-use system is vital. In a first-to-file system, the first person to file a trademark application will generally have the rights to the trademark, regardless of actual use. In contrast, first-to-use countries require the trademark owner to demonstrate use in commerce before claiming rights.

3. **Cultural and Linguistic Considerations**: It's essential to consider cultural and linguistic factors when registering trademarks internationally. A brand name that works well in one language might have negative connotations or be difficult to pronounce in another. This can affect brand perception and marketability.

Research and Preparation for International Registration

1. **Local Trademark Searches**: Conduct comprehensive trademark searches in each target country to ensure that your trademark does not infringe on existing rights. This step can prevent costly legal disputes and rebranding efforts after entering a new market.

2. **Understanding Local Nuances**: Engage with local trademark experts who can provide insights into specific regulatory requirements, potential legal challenges, and the overall trademark registration process in their respective countries. Their expertise can be invaluable in navigating local bureaucratic and legal complexities.

3. **Adapting Trademark Strategies**: Be prepared to adapt your trademark strategy based on local laws and market conditions. This might involve modifying your mark, using different marks in different countries, or even changing your brand name to better fit local markets.

Strategic Planning for Global Expansion

1. **Long-Term Vision**: Develop a long-term trademark strategy that anticipates future expansions and changes in the marketplace. Consider potential global shifts in consumer behavior, emerging markets, and evolving legal landscapes.

2. **Risk Management**: Implement a risk management plan to address potential trademark disputes before they escalate. This includes setting up monitoring systems to watch for trademark misuse and establishing protocols for rapid response.

3. **Continuous Education**: Stay informed about changes in international trademark laws and practices. Regular updates from international IP organizations, legal publications, and your network of local experts can help you keep pace with the dynamic nature of global trademark protection.

Navigating the complex web of international trademark laws requires a deep understanding of local regulations, cultural sensitivities, and strategic adaptation. By thoroughly researching potential markets, engaging with local experts, and planning strategically, you can effectively protect your trademark rights across different jurisdictions and ensure that your brand thrives in the global marketplace.

Leveraging the Madrid Protocol

The Madrid Protocol provides a convenient and cost-effective solution for registering trademarks internationally. As a treaty administered by the World Intellectual Property Organization (WIPO), it allows trademark owners to apply for protection in multiple countries through a single application, filed in one language, with one set of fees. This section explores how businesses can utilize the Madrid Protocol to streamline their international trademark registration process and extend their brand protection globally.

Basics of the Madrid Protocol

1. **Single Application**: Trademark owners can file one application directly with their national or regional trademark office (the "Office of Origin"), which then gets submitted to WIPO. This application can extend trademark protection to over 120 countries that are members of the Madrid System.

2. **Centralized Management**: After registration, any changes such as a change of ownership, address, or renewal of the registration can be made through a single administrative process with WIPO. This central management significantly simplifies the administrative burden associated with maintaining multiple international registrations.

3. **Cost-Effectiveness**: The Madrid System is more cost-effective compared to filing separate trademark applications in each country. Although additional fees may apply based on the number of countries selected and whether additional classes of goods and services are included, the consolidated process results in lower overall costs.

Strategic Use of the Madrid Protocol

1. **Planning Your Application**: Determine which countries are most relevant for your business's international strategy. Not all countries are members of the Madrid System, so additional direct filings might be necessary. Carefully planning which countries to include in your Madrid application is crucial for maximizing your trademark protection while keeping costs in check.

2. **Responding to Provisional Refusals**: While the Madrid System simplifies the application process, individual member countries can still issue "provisional refusals" based on local trademark laws. Be prepared to respond to these refusals, possibly requiring the assistance of local legal counsel to address specific objections within designated timeframes.

3. **Monitoring and Enforcement**: Utilize the global network established through the Madrid System to monitor and enforce your trademark rights efficiently. Leverage the information and resources provided by WIPO

to keep track of your trademark status and any potential infringements internationally.

Collaborating with International Experts

1. **Engaging Local Agents**: In cases where provisional refusals are issued, or where legal complexities arise, working with local trademark agents or attorneys can be invaluable. These experts can navigate local legal systems and ensure compliance with specific country requirements, enhancing the chances of successful registration.

2. **Continuous Learning and Adaptation**: The global trademark landscape is continually evolving. Stay updated on changes within the Madrid System and international trademark laws by attending seminars, workshops, and training provided by WIPO and other international IP organizations.

The Madrid Protocol is an essential tool for businesses looking to protect their trademarks internationally. By understanding and effectively leveraging this system, businesses can extend their brand protection across borders efficiently and cost-effectively. Planning, strategic application, and the ability to respond to challenges within the system are key to harnessing the full potential of the Madrid Protocol in your international trademark strategy.

Post-Registration Timeline – Non-Madrid Protocol
Trademark rights can potentially last indefinitely, but maintaining a federal trademark registration requires active use of the mark in commerce and the timely filing of mandatory maintenance documents. You must submit the first maintenance document between the fifth and sixth year following registration. Subsequent filings are required between the ninth and tenth years after registration, and then every decade thereafter. If these documents are not filed as required, you risk cancellation or loss of your federal registration.

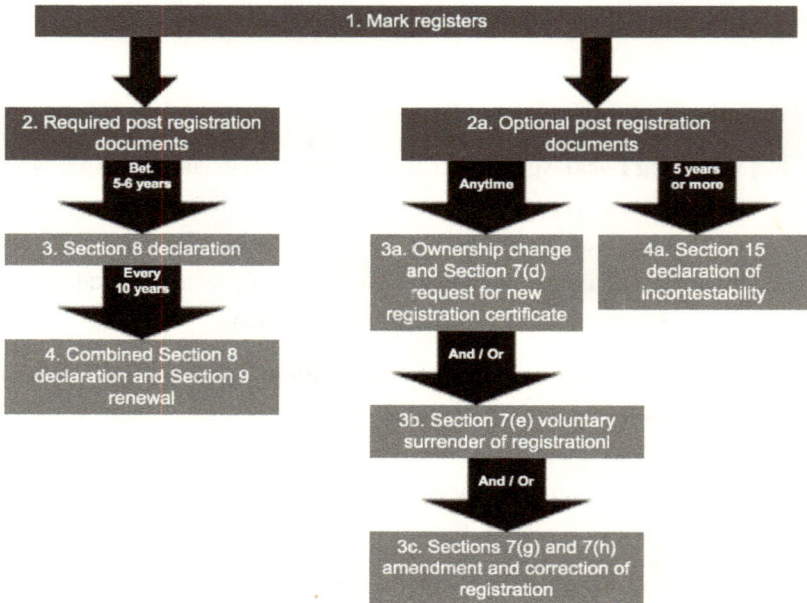

Figure 5: Post-Registration Timeline – Non-Madrid Protocol

Setting Up Global Monitoring Systems

In today's interconnected market, a brand's reputation can be impacted by actions occurring anywhere in the world. Establishing a global monitoring system is essential to safeguard your trademarks across different countries and platforms. This system acts as an early warning radar, detecting potential infringements or misuses of your trademark so you can respond promptly and effectively. This section discusses how to set up an efficient and comprehensive global monitoring system for your trademarks.

Designing a Comprehensive Monitoring Framework

1. **Scope of Monitoring**: Determine the breadth and depth of your monitoring needs based on your brand's geographical reach and market presence. Decide whether to focus on specific regions, key markets, or a worldwide scope. Consider the various channels to monitor, including

online marketplaces, social media platforms, domain registrations, and general web usage.

2. **Choosing the Right Tools**: Select monitoring tools that best suit the scope and scale of your needs. Many software and services specialize in different aspects of trademark monitoring, such as digital media scans, e-commerce listings, and domain name watch services. Tools like MarkMonitor or Corsearch provide extensive capabilities for tracking trademark use globally.

3. **Integration with IP Management**: Ensure that your monitoring system integrates seamlessly with your overall intellectual property management strategy. This includes alignment with your IP database and legal response protocols to enable quick action when infringements are detected.

Implementing the Monitoring System

1. **Setting Up Alerts**: Configure alerts based on specific criteria, such as unauthorized use of your logos, brand names, or other trademarked material. These alerts should be tailored to capture significant infringements while minimizing false positives that can lead to inefficiency.

2. **Regular Reviews and Adjustments**: Continually assess the effectiveness of your monitoring system. This includes reviewing the incidents detected, the response times, and the outcomes of your enforcement actions. Adjust your strategies and tools as necessary to improve efficiency and effectiveness.

3. **Training and Empowerment**: Train relevant team members on how to use monitoring tools and interpret the data they provide. Empowering your team with the right knowledge and tools will enhance their ability to identify and react to potential threats swiftly.

Leveraging Data for Strategic Insights

1. **Analyzing Trends**: Use the data collected from your monitoring efforts to analyze trends in trademark infringement. Understanding where, how,

and by whom your trademarks are being infringed upon can inform broader strategic decisions, such as entering new markets or adjusting marketing strategies.

2. **Reporting and Documentation**: Maintain detailed records of all detected infringements and the actions taken. This documentation can be invaluable for legal proceedings and for refining your trademark protection strategy.

A robust global monitoring system is a cornerstone of effective international trademark management. By setting up a system that continuously scans for trademark misuse across various platforms and regions, you can protect your brand's integrity and value. The right combination of tools, processes, and strategies will not only shield your trademarks from infringement but also provide strategic insights that support broader business objectives.

Enforcing Trademarks Internationally

As businesses expand globally, the task of enforcing trademarks across multiple jurisdictions becomes increasingly complex. Different countries have unique legal frameworks, cultural norms, and enforcement challenges that can significantly affect the protection of intellectual property. Effective international enforcement requires not only a strong legal strategy but also an understanding of local nuances. This section outlines the key considerations and steps for enforcing trademarks internationally.

Establishing a Global Enforcement Framework

1. **Understanding Local Laws**: Begin by gaining a deep understanding of the trademark laws in each country where your trademark is registered. This includes knowing how these laws are applied in practice, not just in theory. Local legal counsel can provide invaluable insights and guidance on specific enforcement mechanisms available in their jurisdiction.

2. **Creating an Enforcement Strategy**: Develop a tailored enforcement strategy for each key market, taking into account the likelihood of infringement, the potential impact on your business, and the

effectiveness of local legal remedies. This strategy should prioritize markets based on risk assessment and align enforcement actions with your overall business goals.

3. **Leveraging International Agreements**: Utilize international agreements and treaties that facilitate cross-border enforcement of intellectual property rights, such as the Agreement on Trade-Related Aspects of Intellectual Property Rights (TRIPS) and regional treaties within the European Union or among ASEAN countries.

Practical Steps for Enforcement

1. **Cease and Desist Letters**: Often, the first step in the enforcement process is sending a cease and desist letter. This letter should be drafted to comply with local legal standards and, where possible, translated into the local language to ensure clear communication.

2. **Collaboration with Local Authorities**: In many countries, local authorities play a crucial role in enforcing anti-counterfeiting laws. Establishing a good working relationship with these authorities can enhance the effectiveness of your enforcement actions, especially in regions where counterfeiting is rampant.

3. **Customs Registration**: Register your trademarks with customs authorities in countries that offer this option. Customs registration enables the authorities to seize counterfeit goods at the border, preventing them from entering the market.

Litigation and Alternative Dispute Resolution

1. **Deciding When to Litigate**: Litigation should be a last resort due to its high cost and unpredictability. Assess the potential benefits against the risks and costs. Litigation may be necessary if the infringement is causing significant damage to your brand or if other enforcement efforts have failed.

2. **Alternative Dispute Resolution (ADR)**: Consider using arbitration or mediation, especially in international disputes where these methods can provide a more efficient resolution than court litigation. ADR can be

particularly effective in jurisdictions where the local courts are slow or less familiar with complex trademark issues.

3. **Working with Local Counsel**: Engage local counsel who specialize in trademark law to navigate the legal system effectively. They can act on your behalf in negotiations, ADR processes, or court proceedings, ensuring that your actions are legally sound and culturally appropriate.

Enforcing trademarks internationally requires a strategic approach that considers the unique challenges of each market. By understanding local legal environments, working collaboratively with local authorities and experts, and choosing the most effective enforcement mechanisms, you can protect your intellectual property rights across borders. This proactive and informed approach will help maintain the integrity and value of your brand worldwide.

Building a Network of International Experts

In the complex landscape of international trademark enforcement, having a network of knowledgeable local experts is invaluable. These professionals provide essential insights into the legal nuances, cultural considerations, and enforcement practices specific to their jurisdictions. Building and maintaining a robust network of international experts is crucial for effectively navigating the challenges of global trademark protection. This section discusses strategies for developing these relationships and leveraging their expertise to enhance your trademark strategy.

Identifying and Engaging Local Experts

1. **Selection Criteria**: Choose experts based on their experience, reputation, and specific knowledge of the intellectual property landscape in their country. This includes lawyers, trademark agents, and consultants who specialize in trademark law and have a proven track record of successful enforcement actions.

2. **Engagement Strategies**: Establish relationships through industry conferences, professional associations, and legal networks. Engage with experts in both formal settings, such as consultations, and informal

settings, such as industry events, to build rapport and mutual understanding.

3. **Continuous Collaboration**: Once relationships are established, maintain regular communication to keep abreast of any changes in local laws, potential risks, and new enforcement strategies. This ongoing dialogue ensures that your network remains active and informed.

Benefits of a Diverse Expert Network

1. **Localized Legal Insight**: Local experts provide specific insights into the legal environment of their countries, including details on court procedures, administrative processes, and effective legal strategies for trademark enforcement.

2. **Cultural Competence**: Experts from different regions bring an understanding of cultural nuances that can influence the effectiveness of your trademark strategy. This includes awareness of local business practices, consumer behavior, and potential cultural sensitivities.

3. **Rapid Response Capability**: Having a network of experts ready to act on your behalf enables quicker responses to infringement issues, which is critical in mitigating damage and enforcing rights effectively across different jurisdictions.

Strategies for Maximizing Network Effectiveness

1. **Regular Updates and Training**: Provide your network with regular updates on your brand's developments, new trademarks, and shifts in strategic focus. Organize training sessions to ensure that all members understand your company's overall international strategy and their role within it.

2. **Shared Resources and Tools**: Facilitate the sharing of resources, such as case studies, legal documents, and enforcement tools, across your network. This not only enhances the expertise within the network but also fosters a collaborative environment.

3. **Performance Reviews and Feedback**: Conduct regular reviews of the network's performance, soliciting feedback on what strategies are

working and where improvements can be made. This helps refine your approach and ensures that your network remains aligned with your goals.

Building a network of international experts is more than just a means to an end in global trademark enforcement; it's a strategic asset that enhances your brand's protection worldwide. By carefully selecting experts, fostering ongoing collaborations, and continuously engaging with them, you can ensure that your trademark strategy is robust, responsive, and respectful of local nuances. This global team becomes a critical component in maintaining the integrity and value of your brand on the international stage.

Quick Tips and Recap

- **Research Local Trademark Laws**: Before entering new markets, thoroughly research local trademark laws to understand registration requirements and protections.

- **Utilize the Madrid Protocol**: Leverage the Madrid Protocol for streamlined, cost-effective trademark registration across multiple countries.

- **Implement Global Monitoring**: Set up a global monitoring system to detect and act on trademark infringements quickly.

- **Engage Local Experts**: Build relationships with local trademark experts in each country to navigate regional legal complexities effectively.

- **Enforce Rights Decisively**: Be prepared to enforce your trademark rights through local legal actions, utilizing cease and desist letters and, if necessary, litigation.

- **Register with Customs**: Use customs registration to prevent counterfeit products from entering key markets.

- **Maintain Regular Communication**: Keep in touch with your network of international experts to stay updated on changes in trademark law and enforcement practices.

- **Adapt Strategies to Local Markets**: Tailor your trademark strategies to fit local cultural and consumer landscapes, ensuring relevancy and compliance.

- **Document All Enforcement Actions**: Keep thorough records of all trademark enforcement actions for legal and strategic review.

- **Evaluate Network Performance**: Regularly assess the effectiveness of your international expert network and make adjustments as needed to improve support and outcomes.

By following these tips, you can ensure a robust international trademark strategy that protects your brand's integrity and facilitates global expansion.

CHAPTER TEN

Conflict Zone:

Managing and Resolving

Trademark Disputes

"In the realm of trademark disputes, success is measured by your ability to secure your intellectual property while maintaining business relationships. It's essential to resolve conflicts in ways that foster cooperation and respect."— URSULA BURNS, FORMER CEO OF XEROX

Welcome to the Conflict Zone—where trademarks clash, tempers flare, and the coffee pot in the legal department never gets a break. Navigating trademark disputes is less like a polite debate and more like a dinner party debate about politics—intense, unpredictable, and nobody wants to give up their seat at the table.

Firstly, consider this: not every skirmish needs to escalate into a full-blown battle. Sometimes, a well-drafted cease-and-desist letter can do the trick, functioning like a polite but firm nudge to back off. Think of it as the corporate equivalent of saying, "You're standing on my foot," with a smile. It's direct, effective, and much more civil than launching into a tirade.

However, if things heat up and you find yourself staring down the barrel of a legal showdown, strategy is key. This is where your inner chess master should emerge. Every move should be calculated, from selecting the right legal team to choosing which battles are worth your while. Remember, the goal is resolution, not annihilation. You want to protect your brand without burning bridges—or your budget.

Mediation and negotiation are your friends here. They're the diplomats in the room when everyone else is ready to declare war. Entering into discussions can often lead to creative solutions that satisfy both parties. Maybe it's a licensing deal, or perhaps a slight adjustment in trademark use. Think outside the box—the goal is to end the dispute with your brand's integrity and your relationships intact.

And remember, the court should be your last resort, like the emergency brake on a train. It's there if you absolutely need it, but it's much smoother if you never have to pull it. Litigation is costly, time-consuming, and unpredictable. It's like flipping a coin where both sides are expense and stress.

So, keep your wits about you and your lawyer on speed dial. With a mix of tact, tenacity, and timely communication, you can navigate through the choppiest of trademark waters and steer your brand back to calmer seas. After all, the best disputes are the ones that are resolved quickly and quietly, leaving you free to focus on what you do best—running a successful brand.

Preventive Measures and Early Detection

In the realm of trademark disputes, prevention is undoubtedly better than cure. Early detection and preventive measures can significantly mitigate the risks of costly and time-consuming legal battles. This section explores strategies to prevent trademark conflicts and detect potential issues early, helping ensure that your brand remains protected and your business operations undisturbed.

Developing a Robust Trademark Strategy

1. **Comprehensive Trademark Searches**: Before adopting and registering a new trademark, conduct thorough trademark searches to identify any potential conflicts with existing trademarks. This includes not only direct matches in your industry but also similar marks in related industries that could pose a conflict.

2. **Clear Brand Guidelines**: Establish and disseminate clear brand usage guidelines within your organization. Ensure that all departments, especially marketing and product development, understand the importance of adhering to these guidelines to prevent unintentional infringements.

3. **Trademark Education**: Regularly educate your employees about the significance of trademarks and the risks of infringement. Understanding the basics of trademark law can empower them to spot potential issues before they escalate into disputes.

Implementing Monitoring Systems

1. **Continuous Monitoring**: Set up a continuous monitoring system to track the use of your trademarks online and in physical markets. Utilize specialized software that alerts you to new trademark filings, publications, or uses of similar marks.

2. **Monitoring Competitors**: Keep an eye on your competitors' trademark activities. Understanding their trademark strategies can help you anticipate potential conflicts and address them proactively.

3. **Engaging External Experts**: Consider hiring external legal experts or trademark watch services that specialize in monitoring trademarks globally. They can provide an additional layer of security by catching issues that internal processes might miss.

Early Detection Tactics

1. **Regular Reviews**: Periodically review your trademark portfolio and the market landscape to ensure your trademarks are not being infringed upon

and are still adequately protected. Adjust your strategy based on new market entries, changes in trademark law, or shifts in industry practices.

2. **Feedback Mechanisms**: Implement mechanisms to gather feedback from customers, partners, and the public regarding the use of your trademarks. Often, these stakeholders can provide first-hand observations of potential infringements.

3. **Legal Checkpoints**: Set up legal checkpoints at key stages of product development, marketing campaigns, and business expansion to ensure that new initiatives comply with existing trademark laws and do not infringe on others' rights.

Proactive trademark management through preventive measures and early detection is crucial for avoiding disputes and maintaining the integrity of your brand. By implementing robust strategies for monitoring and education, you can protect your intellectual property more effectively and ensure that your brand continues to thrive without legal entanglements.

Utilizing Cease and Desist Letters Effectively

Cease and desist letters are a primary tool in the trademark owner's arsenal for addressing potential infringements quickly and directly without immediate recourse to litigation. When crafted and used effectively, these letters can resolve disputes amicably by alerting infringers to the issue and requesting cessation of the infringing activity. This section outlines how to make the most of cease and desist letters as part of a strategic approach to trademark enforcement.

Crafting an Effective Cease and Desist Letter

1. **Clear Identification of the Issue**: Start the letter by clearly identifying the trademark in question and providing a detailed description of the alleged infringement. Include specific examples of the infringing use and explain how it infringes on your trademark rights.

2. **Legal Basis for Claims**: Articulate the legal grounds for your claims. Reference the specific laws and rights under which the infringement

occurs. This not only informs the recipient of the seriousness of the matter but also underscores your readiness to protect your legal rights.

3. **Firm but Professional Tone**: The tone of the letter should be firm enough to convey the seriousness of the infringement while remaining professional. Avoid aggressive or threatening language, as the goal is to resolve the issue amicably and preserve good business relationships when possible.

4. **Demand for Action**: Clearly state what actions you expect the recipient to take. This may include immediately ceasing the infringing activity, removing infringing content from websites, or other specific remedies that will resolve the infringement.

5. **Deadline for Response**: Set a reasonable deadline for the recipient to respond or comply with the demands. This creates a sense of urgency and helps ensure that the issue is addressed promptly.

Strategic Use of Cease and Desist Letters

1. **Tailoring the Approach**: Customize your approach based on the context of the infringement and your knowledge of the infringer. A startup or small business might be unaware they are infringing and may respond positively to a more educational and collaborative approach. In contrast, a letter to a repeat infringer or a larger entity might need to be more stringent.

2. **Escalation Clauses**: Include a statement in the letter that outlines the consequences of failing to comply with the demands, such as potential legal action. This indicates your commitment to taking further steps if necessary while leaving room for negotiation.

3. **Monitoring Compliance**: After sending the letter, actively monitor the situation to ensure compliance with the demands. This may require follow-up communications or adjustments to the strategy based on the recipient's response.

Legal Considerations

1. **Jurisdictional Issues**: Consider the jurisdictional aspects of where the infringement is occurring and where the infringer is based. This may affect the enforceability of your claims and the legal strategies available to you.

2. **Documenting Communications**: Keep detailed records of all communications sent and received regarding the dispute. This documentation will be invaluable if the situation escalates to legal proceedings.

Cease and desist letters are an essential part of managing trademark disputes efficiently. By using these letters judiciously, you can protect your trademarks effectively while minimizing the need for costly and time-consuming litigation. The key is to balance firmness with professionalism, clearly communicate your demands, and be prepared to follow through on legal threats if necessary.

▶ A standard Infringement Demand Letter and Domain Name Infringement Demand Letter can be found in the **Appendix**. **Disclaimer:** Please note that all documents are provided for informational purposes only and should not be construed as legal advice. We recommend consulting with a qualified attorney to ensure that any legal documents or decisions are tailored to your specific circumstances.

Negotiation and Mediation Techniques

In the realm of trademark disputes, litigation is often seen as a last resort due to its potential to drain resources, extend conflict duration, and damage business relationships. Negotiation and mediation serve as vital tools in the alternative dispute resolution (ADR) spectrum, offering more controlled, confidential, and potentially conciliatory paths to resolving conflicts. This section details effective strategies for utilizing these techniques to address and resolve trademark disputes amicably and efficiently.

Preparing for Negotiation

1. **Understanding the Dispute**: Thoroughly assess the nature of the dispute, including the legal and business implications. Identify the core issues and interests at stake for both parties, as this understanding will guide your negotiation strategy.

2. **Setting Objectives**: Define clear, realistic objectives for the negotiation. Determine what concessions you are willing to make and what outcomes are non-negotiable. Establishing these boundaries beforehand helps maintain focus and efficiency during discussions.

3. **Choosing the Right Environment**: Opt for a neutral and private setting for negotiations to facilitate open, confidential discussions. An environment conducive to professional and constructive dialogue can significantly influence the outcome.

Conducting Effective Negotiations

1. **Open Communication**: Engage in open and honest communication, clearly expressing your concerns and listening actively to the other party. This approach fosters mutual understanding and can reveal areas of common interest or potential compromise.

2. **Flexibility and Creativity**: Be flexible in your approach and open to creative solutions. Sometimes, resolving a trademark dispute can involve licensing arrangements, coexistence agreements, or revisions to the trademark use that satisfy both parties' needs.

3. **Use of Facilitators**: In complex disputes, consider using a neutral third party, such as a mediator, who can facilitate discussions and help both sides reach a mutually acceptable solution. Mediators are skilled in navigating difficult conversations and finding the heart of the conflict.

Embracing Mediation

1. **Understanding Mediation's Role**: Recognize that mediation is not about winning or losing but finding a solution that both parties can accept. Unlike in litigation, mediation's success often depends on the willingness of both parties to cooperate and compromise.

2. **Preparation for Mediation**: Prepare comprehensively for mediation by gathering all necessary documentation, understanding the legal precedents, and formulating a strategy aligned with your business objectives. Preparation also involves briefing your mediator on the nuances of the dispute to maximize their effectiveness.

3. **Engaging in the Process**: Actively participate in the mediation process. Be prepared to make decisions in real-time and adapt your strategy based on the flow of mediation. The flexibility to adjust your stance based on new information or proposals is crucial.

Post-Negotiation Follow-Up

1. **Documenting Agreements**: Ensure that any agreement reached is clearly documented in writing. This document should be legally binding and include all specific terms and conditions agreed upon during the negotiation or mediation.

2. **Implementation and Monitoring**: After reaching an agreement, implement the terms effectively and monitor compliance to ensure that all parties uphold their commitments. Regular follow-ups may be necessary to address any issues or adjustments.

Negotiation and mediation are powerful tools in the trademark dispute resolution process, offering paths to resolution that can preserve business relationships and reduce costs. By preparing adequately, engaging openly, and utilizing expert facilitators, parties can navigate the complexities of trademark disputes and arrive at sustainable and mutually beneficial resolutions.

Litigation Strategy

When negotiation and mediation fail to resolve a trademark dispute, litigation may become necessary. Litigation is a powerful tool that involves presenting your case in court to obtain a legally binding decision. This section will outline the critical aspects of formulating a successful litigation strategy, focusing on preparation, execution, and management of a trademark lawsuit.

Preparing for Litigation

1. **Understanding the Legal Grounds**: Before proceeding, ensure you have a solid legal basis for your claim. This includes identifying the specific rights infringed, the nature of the infringement, and the applicable laws and precedents that support your position.

2. **Selecting the Right Legal Team**: Choose attorneys who specialize in trademark law and have experience with similar cases. The right legal team should not only understand the intricacies of trademark law but also be familiar with the court system where the lawsuit will be filed.

3. **Gathering Evidence**: Compile all necessary evidence to support your case. This includes registration details of your trademark, instances of the alleged infringement, any communications with the infringer, and evidence of any harm caused by the infringement such as customer confusion or lost sales.

Formulating the Legal Strategy

1. **Determining the Venue**: Choose the most appropriate jurisdiction to file the lawsuit, considering where the infringement occurred, where the defendant operates, and where the legal environment is most favorable to your case.

2. **Defining the Scope of the Claim**: Clearly define the scope of your claim, including what remedies you are seeking. Remedies can include injunctions to stop further infringement, monetary compensation for damages, and, in some cases, recovery of attorneys' fees.

3. **Anticipating Counterclaims**: Be prepared for potential counterclaims by the defendant, such as challenges to the validity of your trademark. Preparing responses to these counterclaims in advance can significantly strengthen your position.

► A sample Complaint can be found in the **Appendix. Disclaimer:** Please note that all documents are provided for informational purposes only and should not be construed as legal advice. We recommend consulting with a qualified attorney to ensure that any legal documents or decisions are tailored to your specific circumstances.

Managing Litigation

1. **Budgeting**: Establish a clear budget for the litigation process, considering attorney fees, court costs, and potential damages. Litigation can be expensive, so it's crucial to manage financial resources wisely.

2. **Timeline Management**: Understand and plan for the litigation timeline, which can often extend over months or years. Keep stakeholders informed about the expected duration and major milestones in the case.

3. **Communication Strategy**: Maintain an effective communication strategy both internally and externally. Internally, ensure that all team members are informed and aligned with the litigation strategy. Externally, manage communications to protect the brand's reputation, addressing public relations concerns as they arise.

Post-Litigation Actions

1. **Enforcing Judgments**: Once a judgment is obtained, take action to enforce it. This might involve working with law enforcement to seize infringing products or collaborating with financial institutions to collect damages.

2. **Learning from Experience**: After the litigation concludes, review the process and outcomes. Identify what worked well and what could be improved. Use these insights to strengthen your trademark protection strategies going forward.

Litigation is a decisive approach to resolving trademark disputes but comes with significant risks and costs. A well-prepared litigation strategy, backed by a skilled legal team and thorough preparation, can effectively protect your trademark rights and uphold the integrity of your brand in the marketplace.

Post-Dispute Brand Management

After navigating the turbulent waters of a trademark dispute, it's crucial to focus on managing your brand's recovery and enhancement. Whether the dispute ended in a court ruling, settlement, or amicable resolution, the aftermath provides a significant opportunity to strengthen your brand's market position and repair any potential damage to its reputation. This section outlines effective strategies for post-dispute brand management, emphasizing proactive communication, strategic repositioning, and ongoing vigilance.

Rebuilding Brand Reputation

1. **Strategic Communication**: Develop a communication strategy that addresses the resolution of the dispute with your stakeholders, including customers, partners, and investors. This communication should be transparent about the outcomes and reaffirm the brand's commitment to its values and quality standards.

2. **Engaging with Media**: Manage media relations carefully. Prepare press releases or statements that highlight the positive aspects of how the dispute was resolved, focusing on your brand's resilience and dedication to fair business practices. This can help mitigate any negative publicity arising from the dispute.

3. **Customer Engagement**: Reinforce trust with your customer base through targeted campaigns. Consider special promotions, reassurances of quality service, or direct engagement through social media and other channels to reestablish positive relationships and customer loyalty.

Strategic Reinforcement of Trademark Value

1. **Reaffirming Trademark Strength**: Post-dispute, reinforce the value and significance of your trademark by emphasizing its role in representing quality and authenticity. Use marketing and advertising strategies to highlight the trademark's importance to the brand's identity.

2. **Innovative Branding Initiatives**: Launch new products or initiatives that put your trademark at the forefront. This not only diverts attention

from past conflicts but also demonstrates the brand's ongoing innovation and growth.

3. **Enhancing Legal Protections**: Strengthen your trademark's legal protection by reviewing and reinforcing registration details, ensuring all necessary geographical areas are covered and that the trademark is adequately protected against potential future disputes.

Ongoing Vigilance and Adaptation

1. **Continuous Monitoring**: Implement a permanent system for monitoring the use of your trademark in the marketplace to quickly identify and respond to potential infringements or misuses in the future.

2. **Adapting to Market Changes**: Stay informed about changes in trademark law and market conditions that could affect your brand. Regularly update your trademark strategy to adapt to these changes, ensuring continuous relevance and protection.

3. **Learning from Experience**: Analyze the dispute and your company's response to it. Identify key learnings regarding both legal strategy and brand management. Apply these insights to improve both preventive measures and response strategies for future issues.

The end of a trademark dispute marks the beginning of an important phase for brand management. By focusing on strategic communication, reinforcing the trademark's value, and maintaining vigilance, you can turn the challenge of a dispute into an opportunity to enhance your brand's strength and market position. Effective post-dispute management not only repairs any damage but also positions the brand for future growth and success.

Quick Tips and Recap

- **Prioritize Prevention**: Implement proactive measures to prevent disputes through comprehensive trademark searches and clear internal guidelines.

- **Utilize Cease and Desist Letters**: Employ cease and desist letters effectively as a first response to potential infringements, balancing firmness with professionalism.

- **Engage in Mediation**: Consider mediation and negotiation as cost-effective and relationship-preserving approaches to resolving trademark disputes.

- **Prepare for Litigation**: If litigation is necessary, carefully select a specialized legal team, and meticulously prepare your case with a focus on gathering solid evidence.

- **Communicate Strategically Post-Dispute**: After a dispute, communicate transparently with stakeholders about the outcome and what it means for the brand.

- **Rebuild and Reinforce Brand Reputation**: Use strategic marketing and public relations to reinforce the brand's value and rebuild customer trust.

- **Enhance Legal Protections**: Strengthen your trademark's legal protections by reassessing and updating registrations and monitoring strategies.

- **Learn from Every Dispute**: Analyze each dispute to glean insights that can refine your approach to trademark management and dispute resolution.

- **Stay Informed on Legal Developments**: Keep abreast of changes in trademark laws and international agreements that could impact your brand's protection strategies.

- **Maintain Vigilance**: Continue monitoring the use of your trademark in the market to quickly address any new threats or infringements.

By following these tips, you can effectively manage and resolve trademark disputes, safeguarding your brand's integrity and promoting its continued growth and success.

PART THREE

Trademark Deep Dive

Diving into the world of trademarks is akin to plunging into the deep end of a pool, except this pool is filled not with water, but with legalese, paperwork, and potential pitfalls. It's a realm where the unassuming "@" and "™" reign supreme, guarding their brand kingdoms with ferocity. Here, every mark tells a tale, every label carries weight, and if you're not careful, you might just get tangled in a web of costly disputes. So, strap on your intellectual property floaties and get ready to navigate the choppy waters of trademark law, where vigilance is your lifeguard and a good attorney is worth their weight in gold—or at least in registered trademarks.

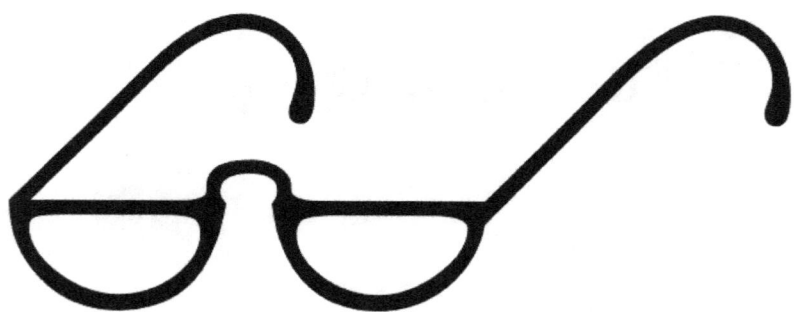

CHAPTER ELEVEN

The Battle Against Dilution

and Genericide

"Protecting a trademark from becoming generic is an ongoing battle of education and enforcement. It's about ensuring your brand doesn't become a victim of its own success."— PHIL KNIGHT, CO-FOUNDER OF NIKE

Welcome to the frontline of trademark warfare, where the enemies are insidious and the battles are fought not with swords, but with semantics and consumer perceptions. This is the arena of dilution and genericide, where even the mightiest of trademarks can fall victim to their own success.

Dilution is the sneaky little gremlin that nibbles away at the uniqueness of a trademark, gradually diminishing its power as others use similar marks for different products. Imagine your trademark is a bright, shining star in the consumer cosmos. Now picture tiny little stars popping up around it, stealing its light and sparkle. That's dilution—death by a thousand cuts, or in this case, a thousand little trademarks.

Then there's the bigger beast: genericide. It sounds like something you'd want to avoid just from the name alone, right? This is where a trademark becomes so popular that it transforms from a brand into a generic term for a type of product. Congratulations, your brand is now so famous that it's no longer yours! You've become the caretaker of a linguistic zombie that everyone uses, from the toddler demanding a tissue to the grandpa referring to every tablet as an iPad. It's the brand equivalent of a hit song going viral and then being played so often that people start changing the station.

The battle against these foes requires vigilance, strategy, and a hefty dose of legal savvy. Think of it as playing a high-stakes game of Whac-A-Mole, where every incorrect usage of your brand that pops up could be the next strike against your trademark's integrity. Your weapons? A solid set of trademark guidelines, an army of eagle-eyed lawyers, and an ongoing public education campaign to remind everyone that your brand is not the name for every similar product out there.

So, suit up and prepare to defend your brand's honor. Remember, in the world of trademarks, it's not just about making a mark—it's about making sure it stays yours.

Understanding Trademark Dilution

Trademark dilution represents a subtle yet significant threat to well-known brands, occurring when the distinctiveness of a famous mark is weakened, regardless of the presence of competition or likelihood of confusion. This erosion can diminish a brand's identity and consumer impact over time, making it crucial for trademark holders to understand and address dilution proactively.

Types of Trademark Dilution

1. **Dilution by Blurring**: Blurring happens when a trademark loses its uniqueness and becomes less associated with the original product or service due to its use by others. For example, if a famous mark like "Xerox" is used by other companies for products unrelated to its core

business, it could weaken its association with photocopiers and related services.

2. **Dilution by Tarnishment**: Tarnishment occurs when a trademark is associated with inferior or unseemly products or services, which can harm the reputation of the brand. For instance, if a luxury brand's trademark is used without permission on cheap, low-quality merchandise, it could tarnish the public's perception of the brand's quality and luxury status.

Factors Contributing to Dilution

1. **Widespread Unauthorized Use**: The more extensively a trademark is used without the owner's permission, the higher the risk of dilution. This unauthorized use can occur in various forms, including products, services, and even domain names.

2. **Similarity and Overlap**: The degree of similarity between the infringing mark and the famous mark can accelerate dilution, especially if the marks are used in overlapping or closely related markets.

3. **Brand Recognition and Fame**: The level of a brand's fame plays a critical role in dilution. Highly recognizable and famous trademarks are more susceptible to dilution as their widespread recognition makes them more likely targets for unauthorized use.

Legal Protections Against Dilution

1. **Federal Trademark Dilution Act (FTDA)**: In the United States, the FTDA provides an avenue for owners of famous trademarks to seek an injunction against uses of their marks that would cause dilution, regardless of the presence of competition or the likelihood of confusion.

2. **Proving Dilution**: To prove dilution by blurring, trademark owners must demonstrate that the distinctiveness of the mark has been impaired by its association with different products. For dilution by tarnishment, it must be shown that the mark's reputation has been harmed by its association with inferior or unsuitable products.

3. **Remedies**: Typical remedies for trademark dilution include injunctions preventing further use of the mark, monetary compensation for damages, and in some cases, recovery of profits made from the unauthorized use of the diluted trademark.

Understanding trademark dilution is crucial for maintaining the integrity and value of a brand. By recognizing the signs of dilution early and utilizing available legal protections, trademark owners can take decisive action to safeguard their intellectual property. This not only prevents the erosion of brand identity but also ensures that the trademark continues to hold significant value in the marketplace.

Legal Framework for Fighting Dilution

Protecting a trademark from dilution requires a robust understanding of the legal framework designed to safeguard brands against the weakening of their distinctive quality. This section explores the key legal instruments and doctrines that provide the basis for fighting dilution, offering trademark owners the tools needed to defend their marks effectively.

Key Legal Provisions

1. **Federal Trademark Dilution Act (FTDA)**: In the United States, the FTDA, amended by the Trademark Dilution Revision Act of 2006, specifically targets the protection of famous marks from dilution. This act allows the owners of well-known trademarks to take action against any use of a mark that dilutes the distinctive quality of the trademark, either by blurring or tarnishment.

2. **Requirements for Protection**: To qualify for protection under the FTDA, a trademark must be nationally recognized as famous. The criteria for fame include the duration, extent, and geographic reach of advertising and publicity of the mark, the amount, volume, and geographic extent of sales, and the extent of actual recognition of the mark.

3. **International Frameworks**: Different countries have varied approaches to trademark dilution. The European Union, for example, provides

protection against dilution under the Community Trademark Regulation, which requires that a trademark must be known by a significant part of the public concerned by the products or services covered by the trademark within the Community.

Implementing the Law

1. **Establishing Fame**: The first step in a dilution claim is to prove that the trademark is indeed famous and distinctive. This involves presenting evidence such as surveys, sales figures, advertising expenditures, and the duration of use to establish the mark's widespread recognition.

2. **Demonstrating Dilution**: Once fame is established, the trademark owner must demonstrate actual dilution. For blurring, this might involve showing that the distinctiveness of the mark has been compromised. For tarnishment, evidence must show that the mark's reputation has been harmed by association with inferior or unsavory goods or services.

3. **Seeking Remedies**: If dilution is proven, the remedies typically include injunctions to prevent further misuse of the trademark, monetary relief for damages suffered, and sometimes orders for the destruction of infringing goods.

Challenges in Fighting Dilution

1. **Proving Dilution**: Unlike infringement, where confusion must be demonstrated, dilution does not require proof of confusion. However, proving that a mark has been diluted can still be challenging, as it requires demonstrating a change in the public's perception of the mark.

2. **International Variability**: The protection against dilution varies significantly from one jurisdiction to another. Navigating international laws can be complex, as each country has its own standards for what constitutes a famous mark and how dilution is assessed.

The legal framework for fighting dilution provides a critical means by which trademark owners can protect their brands. Understanding and effectively leveraging these laws is essential for maintaining the integrity and value of famous trademarks. While the battle against dilution can be challenging, especially on an international scale, well-prepared trademark owners can navigate these complexities with the right legal strategies and expert guidance.

Strategies to Prevent Genericide

Genericide occurs when a trademark becomes so commonly used to refer to a type of product or service that it loses its legal protection as a distinctive brand identifier. This transformation from a proprietary name to a generic term can erode a brand's legal rights, making it crucial for companies to proactively protect against this risk. This section outlines effective strategies to prevent genericide and maintain the distinctiveness of trademarks.

Education and Branding Initiatives

1. **Proactive Brand Education**: Regularly educate both internal staff and external stakeholders on the importance of using the trademark correctly. This includes training employees, distributors, and marketing partners to use the trademark as an adjective followed by a generic term (e.g., "KLEENEX tissues" instead of just "Kleenex").

2. **Public Awareness Campaigns**: Implement public awareness campaigns to reinforce the proper use of the trademark. These campaigns can utilize various media channels to remind consumers of the brand's proper usage and its status as a registered trademark.

3. **Corrective Advertising**: When incorrect usage starts to become widespread, corrective advertising can help reclaim the trademark's brand identity. This type of advertising explicitly addresses the misuse and educates the public on the correct reference, emphasizing that the name is a brand, not a generic term.

Legal and Marketing Tactics

1. **Trademark Guidelines**: Publish clear trademark usage guidelines that detail how third parties, including the media and bloggers, should use the brand name. These guidelines should specify that the trademark is not to be used as a noun or a verb, which are common pathways to genericide.

2. **Monitoring and Enforcement**: Vigilantly monitor the use of the trademark in all forms of media and take swift action to correct misuses. This can involve sending out reminders or cease-and-desist letters to those who misuse the brand, emphasizing the need to maintain its trademark status.

3. **Distinctive Packaging and Advertising**: Use distinctive packaging and advertising to differentiate your product from generic products. This reinforces the association between the trademark and the specific characteristics of your product, helping prevent the name from becoming a generic term.

Legal Precautions and Responses

1. **Register the Trademark**: Ensure the trademark is registered and maintain the registration with the appropriate trademark offices. Regularly renew these registrations and keep them active to bolster legal protections.

2. **Legal Challenges and Litigation**: Be prepared to take legal action if necessary to prevent misuse of the trademark. This could include suing for trademark infringement to stop unauthorized uses that contribute to the risk of genericide.

3. **Documentation of Trademark Protection Efforts**: Maintain thorough documentation of all efforts to protect the trademark from becoming generic. This documentation can be invaluable in legal proceedings to demonstrate the active steps taken to preserve the trademark's distinctiveness.

Preventing genericide is an ongoing challenge that requires a multi-faceted approach combining education, legal action, and vigilant enforcement. By actively managing how a trademark is used in public discourse and reinforcing its association with a specific product or service, companies can protect their valuable trademarks from falling into generic use, thus preserving their unique brand identity and legal protections.

Examples of Proper Usage

The subsequent examples of correct usage are drawn from the former 3Com Corporation trademarks, but any company investing in trademarks and branding should apply similar practices to their own trademark portfolio.

Incorrect	Rule	Correct
Configurations using 3-Com-based products.	Never hyphenate a trademark.	Configurations using 3Com® products.
Widgeteer software is compatible with the Palm V.™	Always use a generic noun with a trademark.	Widgeteer software is compatible with the Palm V™ connected organizer.
3Com® Corporation announces a new U.S. Robotics® modem.	Never use a symbol when using "3Com" as part of the legal corporate name.	3Com Corporation announces a new U.S. Robotics® modem.
XYZ company announces the purchase of new 3Com servers.	Use a trademark symbol when using "3Com" as a brand name. If you can mentally use "brand" after 3Com, you are using the name as a brand name as opposed to using it as the company name.	XYZ company announces the purchase of new 3Com® servers.
You can access the dynamic infrared beaming feature on the Palm IIIs™.	Never use trademarks in a plural form.	You can access the dynamic infrared beaming feature on the Palm III™ organizers.
3Com announces its award-winning CoreBuilder® High-Function Switch for LAN routing.	Don't capitalize the generic noun, as the emphasis should be placed on the brand, not the noun.	3Com announces its award-winning CoreBuilder® high-function switch for LAN routing.
The Impact® IQ modem is easier to install than the xyz modem.	Never abbreviate a trademark as it must be used consistently in the way it was intended to be used.	The 3ComImpact® IQ modem is easier to install than the xyz modem.
Hotsyncing your data ensures a two-way data exchange between your PC and the product.	Never alter a trademark (a trademark is never a verb).	Synchronization, using HotSync® technology, allows two-way data exchange between your PC...
Use a Megahertz PC Card modem.	Use a trademark symbol on first reference.	Use a Megahertz® PC Card modem.
The PathBuilder's key selling feature is...	Never use trademarks as possessives.	The PathBuilder™ platform's key selling feature is...
TNM software.	Never turn a trademark into an acronym. Not only does the acronym dilute the brand, but it could also be another company's registered trademark.	Transcend® network management software.
The new OfficeConnect® delivers flexible, high-speed solutions for small offices.	Never use a trademark as the noun or 3Com risks losing the trademark.	New OfficeConnect® switches deliver flexible, high-speed solutions for small offices.

Figure 6: Examples of Proper Trademark Usage

The magazine cited the U.S. robtoics® modem as the best.	Always use the proper capitalization of a trademark.	The magazine cited the U.S. Robotics® modem as the best.
PACE-enabled® network interface cards enhance…	Never use a hyphen in conjunction with a trademark.	Network interface cards with PACE® technology enhance…
The SuperStack II NETBuilder® router is price competitive.	When compound trademark uses occur, apply the appropriate trademark symbol ™ or ® to both trademarks.	The SuperStack® II NETBuilder® router is price competitive.
Transcend Networking® framework.	Place symbols correctly. "Networking" is not part of the registered trademark.	Transcend® networking framework.
CoreBuilder® 12-slot chassis.	Avoid placing descriptors between a trademark and its noun.	12-slot CoreBuilder® chassis.
SuperStack® II Hub 10 hubs get positive praise at the world's most attended tradeshow this month.	When a product name includes the generic noun, it's not necessary to repeat the noun.	SuperStack® II Hub 10s get positive praise at the world's most attended tradeshow this month.
HomeConnect™ NC.	Avoid using acronyms as the noun; the generic noun must tell the consumer what the product (brand) is or does.	HomeConnect™ network interface card.
3Com® delivers third-party Web software to U.S. Robotics® modem users.	Never use a trademark symbol on "3Com" when using the name as a trade name.	3Com delivers third-party Web software to U.S. Robotics® modem-users.
TokenLink® network interface card.	Never abbreviate a full trademarked name.	TokenLink Velocity® network interface card.

Figure 7: Examples of Proper Trademark Usage

Public Education and Branding Efforts

To prevent genericide and ensure a trademark maintains its distinctiveness, public education and consistent branding efforts are crucial. This section focuses on how brands can engage effectively with the public and stakeholders to reinforce the proper use of trademarks and educate consumers about their significance as brand identifiers rather than generic terms.

Key Strategies for Public Education and Branding

1. **Educational Campaigns**: Develop and deploy educational campaigns that focus on the proper use of your trademark. These campaigns can utilize various media platforms—social media, print ads, TV commercials, and online videos—to communicate the importance of recognizing the trademark as a brand name and not a generic term.

2. **Collaborations with Influencers and Educators**: Partner with influencers, industry experts, and educators who can help disseminate the correct usage of your trademark. These partnerships can amplify your message and reach a broader audience more effectively.

3. **Direct Consumer Engagement**: Engage directly with consumers through workshops, webinars, and interactive online content. Direct engagement not only educates consumers but also builds a stronger relationship between them and your brand, fostering loyalty and proper usage.

Branding Efforts to Reinforce Trademark Use

1. **Consistent Visual Identity**: Ensure that all marketing materials, packaging, and advertising consistently use the trademark in a way that emphasizes its status as a registered brand. This includes the use of the ® symbol to signify registered trademark status and using the trademark in a distinctive typeface or color that sets it apart from generic terms.

2. **Corrective Branding**: Implement corrective branding strategies when instances of generic usage are detected. This might involve revising advertising slogans, taglines, or packaging to reinforce the trademark's proper usage and distinctiveness.

3. **Consumer Feedback Mechanisms**: Establish mechanisms for consumers to provide feedback on how they perceive and use the brand. This feedback can offer valuable insights into potential areas where confusion might occur, allowing the brand to adjust its educational and branding strategies accordingly.

Utilizing Educational Content

1. **Content Marketing**: Create content that not only promotes the brand but also educates the audience about the importance of trademarks. Blog posts, infographics, and informational videos can help clarify the distinction between brand names and generic terms.

2. **Training Retail Partners**: Work with retailers and distributors to ensure that they understand and communicate the trademark's significance to

consumers. Providing training sessions and informational materials can help maintain consistency in how the trademark is presented and discussed at the point of sale.

3. **Monitoring and Responding**: Actively monitor how the trademark is used in public domains, including online forums, retail environments, and media. Respond promptly to correct inaccuracies to prevent them from becoming widespread.

Effective public education and strategic branding are vital components of protecting a trademark from becoming generic. By actively engaging with consumers and stakeholders, ensuring consistent use in all forms of communication, and correcting misuses proactively, companies can safeguard their trademarks, maintain their distinctiveness, and ensure their long-term value. These efforts not only prevent genericide but also strengthen the overall brand identity in the marketplace.

Monitoring and Enforcement

Effective monitoring and enforcement are crucial to preventing both dilution and genericide, ensuring that a trademark retains its distinctive identity and legal protections. This final section outlines strategies for vigilant oversight of trademark usage across various platforms and markets, coupled with assertive enforcement actions to address violations promptly.

Establishing a Robust Monitoring System

1. **Comprehensive Monitoring Tools**: Invest in advanced monitoring tools that can scan a wide range of media, including online platforms, print media, and broadcast channels, for unauthorized use of your trademark. These tools should be capable of detecting both exact and similar uses of your trademark.

2. **Regular Audits and Reviews**: Schedule regular audits of how your trademarks are being used in the marketplace. This includes reviewing marketing materials, third-party websites, and any licensed uses of your trademark to ensure compliance with your brand guidelines.

3. **Global Watch Services**: Employ global watch services that notify you of new trademark filings that are similar to yours anywhere in the world. These services can help you act swiftly against potential conflicts or infringements.

Strategies for Effective Enforcement

1. **Cease and Desist Communications**: When unauthorized uses are detected, a well-crafted cease and desist letter can be the first step in the enforcement process. These communications should be clear, firm, and respectful, urging the infringer to stop the unauthorized use immediately.

2. **Legal Action for Non-Compliance**: If cease and desist efforts are ignored or fail, be prepared to take legal action. This can include filing for injunctions to prevent further misuse, pursuing damages if applicable, and working with local authorities in various jurisdictions to enforce your rights.

3. **Collaboration with Online Platforms**: Build relationships with major online platforms to facilitate faster takedowns of infringing content. Many platforms have procedures in place for trademark holders to report violations, which can expedite the removal process.

Leveraging Partnerships and Alliances

1. **Industry Coalitions**: Join or form coalitions with other trademark holders to combat common issues related to trademark dilution and genericide. These groups can provide support, share resources, and collectively advocate for stronger trademark protections.

2. **Engaging with Customs Authorities**: Register your trademarks with national customs authorities where available. This registration allows customs officers to seize counterfeit goods at borders, significantly reducing the circulation of infringing products.

3. **Training and Empowering Stakeholders**: Provide training for employees, partners, and even consumers on the importance of trademark protection. Educated stakeholders can act as additional eyes and ears, reporting potential infringements for further investigation.

Monitoring and enforcement are dynamic components of trademark protection that require continuous attention and adaptation. By implementing a comprehensive monitoring system, enforcing rights decisively, and leveraging partnerships, companies can effectively safeguard their trademarks against dilution and genericide. These efforts not only protect the legal status of the trademarks but also maintain their value and significance in the market, ensuring the brand's longevity and success.

Quick Tips and Recap

- **Implement Advanced Monitoring**: Utilize sophisticated tools to monitor the use of your trademark across various platforms, ensuring you catch potential infringements early.

- **Educate Internally and Externally**: Regularly educate employees, partners, and the public on the correct use of your trademark to prevent accidental misuse and dilution.

- **Use Cease and Desist Letters Wisely**: Send cease and desist letters as a first response to infringement, ensuring they are clear, firm, and legally sound.

- **Stay Proactive in Legal Enforcement**: Be ready to take legal action if informal resolutions fail, ensuring you protect your trademark rights vigorously.

- **Engage with Online Platforms**: Build relationships with online platforms for quicker response and removal of infringing content.

- **Register with Customs Authorities**: Register your trademark with customs authorities to help prevent the importation of counterfeit goods.

- **Form Industry Coalitions**: Join or form coalitions with other brands to address common trademark protection challenges and advocate for stronger enforcement.

- **Document All Actions**: Keep detailed records of all monitoring and enforcement activities to support any potential legal actions and to refine strategies over time.

- **Review and Adapt Strategies**: Continuously evaluate the effectiveness of your trademark protection strategies and make adjustments as necessary to address new challenges.

- **Promote Public Awareness**: Implement public awareness campaigns to educate consumers on recognizing genuine products and understanding the importance of trademarks.

By following these tips, you can effectively combat trademark dilution and genericide, ensuring your brand maintains its unique identity and legal protections.

CHAPTER TWELVE

The Long Haul: Trademark Renewals and Portfolio Management

"Managing your trademark portfolio with regular renewals is akin to navigating a ship through ever-changing waters; it requires constant vigilance and strategic foresight to ensure your brand remains protected and powerful."—GINNI ROMETTY, Former CEO of IBM

Buckle up, dear reader, for the long haul of trademark renewals and portfolio management—a journey not unlike a cross-country road trip, only with less roadside attractions and more paperwork. Think of it as the marathon of the legal world: stamina is required, snacks are recommended, and the rewards are worth the slog.

Trademark renewals are the pit stops of this journey. Miss one, and your trademark could run out of gas, stranded on the side of the intellectual property highway. These renewals aren't just bureaucratic checkboxes; they're affirmations of your ongoing commitment to your brand's identity and legal safety net. Remember, a well-maintained trademark is like a classic car—it only increases in value over time, provided you don't ignore those pesky service lights.

Now, onto portfolio management, the GPS guiding your trademarks through the complex terrain of markets and legal landscapes. A well-managed trademark portfolio is like a finely tuned orchestra—each mark plays its part, contributing to the symphony of your brand's global presence. But beware, this is no set-it-and-forget-it cruise control; active management involves strategic acquisitions, vigilant enforcement, and sometimes, the tough decision to let go of marks that no longer serve your route.

So, keep your eyes on the road and your hands on the legal documents. With diligence, foresight, and a bit of legal elbow grease, your trademark portfolio will not just endure but thrive, powering your brand forward through the years like a well-oiled machine. Let's hit the road—there's a horizon full of brand opportunities waiting to be claimed!

Understanding Trademark Renewals

Trademark renewals are crucial checkpoints that ensure the continued legal protection of your brand's identity. Like a car requires regular maintenance to keep running, trademarks need timely renewals to remain active and enforceable. Neglecting these renewals can lead to the expiration of trademark rights, leaving your brand vulnerable to infringement and potentially losing exclusive rights to your mark. This section guides you through the renewal process, highlighting its importance and providing a strategic approach to managing renewals effectively.

The Renewal Process

1. **Understanding Renewal Timelines**: Trademarks in the United States are initially registered for ten years and can be renewed every ten years thereafter. The renewal process involves submitting a declaration of continued use and an application for renewal with the United States Patent and Trademark Office (USPTO) within a specific time frame before expiration.

2. **Requirements for Renewal**: To renew a trademark, you must demonstrate that the mark is still in use in commerce. This involves submitting evidence of the trademark's ongoing use, such as examples of advertising, packaging, or sales receipts that feature the trademark. Failure to provide proof of continued use can result in the cancellation of the registration.

3. **Grace Periods and Late Renewal**: The USPTO offers a grace period after the expiration of a trademark during which the trademark can still be renewed with additional fees. Understanding these grace periods is essential to avoid unintentional lapses that could complicate the renewal process or lead to higher costs.

Strategic Management of Renewals

1. **Renewal Alerts and Calendars**: Implement a system of alerts to track renewal deadlines for each trademark in your portfolio. This might involve dedicated software or a simple calendar system, but it should provide ample warning to prepare renewal applications well in advance.

2. **Audit Trademark Use**: Regularly review how each trademark is being used in your business operations. This helps ensure that you can provide necessary evidence of use and make informed decisions about which trademarks are valuable and should be renewed.

3. **Legal and Professional Assistance**: Consider engaging trademark attorneys or intellectual property professionals to manage renewal filings. Their expertise can help navigate the complexities of the renewal process and ensure that all legal requirements are met efficiently.

Common Pitfalls in Renewal

1. **Documentation Errors**: Incorrect or incomplete submission of evidence or forms can lead to delays or rejections of renewal applications. Double-check all documents for accuracy before submission.

2. **Overlooking Non-Use**: If a trademark has not been in active use, assess whether to revive its use in commerce or potentially abandon the renewal to focus resources on more active elements of your trademark portfolio.

3. **Misjudging the Scope of Use**: Ensure that the evidence of use submitted accurately reflects the current scope of the trademark's use in commerce. Expansions or reductions in the goods and services associated with the trademark should be appropriately documented and reflected in renewal applications.

Timely and strategic management of trademark renewals is vital for maintaining the legal protections necessary for your brand's success. By understanding the renewal process, setting up effective management systems, and avoiding common pitfalls, you can ensure that your trademarks continue to serve as valuable assets for your business.

Strategic Portfolio Management

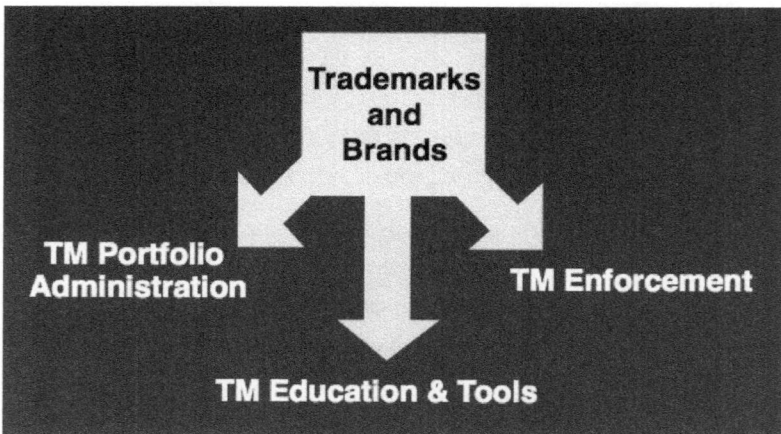

Figure 8: Trademarks and Brand Flowchart

Effective trademark portfolio management is akin to navigating a complex financial portfolio; it requires strategic planning, ongoing assessment, and timely decision-making. For businesses that hold multiple trademarks, managing these assets strategically ensures not only protection but also the maximization of their value. This section will explore the key components of strategic trademark portfolio management and how they can be implemented to support your business's growth and branding strategy.

Assessing Portfolio Health

1. **Regular Portfolio Reviews**: Conduct periodic reviews of your trademark portfolio to assess the health and strategic alignment of each mark with your business objectives. This involves evaluating the legal status, market relevance, and financial performance of each trademark.

2. **Identifying Underperforming Assets**: Identify trademarks that are underperforming or no longer align with your business strategy. Consider whether these marks should be maintained, sold, or allowed to lapse, based on their cost versus benefit to your business.

3. **Market and Competitor Analysis**: Keep abreast of market trends and competitor activities. Understanding how your trademarks stack up against competitors and shifting market demands can inform strategic decisions, such as the need for new trademarks or the repositioning of existing ones.

Enhancing Portfolio Value

1. **Strategic Registrations**: Identify gaps in your trademark coverage and consider new registrations to fill these gaps. This may involve expanding into new geographical markets or product lines. Ensure that each new registration adds value and supports the broader strategic goals of your company.

2. **Licensing Opportunities**: Explore opportunities to license your trademarks to other entities. Licensing can be a lucrative way to expand your brand's reach and generate revenue without significant additional investment.

3. **Enforcement Strategy**: Develop and maintain a robust enforcement strategy to protect your trademarks from infringement. Regular monitoring and decisive action against infringers not only protect your individual marks but also strengthen the overall portfolio.

Rationalizing the Portfolio

1. **Cost-Benefit Analysis**: Regularly perform cost-benefit analyses to determine the economic viability of maintaining each trademark. Factor in renewal fees, enforcement costs, and potential market expansion against the revenue each mark generates.

2. **Pruning the Portfolio**: Decide which trademarks are non-essential and can be pruned from the portfolio. This reduces costs and focuses your resources on trademarks that are most valuable to your business.

3. **Integrating Business and IP Strategy**: Ensure that your trademark portfolio management is integrated with your overall business strategy. This alignment helps in making informed decisions that reflect both current business needs and future growth plans.

Leveraging Technology and Expertise

1. **Utilizing IP Management Software**: Invest in intellectual property management software to track registration deadlines, renewal dates, and enforcement actions. This technology can also provide analytics to support decision-making.

2. **Engaging with IP Professionals**: Work with intellectual property attorneys or consultants who specialize in trademark law. Their expertise can be invaluable in navigating complex legal landscapes, especially when entering new markets or dealing with complicated disputes.

Strategic portfolio management is essential for maximizing the value of your trademark assets. By assessing the health of your portfolio, enhancing its value through strategic actions, and rationalizing assets based on performance, you can ensure that your trademarks continue to support and drive your business's success in a competitive marketplace.

Monitoring Market Changes

In the fast-paced global marketplace, staying informed about evolving trends, technological shifts, and competitive maneuvers is critical for maintaining the relevance and effectiveness of your trademark portfolio. Vigilant monitoring of these changes allows you to anticipate market needs, capitalize on emerging opportunities, and mitigate potential threats. This section delves deeper into the importance of continuous market surveillance and outlines strategies to integrate these insights into your trademark strategy effectively.

Comprehensive Monitoring: Key Focus Areas

1. **Consumer Behavior and Preferences**: Understanding consumer trends is pivotal. Regularly engage in detailed market research, including surveys, focus groups, and social media monitoring, to gauge changing consumer desires and expectations. This ongoing analysis helps in identifying how these shifts could influence the perception and effectiveness of your trademarks.

2. **Technological Innovations**: Technological advancements can redefine industries overnight, creating new product categories and obsoleting others. Stay abreast of technological trends not only within your industry but also in areas that could indirectly affect your business. This proactive approach ensures that your trademarks evolve in tandem with relevant technological innovations, maintaining their alignment with current products and services.

3. **Competitive Analysis**: Keeping an eye on your competitors is crucial. Monitor their trademark filings, product launches, brand strategies, and market expansions. Tools like competitor benchmarking and SWOT analysis can provide strategic insights into your competitors' strengths and weaknesses, helping you to position your trademarks more strategically in the marketplace.

Strategies for Effective Market Monitoring

1. **Advanced Analytical Tools**: Utilize cutting-edge analytics tools to process and analyze large datasets. These tools can detect emerging patterns, predict market trends, and provide insights that are not immediately obvious through traditional analysis methods.

2. **Industry Engagement**: Actively participate in industry forums, workshops, and seminars. These platforms offer valuable insights into

upcoming regulatory changes, market trends, and innovative practices that could impact your trademark strategy.

3. **Global Trade Shows and Expositions**: Attend international trade shows and expositions to gather firsthand information about global market trends and consumer preferences. These events are also excellent for observing how competitors are positioning their brands and for identifying potential risks and opportunities for your trademarks.

Adaptive Strategies for Trademark Management

1. **Forward-Looking Trademark Registrations**: Based on the intelligence gathered, proactively register trademarks in categories or regions where future expansion is anticipated. This not only protects your brand but also prevents competitors from encroaching on new market segments you plan to enter.

2. **Realigning Trademark Usage**: As markets evolve, so should the application and representation of your trademarks. Adjust your branding materials, marketing strategies, and even the trademarks themselves to better resonate with current consumer expectations and market realities.

3. **Defensive and Offensive Legal Postures**: Prepare to defend your trademarks against potential infringements that become apparent through market monitoring. Simultaneously, adopt an offensive posture by challenging competitor actions that threaten your market position or dilute your brand's strength.

Effective market monitoring is an indispensable component of strategic trademark management. By keeping a finger on the pulse of market dynamics, technological advancements, and competitive activities, you can ensure that your trademark portfolio remains robust and adaptive. This proactive approach not only safeguards your intellectual property but also enhances your brand's agility and competitiveness in the global marketplace.

Enforcement and Defense

Effective enforcement and defense are critical components of maintaining the integrity and value of your trademark portfolio. As markets evolve and new threats emerge, having a proactive strategy for enforcing your trademark rights and defending against potential infringements is essential. This section outlines practical steps and strategies for robust trademark enforcement and defense, ensuring that your intellectual property remains protected across all markets.

Building a Comprehensive Enforcement Strategy

1. **Monitoring for Infringements**: Establish a rigorous system to continuously monitor the use of your trademarks globally. Utilize technology to scan the internet, social media, marketplaces, and other platforms for unauthorized use of your marks. This proactive surveillance allows for immediate detection of potential infringements.

2. **Cease and Desist Letters**: As a first line of defense, sending a well-drafted cease and desist letter can effectively address many infringement issues. These letters should clearly outline the infringement, assert your rights, and demand immediate cessation of the unauthorized use. Tailor your communication to the context and severity of the infringement to maximize its impact.

3. **Legal Actions**: When infringement persists despite initial warnings, be prepared to escalate to legal action. This can involve filing for injunctions to prevent further misuse, seeking damages for losses incurred, and, in some cases, demanding the destruction of infringing goods.

Defensive Tactics Against Challenges

1. **Handling Oppositions and Cancellations**: Be prepared to defend your trademarks against oppositions or cancellation actions. This includes gathering substantial evidence of your trademark's use, distinctiveness, and consumer recognition to support your case.

2. **Engaging Expert Legal Representation**: Partner with experienced intellectual property lawyers who specialize in trademark law. Their expertise will be invaluable in navigating complex legal challenges and developing effective strategies for both enforcement and defense.

3. **Using Alternative Dispute Resolution (ADR)**: Consider using mediation or arbitration to resolve disputes when appropriate. ADR can offer a more cost-effective and confidential means of settling disputes compared to traditional litigation.

Strategies for Global Enforcement

1. **Understanding International Laws**: Since trademark laws vary significantly by country, develop a clear understanding of the legal frameworks in all jurisdictions where your trademarks are registered. This knowledge is crucial for effective global enforcement and can help avoid legal pitfalls.

2. **Collaboration with International Agencies**: Work with local and international agencies, including customs authorities and trade organizations, to enforce your trademarks. These agencies can act against counterfeit goods and help enforce rulings on trademark infringements.

3. **Cross-Border Legal Coordination**: Coordinate enforcement actions across borders when dealing with international infringements. This may involve working with legal teams in multiple countries to ensure consistent and effective action.

Maintaining Vigilance and Adaptability

1. **Regular Training for Teams**: Conduct regular training sessions for your legal, marketing, and sales teams to ensure they are up to date on the latest trademark enforcement practices and legal developments.

2. **Review and Adapt Strategies**: Continually review the effectiveness of your enforcement strategies and be ready to adapt them in response to new challenges and market changes.

3. **Leveraging Technology**: Invest in the latest technology for monitoring and enforcement, including artificial intelligence and blockchain, which can enhance the efficiency and effectiveness of your efforts.

A proactive and well-structured approach to trademark enforcement and defense is essential for protecting your brand's reputation and market position. By implementing robust monitoring systems, engaging in decisive legal actions, and maintaining adaptability in your strategies, you can effectively safeguard your trademarks against infringement and uphold their value in the marketplace.

Future-Proofing Your Trademarks

In the ever-evolving business landscape, future-proofing your trademarks is essential to ensure they continue to support and drive your brand's success. This involves anticipating future challenges, adapting to changes in the market, and employing strategies that maintain the relevance and legal protection of your trademarks over time. This section explores how to effectively future-proof your trademarks, ensuring they remain a robust asset for your company.

Strategic Planning for Trademark Longevity

1. **Regular Portfolio Assessment**: Conduct periodic assessments of your trademark portfolio to ensure each mark remains aligned with current and future business strategies. This includes evaluating the effectiveness of your trademarks in new markets, technologies, and consumer trends.

2. **Adaptive Trademark Practices**: Stay flexible in your trademark strategies to accommodate shifts in your business model or product lines. This may involve updating the visual elements of a trademark, expanding or narrowing the goods and services it covers, or even retiring certain marks that no longer serve your business objectives.

3. **Technological Integration**: Leverage technology to enhance the management and protection of your trademarks. Tools like blockchain for registration and AI-powered monitoring systems can provide more efficient and secure ways to manage your trademarks.

Legal and Regulatory Vigilance

1. **Monitor Legal Changes**: Keep abreast of changes in trademark laws and regulations, both domestically and internationally. Changes in intellectual property law can affect how your trademarks are protected and enforced, requiring adjustments to your strategy.

2. **International Compliance**: As your brand expands globally, ensure that your trademarks comply with international laws and conventions. This involves not only securing registrations in new markets but also understanding and adhering to local trademark practices and challenges.

3. **Renewal Discipline**: Maintain strict discipline around the renewal of your trademarks. Overlooking a renewal can lead to a lapse in protection, which could be exploited by competitors or result in losing exclusive rights to the mark.

Enhancing Trademark Enforcement

1. **Proactive Infringement Monitoring**: Continuously monitor the market for potential infringements or misuses of your trademarks. Early detection allows for timely enforcement actions to prevent erosion of your brand's distinctiveness and value.

2. **Collaborative Enforcement Strategies**: Work collaboratively with other brands and industry groups to combat common threats such as counterfeiting and piracy. Collective actions can often be more effective than individual efforts.

3. **Legal Action Readiness**: Maintain readiness to take legal action when necessary. This includes having a legal team familiar with your business and intellectual property strategy, as well as setting aside resources for potential litigation.

Leveraging Trademark Education

1. **Internal Training**: Regularly train new employees and refresh existing staff on the importance of trademarks and the role they play in the company's success. This helps ensure consistent application and enforcement of your trademark policies internally.

2. **Public Awareness**: Engage in public education campaigns to inform consumers and the industry about the significance of your trademarks. This helps build a strong brand identity and reduces the likelihood of genericide.

Future-proofing your trademarks involves a blend of strategic foresight, legal vigilance, and proactive management. By continually assessing and adapting your trademark strategies to meet the demands of a changing market and legal environment, you can ensure that your trademarks remain effective and enforceable, supporting your brand's growth and innovation for years to come.

Quick Tips and Recap

- **Conduct Regular Portfolio Reviews**: Periodically assess your trademark portfolio to ensure each mark continues to align with your current business strategy and market trends.

- **Stay Informed on Legal Changes**: Keep up-to-date with changes in trademark laws and regulations both domestically and internationally to ensure compliance and optimal protection.

- **Leverage Technology**: Utilize advanced technologies such as AI and blockchain for efficient management and enhanced protection of your trademarks.

- **Implement Renewal Reminders**: Set up a systematic reminder process for trademark renewals to avoid unintentional lapses that could result in loss of protection.

- **Monitor Market Changes**: Actively monitor the marketplace for shifts in consumer behavior, new technological advancements, and competitor activities that may impact your trademarks.

- **Maintain Enforcement Vigilance**: Continuously monitor for potential infringements and enforce your trademark rights promptly to protect against dilution and unauthorized use.

- **Educate Employees and the Public**: Regularly train employees on the importance of trademarks and conduct public awareness campaigns to ensure proper use and recognition of your trademarks.

- **Engage Legal Expertise**: Work with experienced intellectual property lawyers to navigate complex trademark issues, especially in international markets.

- **Plan for the Future**: Anticipate future changes and challenges by adapting your trademarks and strategies accordingly to maintain relevance and effectiveness.

- **Collaborate with Industry Groups**: Partner with other companies and industry organizations to combat common threats such as counterfeiting and piracy more effectively.

By following these tips, you can ensure that your trademark portfolio is not only protected but also poised for growth as it supports your brand's strategic objectives over the long haul.

CHAPTER THIRTEEN

Beyond the Basics: Service Marks and Promotional Strategies

"Going beyond the basics with service marks and promotional strategies is about creating a distinct identity that communicates value and builds lasting connections with your audience."— SETH GODIN, AUTHOR, ENTREPRENEUR, AND MARKETING EXPERT

Strap in, because we're taking a scenic detour from the well-trodden path of trademarks to the exciting backroads of service marks and promotional strategies. Think of trademarks as the flashy billboards along the highway, while service marks are the high-flying banners towed by planes, signaling who's who in the service industry. Both mark your territory, but service marks do it with a flair for the dramatic, focusing on the *experience* rather than the *product*.

First, let's decode the mystique of service marks. If trademarks are the superheroes of the product world, service marks are their charming, sophisticated cousins in the service sector. They're the tuxedos to trademarks' superhero capes—equally powerful but playing the game with a touch more subtlety. Whether you're a five-star hotel, a bank with customer service that actually understands humans, or a courier service that's more reliable than your alarm clock, your service mark is your silent herald.

Now, onto the art of promotional strategies. Here, creativity is your currency, and your service mark is the mint. The goal? To embed your mark not just on billboards but into the hearts and minds of your audience. It's about making your mark synonymous with memories, feelings, and experiences. Think of it as branding with a side of storytelling, where every interaction is an opportunity to reinforce your narrative.

The trick is to keep your strategies as dynamic as the markets you serve. Innovate promotions that break the mold. Ever thought about a loyalty program that actually feels rewarding? Or how about service previews that turn first-time clients into lifelong fans? Your service mark can be the star of the show, but your promotional strategies are the scriptwriters, directors, and sometimes, the stunt doubles.

In this chapter, we strap on our marketing jetpacks and soar beyond the basics, where service marks and bold promotional strategies create not just visibility but lasting impressions. Buckle up; it's going to be an exhilarating ride!

Understanding Service Marks

Service marks, often overshadowed by their more discussed counterpart, trademarks, play a pivotal role in distinguishing the services of one entity from those of another. Unlike trademarks, which are associated with products, service marks are exclusively linked to services, offering a unique form of identity and legal protection in the service sector. This section will delve into the definition, importance, and legal underpinnings of service marks, setting the stage for their strategic use in business.

Definition and Distinction

1. **What is a Service Mark?**: A service mark is a symbol, name, or logo used in commerce to identify and distinguish the services of one provider from those of others. Unlike trademarks, which cover goods and products, service marks specifically relate to services such as banking, transportation, or hospitality.

2. **Examples of Service Marks**: Examples include the distinctive logos and names used by financial institutions, airlines, or hotel chains. These marks are not just logos but identifiers that promise a certain quality of service and customer experience.

Legal Framework for Service Marks

1. **Registration Process**: In many jurisdictions, the process for registering a service mark is similar to that for trademarks. This involves filing an application with the relevant intellectual property office, demonstrating use in commerce, and specifying the services class under which the mark will be registered.

2. **Protection Offered**: Registered service marks are protected from being used by other entities within the same or similar service categories where such use might cause confusion among consumers. This protection is crucial for maintaining a service provider's reputation and market position.

3. **Duration and Renewal**: Like trademarks, service marks are typically granted protection for a finite period, often ten years, with the option to renew. The holder must continue to use the mark in commerce and adhere to renewal deadlines to maintain protection.

Importance of Service Marks in Business

1. **Brand Identity**: Service marks are integral to building and maintaining a strong brand identity. They help consumers identify the source and expected quality of a service, thereby building trust and loyalty.

2. **Competitive Edge**: In competitive industries, a well-recognized service mark can be a significant differentiator, helping to attract and retain customers by assuring them of consistent service quality.

3. **Legal Safeguard**: Registering a service mark provides legal recourse against unauthorized use, which is essential in preventing other businesses from diluting your brand's value or misleading consumers.

Challenges in Managing Service Marks

1. **Market Perception**: The perception of a service mark directly impacts a brand's image and consumer loyalty. Mismanagement of the mark or poor service delivery can tarnish the brand's reputation.

2. **Global Consistency**: For businesses operating in multiple jurisdictions, ensuring that service marks are consistently protected and recognized across borders can be challenging due to varying laws and registration requirements.

Understanding service marks is the first step toward leveraging them effectively within a business strategy. They not only signify the source and quality of services but also serve as legal tools that protect a business's intangible assets. As markets evolve and competition intensifies, the strategic use of service marks becomes increasingly important in maintaining a brand's visibility and reputation in the service sector.

Developing Effective Service Mark Strategies

Effectively managing service marks is a critical aspect of establishing and maintaining a strong presence in the service industry. Beyond mere symbols, service marks encapsulate the reputation and identity of a business, making their strategic development, protection, and use essential for long-term success. This section provides detailed strategies for selecting, deploying, and safeguarding service marks that not only ensure legal compliance but also strengthen market position.

Selection and Refinement of Service Marks

1. **Criteria for Choosing Service Marks**: Begin by identifying service marks that resonate deeply with the core offerings and ethos of your business. The chosen mark should be distinct, memorable, and reflective of the service quality and experience your business aims to provide. It should resonate with your target audience, reinforcing the perceived value of your services.

2. **Distinctiveness and Memorability**: A service mark should stand out from competitors and stick in the minds of consumers. Consider factors such as linguistic appeal, cultural relevance, and visual impact when choosing a mark. Employing branding professionals can provide valuable insights into creating a mark that is both unique and appealing.

3. **Comprehensive Searches and Clearance**: Prior to adopting a service mark, perform extensive searches to avoid potential legal conflicts with existing marks. This involves checking national and international trademark databases and assessing the mark's viability across all intended markets. Early identification of potential conflicts can prevent costly disputes and rebranding efforts.

Legal Framework and Protection Strategies

1. **Securing Registration**: Actively pursue registration of the service mark in pertinent jurisdictions to secure legal protection. This grants you exclusive rights to use the mark in connection with the registered services and forms the basis for any future infringement actions.

2. **Defining the Scope of Services**: When registering, accurately define the scope of services to ensure broad protection. Consider potential future expansions and ensure the registration encompasses all relevant service categories to avoid gaps in protection.

3. **Global Protection Considerations**: For businesses operating internationally or planning to expand, strategize for global mark protection. Utilize international treaties such as the Madrid Protocol for efficient multi-country registration and protection.

Operational Integration and Usage Compliance

1. **Brand Alignment**: Integrate the service mark consistently across all business operations and marketing channels. Use the mark in accordance with the established brand guidelines to reinforce brand identity and avoid dilution of the mark's distinctiveness.

2. **Training and Compliance**: Educate all employees about the importance and proper usage of the service mark. Regular training ensures that the mark is used correctly in communications, advertisements, and digital media, which helps in maintaining its legal strength.

3. **Ongoing Monitoring and Enforcement**: Implement monitoring mechanisms to detect unauthorized use of the service mark both within and outside the organization. This proactive surveillance allows for timely enforcement actions to protect the mark from infringement and misuse.

Strategic Evaluation and Market Adaptation

1. **Regular Performance Audits**: Conduct periodic evaluations of how effectively the service mark is supporting brand recognition and customer engagement. Utilize customer feedback, brand penetration metrics, and competitive analysis to measure the mark's impact.

2. **Adaptability to Market Dynamics**: Be ready to refine or evolve your service mark strategy in response to changing market conditions, consumer trends, or competitive pressures. Flexibility in strategy can involve minor adjustments to the mark or more substantial rebranding initiatives to better meet market demands.

Developing a robust strategy for service marks involves thoughtful selection, meticulous legal planning, consistent operational integration, and continuous market responsiveness. By embracing these strategies, businesses can ensure that their service marks not only comply with legal standards but also dynamically contribute to building a strong, enduring brand identity in the competitive service sector.

Creative Promotional Tactics

In the highly competitive landscape of the service industry, standing out requires more than just traditional advertising; it requires innovative, memorable promotional tactics that make a lasting impression. These strategies not only elevate the visibility of your service mark but also engage customers on a deeper level, transforming them from one-time users into loyal advocates. This section explores a variety of creative approaches to promote your service mark effectively, aiming to enhance both recognition and engagement.

Embracing Digital Innovations

1. **Social Media Engagement**: Harness the power of social media platforms to launch targeted campaigns that highlight your service mark. Design interactive and shareable content such as viral challenges, polls, and themed posts that encourage user participation and discussion. Incorporate your service mark creatively in these initiatives to reinforce brand recognition.

2. **Influencer Collaborations**: Partner with influencers who resonate with your brand values and have a significant following within your target demographic. These influencers can introduce your service mark to new audiences through authentic storytelling, personalized experiences, and genuine endorsements, adding a layer of trust and relatability to your brand.

3. **Content Marketing Excellence**: Create a comprehensive content marketing strategy that consistently delivers valuable information while subtly incorporating your service mark. This could involve producing expert articles, insightful video content, and informative podcasts that not only entertain but also educate your audience about your service offerings.

Utilizing Experiential Marketing

1. **Live Brand Activations**: Organize and participate in live events such as pop-up shops, interactive workshops, or immersive exhibitions where participants can experience your services firsthand. These events should

be branded heavily with your service mark, ensuring that every aspect of the experience is associated with your brand.

2. **Technological Interactions**: Deploy cutting-edge technologies like augmented reality (AR) or virtual reality (VR) to create unique, immersive experiences that highlight your services. For instance, an AR app could allow customers to visualize your service in their own life before purchase, effectively using your service mark within an engaging, technological context.

Revitalizing Traditional Tactics

1. **Direct Mail Campaigns**: Leverage the personalized touch of direct mail by sending out well-designed, thoughtful communications that feature your service mark prominently. Include special offers, membership perks, or personalized messages that make recipients feel valued and more connected to your brand.

2. **Branded Merchandise**: Develop high-quality merchandise that prominently features your service mark. This approach not only serves as a marketing tool but also as a revenue stream if customers are keen to purchase branded products. Ensure that the merchandise is practical and aesthetically pleasing, encouraging daily use and constant exposure.

Strengthening Through Collaborations

1. **Strategic Business Partnerships**: Form alliances with non-competing businesses that share your target market. Joint promotions or co-branded services can expose your service mark to new audiences in a context that adds value to their experience, enhancing the perception of your brand.

2. **Community and Charity Engagements**: Actively participate in community events or support local charities. Sponsorships or participation in community projects can position your service mark as a positive contributor to the community, building goodwill and brand affinity.

Crafting creative promotional tactics is crucial for differentiating your service mark in a saturated market. By blending innovative digital strategies, experiential marketing, revitalized traditional methods, and collaborative efforts, you can significantly enhance the prominence and attractiveness of your service mark. Each strategy should not only aim to amplify visibility but also to imbue your service mark with meaningful interactions and positive experiences that resonate with and retain customers.

Integrating Service Marks in Customer Experience

Effective integration of your service mark into the customer experience is vital for establishing a strong, memorable brand identity. This strategic incorporation should transcend mere visual representation, embedding the service mark into the essence of every customer interaction. Doing so not only reinforces brand recognition but also strengthens customer loyalty by providing a consistent and engaging brand experience. This section delves into advanced strategies for weaving your service mark seamlessly into various aspects of the customer journey, ensuring that it resonates deeply and enriches the customer's interaction with your brand.

Comprehensive Visibility and Design Integration

1. **Consistent Presence Across All Touchpoints**: Your service mark should be prominently displayed across all customer interaction points. This includes physical spaces like offices or stores, digital platforms such as websites and social media, customer service interactions, and all marketing materials. Consistency is key to reinforcing brand recognition and supporting a unified brand narrative.

2. **Aesthetic and Functional Integration**: Design your customer environments—both physical and digital—to naturally incorporate your service mark. This integration should enhance the aesthetic appeal and contribute to the functionality of the design, whether it's through thematic decor elements, staff uniforms, digital interface layouts, or even the architectural features of your business premises.

3. **Dynamic Use in Multimedia**: Employ your service mark dynamically across various media formats to ensure it becomes a staple of your brand identity. Feature it in video content, mobile apps, audio signatures, and interactive digital experiences. This varied and repeated exposure helps cement the service mark in the customer's memory across different contexts and platforms.

Enhancing Direct Customer Interactions

1. **Personalization of Services**: Use your service mark to personalize the customer experience. Incorporate it into email communications, membership cards, loyalty programs, and personalized marketing efforts. This reminds customers of your brand's value and presence in their everyday interactions with your service.

2. **Mapping the Customer Journey**: Carefully map out the customer journey to identify strategic points where your service mark can be emphasized to enhance the customer experience. Look for opportunities to feature the mark during crucial interactions, such as during service delivery, in confirmation emails, or within loyalty app notifications.

3. **Adaptive Feedback Utilization**: Continuously collect and analyze customer feedback regarding their experiences with your service mark. Use this invaluable insight to adapt and refine how your service mark is presented, ensuring it remains a positive and value-adding element of the customer experience.

Building Emotional and Experiential Connections

1. **Narrative and Storytelling**: Develop compelling stories that revolve around your service mark, illustrating your brand's history, mission, and core values. Disseminate these stories through your marketing channels to build an emotional connection with your audience, making your service mark a symbol of your brand's larger story.

2. **Designing Signature Experiences**: Create unique, signature experiences that are distinct to your brand and feature your service mark prominently. These should be memorable, enjoyable, and sharable,

encouraging customers to associate these positive experiences directly with your service mark.

3. **Cultivating Brand Rituals**: Establish brand rituals that involve your service mark in a meaningful way. These could include special ways of packaging, unique service delivery methods, or customer interaction styles that are consistent and memorable, reinforcing the service mark as an integral part of the customer experience.

Integrating your service mark into the customer experience requires thoughtful strategy and creative execution. By ensuring your mark is visible and vibrant across all touchpoints, enhancing personal interactions, and forging strong emotional connections, you transform your service mark from a simple brand identifier into a powerful emblem of customer trust and loyalty. This holistic approach not only strengthens your brand's identity but also significantly boosts its presence and influence in the competitive service market.

Evaluating the Impact of Service Marks and Promotions

To ensure that your service marks and promotional strategies are not only reaching but also resonating with your target audience, it is essential to evaluate their effectiveness systematically. This evaluation helps you understand the return on investment (ROI) and adjust your strategies to maximize impact. This section discusses methods and metrics for assessing the performance of your service marks and the efficacy of associated promotional activities.

Establishing Key Performance Indicators (KPIs)

1. **Brand Awareness**: Measure how well your service mark is recognized within your target market. Surveys, social media monitoring, and market research can provide insights into the level of brand awareness and the degree to which your service mark is associated with your specific services.

2. **Brand Equity**: Evaluate changes in brand perception before and after promotional campaigns. Tools like brand equity models assess

consumers' value perception, loyalty, and preference for your brand over competitors.

3. **Customer Engagement**: Track engagement metrics from your promotions, including interaction rates on social media, click-through rates on digital ads, and participation in events or contests. High engagement rates often indicate effective use of the service mark in promotions.

Utilizing Analytical Tools

1. **Digital Analytics**: Use digital analytics platforms to track online interactions related to your service mark. Google Analytics and social media analytics tools can provide detailed data on how users interact with your content that features the service mark.

2. **Market Research**: Conduct periodic market research to gather qualitative and quantitative data on how your service mark and promotions are perceived. This might include focus groups, customer satisfaction surveys, and brand health checks.

3. **Competitive Analysis**: Regularly compare your brand's performance with that of your competitors. This helps identify strengths to be leveraged and weaknesses to be addressed, positioning your service mark more strategically in the marketplace.

Assessing Promotional Campaign Effectiveness

1. **Campaign ROI**: Calculate the ROI for each promotional campaign involving your service mark. Analyze sales data, customer acquisition costs, and overall profitability to determine the financial success of your promotions.

2. **Conversion Rates**: Monitor conversion rates from campaigns that feature your service mark. High conversion rates indicate that the promotional strategy effectively drives customer actions, such as purchases, sign-ups, or inquiries.

3. **Long-Term Impact**: Look beyond immediate campaign results to assess the long-term impact on brand loyalty and customer retention. Effective

service mark promotions should contribute to sustained business growth and customer base expansion.

Strategic Adjustments Based on Insights

1. **Iterative Improvements**: Use insights gained from assessments to make iterative improvements to your service mark utilization and promotional strategies. This might involve refining the messaging, targeting different audience segments, or altering the visual presentation of the service mark.

2. **Budget Reallocations**: Based on performance metrics, consider reallocating budgets to more effective promotional channels or scaling successful campaigns to maximize impact.

3. **Stakeholder Feedback**: Engage with key stakeholders, including marketing teams, sales staff, and customers, to gather feedback on the service mark's effectiveness and promotional activities. This direct feedback can provide actionable insights for refining strategies.

Evaluating the impact of your service marks and promotional strategies is crucial for ensuring that your branding efforts contribute positively to your business objectives. By establishing clear metrics, utilizing robust analytical tools, and continuously refining your approach based on data-driven insights, you can enhance the visibility and effectiveness of your service marks, driving meaningful engagement and sustainable business growth.

Assignment of Service Marks and Trademarks

The assignment of service marks and trademarks involves the transfer of ownership of these marks from one party to another. This process is crucial for businesses undergoing restructuring, mergers, acquisitions, or those simply looking to sell their marks. An assignment transfers all rights of the mark to the new owner, enabling them to use, sell, and license the mark as they see fit.

Key Considerations for Assignment

1. **Legal Requirements**: For an assignment to be valid, it must generally be in writing and include the specific rights being transferred. The

document should clearly identify the mark, the associated goods or services, and the parties involved.

2. **Intent and Use**: The transfer of a trademark or service mark must include the transfer of the goodwill associated with the mark. This means the mark must continue to be used in the same way by the new owner to prevent misleading or confusing consumers about the origin of the goods or services.

3. **Recording the Assignment**: To solidify the transfer legally, the assignment should be recorded with the relevant governmental body, such as the United States Patent and Trademark Office (USPTO) in the U.S. Recording an assignment provides public notice of the change in ownership and is necessary to maintain the mark's protection and enforceability.

Types of Assignments

- **Complete Assignment**: Transfers all rights of the mark to another entity. The original owner retains no rights to the mark or its use.

- **Partial Assignment**: Involves transferring rights to use the mark in a specific geographical area or for a particular product or service.

Post-Assignment Considerations

Following the assignment, the new owner should ensure that the mark is used consistently with its established goodwill and reputation. Additionally, it is advisable for the new owner to monitor the use of the mark and enforce its rights to prevent unauthorized use, which could dilute the mark's value.

Conclusion

Assigning trademarks and service marks is a strategic business decision that can have significant legal and financial implications. Proper handling of the assignment process is essential to ensure that the rights and value of the mark are preserved and that both parties benefit from the transfer. Consulting with an intellectual property attorney is recommended to navigate the complexities of this process effectively.

▶ An Assignment of Service Marks and Trademarks Agreement can be found in the **Appendix**. If you are interested in receiving an electronic copy of this document, please email us at documents@AuthorsDoor.com with the subject line "Request for Assignment of Service Marks and Trademarks Agreement." Upon receiving your email, we will promptly send you a Microsoft Word copy of the document. **Disclaimer:** Please note that all agreements are provided for informational purposes only and should not be construed as legal advice. We recommend consulting with a qualified attorney to ensure that any legal documents or decisions are tailored to your specific circumstances.

Quick Tips and Recap

- **Consistency is Key**: Ensure your service mark is consistently used across all marketing channels and customer touch points to reinforce brand recognition.

- **Engage Creatively**: Leverage creative promotional tactics that make your service mark memorable and engaging, helping to embed it in the minds and hearts of your audience.

- **Monitor Regularly**: Keep a vigilant eye on how your service mark is perceived and used in the marketplace through regular monitoring and analytics.

- **Assess Impact**: Regularly evaluate the effectiveness of your service mark and promotional strategies using established KPIs like brand awareness, customer engagement, and ROI.

- **Use Digital Tools**: Implement digital analytics tools to track interactions and engagement with your service mark online, gaining insights into customer behavior and campaign performance.

- **Gather Feedback**: Continuously collect feedback from customers and internal stakeholders to understand the strengths and weaknesses of your service mark's impact.

- **Adapt Strategies**: Be prepared to adapt your promotional strategies based on data-driven insights and market trends to ensure your service mark remains relevant and effective.

- **Focus on Experience**: Integrate your service mark into the customer experience at every opportunity, ensuring it represents positive interactions and high-quality service.

- **Leverage Partnerships**: Use strategic partnerships to enhance the reach and visibility of your service mark, accessing new audiences and resources.

- **Plan for the Future**: Future-proof your service mark by staying ahead of industry changes and being ready to evolve your strategies to meet new market demands.

By following these tips, you can ensure that your service mark not only gains visibility but also builds a strong, positive association with your brand, driving long-term success and customer loyalty.

CHAPTER FOURTEEN

The Art of Licensing: Maximizing the Value of Your Trademarks

"Licensing your trademark is not just about lending your name; it's about strategically extending your brand's reach and influence while ensuring it aligns with partners who uphold its values and promise."—
ANNA WINTOUR, EDITOR-IN-CHIEF OF VOGUE

Welcome to the Art of Licensing, where your trademarks aren't just symbols of your business—they're hardworking assets ready to be leased out like beachfront properties. This isn't just about putting your logo on a mug or a t-shirt; it's about turning your brand into a veritable gold mine.

Think of licensing as the corporate equivalent of playing matchmaker. You've got this attractive, well-established trademark that's caught the eye of many suitors (other businesses and products), all eager to associate with your brand's charm and reputation. Your job? Pairing your trademark with the right partners who can respect and enhance your brand's image, not take it on a dubious blind date.

Navigating the world of licensing agreements is akin to walking through a minefield while juggling flaming torches. It's an art form. You'll need a keen eye for details and a knack for foreseeing potential pitfalls. It's about knowing who to trust, determining how far to extend your brand, and ensuring that every licensing deal aligns perfectly with your brand's values and vision.

But beware, the path of licensing is littered with tales of mismatched partnerships and dilution disasters. For every successful Disney and Marvel pairing, there's a cautionary tale waiting in the wings. Your mission, should you choose to accept it, is to weave through these challenges with the grace of a ballet dancer and the precision of a sniper.

So, roll up your sleeves and get ready to turn your trademarks into team players on the global stage. With the right strategy, a solid contract, and a bit of licensing savvy, your trademarks can go from being mere identifiers to superstar earners in your business portfolio. Let's make it rain royalties!

Understanding Trademark Licensing

Trademark licensing is a powerful strategy that allows businesses to expand their brand's reach and generate additional revenue without directly managing new product lines or markets. By granting legal permission to another entity to use your trademark, you can capitalize on established brand equity and recognition, allowing your business to grow in diverse and dynamic ways.

Definition and Scope of Trademark Licensing

1. **What is Trademark Licensing?**: Trademark licensing involves a trademark owner (licensor) granting permission to another party (licensee) to use the trademark under specific conditions. This agreement allows the licensee to legally utilize the mark on products, in advertising, or in association with services, typically in exchange for a royalty fee.

2. **Types of Licensing Agreements**: Licensing agreements can vary significantly based on their scope and terms. Common types include:

   o **Exclusive Licensing**: Only the licensee has the rights to use the trademark in a particular region or sector.

   o **Non-exclusive Licensing**: Multiple licensees can use the trademark simultaneously under similar terms.

   o **Sole Licensing**: The licensor retains the right to use the trademark but can also grant usage rights to a single licensee.

Benefits of Trademark Licensing

1. **Revenue Generation**: Licensing is a lucrative way to monetize a trademark. Royalties from licensing agreements provide a steady income stream without the overhead costs associated with product development and market expansion.

2. **Brand Expansion**: Licensing allows brands to expand into new markets and product categories more rapidly and with less risk. It leverages the licensee's existing distribution channels and market knowledge.

3. **Enhanced Brand Visibility and Reputation**: Strategic licensing can enhance brand visibility and reinforce brand reputation by associating with high-quality products and reputable companies in different markets.

Legal Foundations of Licensing

1. **Intellectual Property Rights**: Understanding the intellectual property rights involved in trademark licensing is crucial. The licensor must ensure the trademark is registered and the rights to use it are clear and enforceable.

2. **Compliance and Protection**: Every licensing agreement must comply with local and international trademark laws. Agreements should clearly delineate the terms of use, geographical areas, duration, and the nature of products or services covered to protect the trademark from misuse or dilution.

3. **Quality Control**: Licensors must establish and enforce quality control measures to maintain the standard of the products or services associated with their trademark. This helps protect the integrity of the brand and ensure consumer trust.

Understanding the fundamentals of trademark licensing is essential for any business looking to leverage its brand through strategic partnerships. Effective licensing not only provides financial benefits but also enhances market presence and brand equity. By carefully crafting licensing agreements and managing them diligently, businesses can maximize the value of their trademarks and achieve sustained growth and success.

Identifying Potential Licensing Opportunities

Expanding your brand through licensing starts with identifying the right opportunities. This strategic exploration involves analyzing market trends, evaluating your brand's strength and appeal, and determining where your trademark can be most effectively leveraged. Here, we'll guide you through the process of spotting potential licensing ventures that align with your business objectives and brand identity.

Assessing Your Trademark's Market Potential

1. **Brand Evaluation**: Conduct a thorough analysis of your brand to understand its unique strengths and market appeal. This includes evaluating the recognition, customer loyalty, and the emotional connection your brand establishes with its audience. Understanding these factors can help pinpoint industries or sectors where your trademark could have significant impact.

2. **Market Research**: Dive into extensive market research to identify trends and consumer behaviors that align with your brand's values and offerings. Look for underserved markets or segments where your trademark can fill a niche or meet a growing demand.

3. **Competitor Analysis**: Study your competitors' licensing activities to gain insights into successful strategies and potential gaps in the market.

Analyzing where your competitors have not yet reached or markets they may be underserving can provide valuable opportunities for your brand.

Strategic Considerations for Licensing

1. **Synergistic Partnerships**: Look for potential licensees who not only have the capability to produce and market products under your trademark but also share similar brand values and quality standards. The right partner should enhance your brand's image and reputation through their offerings.

2. **Geographical Expansion**: Consider geographical areas where your brand has potential to grow. Licensing can be a strategic move to enter new markets, especially international ones, without the need for substantial capital investment in local operations.

3. **Diversification Opportunities**: Evaluate different product or service categories that resonate with your brand's identity but are outside your current offerings. This can include adjacent industries or completely new areas where your trademark can add value and recognition.

Tools and Methods for Identifying Opportunities

1. **Licensing Shows and Expos**: Attend industry-specific licensing expos, trade shows, and conferences to network with potential partners and gain insights into the latest trends and opportunities in licensing.

2. **Licensing Agents and Consultants**: Engage with professional licensing agents or consultants who specialize in your industry. They can provide expert advice, market insights, and introductions to potential licensees.

3. **Online Marketplaces and Platforms**: Utilize online platforms that connect licensors and licensees. These platforms can offer a broad view of the licensing landscape, including what types of products and services are being licensed and by whom.

Identifying the right licensing opportunities requires a strategic blend of market insight, brand evaluation, and industry networking. By understanding where your trademark can be most effectively utilized and finding partners that align with your brand's standards and goals, you can maximize the benefits of licensing. This proactive approach ensures that each licensing agreement contributes positively to your brand's growth, visibility, and profitability.

Negotiating Licensing Agreements

Negotiating licensing agreements is a critical step in the process of leveraging your trademarks. Effective negotiations ensure that both parties—the licensor and the licensee—benefit from the partnership. This section outlines key considerations and strategies for negotiating agreements that protect your interests and maximize the potential of your trademark.

Preparing for Negotiations

1. **Understand Your Objectives**: Clearly define what you want to achieve through the licensing agreement. Consider aspects such as revenue goals, market expansion, brand exposure, and strategic partnerships. Understanding your objectives will guide your negotiation tactics and help you prioritize terms.

2. **Know Your Value**: Assess the value of your trademark in the context of the proposed licensing deal. Consider the brand's market recognition, previous successful uses, and how well it aligns with the licensee's offerings. This valuation will form the basis for royalty rate discussions and other financial terms.

3. **Research the Licensee**: Gain a thorough understanding of the potential licensee's business model, market presence, and reputation. This information will help you assess their capability to effectively leverage your trademark and adhere to your brand standards.

Key Elements of Licensing Agreements

1. **Scope of License**: Define the scope of the license, including the geographical areas, specific products or services covered, and whether the license will be exclusive or non-exclusive. These terms determine how broadly the licensee can use the trademark.

2. **Duration and Renewal Terms**: Set clear terms regarding the duration of the license and conditions under which it can be renewed. This includes aligning the agreement's duration with your strategic business plans.

3. **Financial Terms**: Negotiate financial aspects such as upfront fees, minimum guarantees, royalty rates, and payment schedules. Ensure these terms are competitive yet fair, reflecting the trademark's value and the licensee's capacity to generate revenue from its use.

4. **Quality Control Measures**: Establish stringent quality control measures to maintain the integrity of the trademark. Specify the standards that the licensee must meet in the production and marketing of the licensed products or services. Include mechanisms for regular reviews and audits.

5. **Intellectual Property Protection**: Ensure the agreement includes clauses that protect your intellectual property rights and outline the measures to address infringement or misuse. This protects not only the legal rights but also the brand's reputation and market position.

Negotiation Tactics

1. **Flexibility and Creativity**: While it's important to have clear goals, being flexible and creative in how you achieve them can lead to more beneficial agreements. Consider alternative deal structures or value-adds that can make the agreement more attractive without compromising your key interests.

2. **Use of Legal Counsel**: Engage experienced intellectual property lawyers to review and advise on all aspects of the agreement. Their expertise can help navigate complex legal issues and ensure the agreement is enforceable and compliant with relevant laws.

3. **Building Relationships**: Approach negotiations as an opportunity to build a long-term relationship rather than just a contractual agreement. Establishing trust and mutual understanding can lead to more collaborative and successful licensing partnerships.

Negotiating a licensing agreement is a complex but critical process in maximizing the value of your trademarks. By carefully preparing for negotiations, focusing on key elements of the contract, and employing effective negotiation tactics, you can secure agreements that meet your business objectives and foster profitable and enduring partnerships.

► A Trademark Ownership and License Agreement can be found in the **Appendix**. If you are interested in receiving an electronic copy of this document, please email us at documents@AuthorsDoor.com with the subject line "Request for Trademark Ownership and License Agreement." Upon receiving your email, we will promptly send you a Microsoft Word copy of the document. **Disclaimer:** Please note that all agreements are provided for informational purposes only and should not be construed as legal advice. We recommend consulting with a qualified attorney to ensure that any legal documents or decisions are tailored to your specific circumstances.

Managing Licensing Relationships

Effective management of licensing relationships is critical for maintaining brand integrity and ensuring continued profitability from licensed agreements. This involves ongoing communication, regular compliance checks, and adapting to changes in the market or business objectives. This section offers strategies for managing licensing relationships effectively, ensuring they remain beneficial and align with your brand's reputation and goals.

Establishing Clear Communication Channels

1. **Regular Updates and Meetings**: Establish routine communication schedules with your licensees to discuss progress, address challenges, and share updates. Regular interactions help keep both parties aligned with the agreement's terms and objectives.

2. **Transparent Reporting Systems**: Implement transparent reporting systems that allow for the tracking and sharing of sales data, marketing efforts, and other relevant metrics. This ensures that all parties are informed about the performance and can make data-driven decisions.

3. **Dedicated Support and Resources**: Provide licensees with adequate support such as marketing materials, brand guidelines, and any necessary training. Supporting your licensees in understanding and leveraging your brand will help maximize the success of the partnership.

Monitoring Compliance and Quality

1. **Quality Control Checks**: Conduct regular quality control checks to ensure that the products or services offered by the licensee meet your brand's standards. This may involve random sampling, customer feedback analysis, or on-site inspections.

2. **Performance Reviews**: Periodically review the licensee's performance against the contract terms. This includes assessing their adherence to financial obligations, marketing commitments, and any other contractual stipulations.

3. **Legal and Regulatory Compliance**: Monitor the licensee's compliance with relevant legal and regulatory requirements. This is crucial for avoiding legal disputes that could tarnish the brand's reputation and financial standing.

Nurturing the Partnership

1. **Recognition and Incentives**: Recognize and reward licensees for outstanding performance or particularly innovative approaches to the market. Incentives can motivate higher performance and deeper commitment to the brand.

2. **Handling Conflicts and Resolutions**: Establish a fair and effective process for handling disputes or conflicts. Quick and equitable resolution of issues maintains trust and prevents minor disagreements from escalating into major disputes.

3. **Adaptive Contract Adjustments**: Be open to revising the terms of the agreement as the market conditions or business objectives change. Flexible and adaptive management can lead to a more successful long-term partnership.

Leveraging Technology in Licensing Management

1. **Utilize Licensing Management Software**: Implement specialized software to streamline tracking and management of licensing agreements. These tools can help manage contracts, monitor compliance, and analyze performance metrics efficiently.

2. **Digital Communication Tools**: Leverage digital tools for communication and collaboration, such as shared online workspaces, real-time data dashboards, and digital file sharing. These tools enhance transparency and facilitate smoother cooperation between parties.

Managing licensing relationships requires a proactive and structured approach that goes beyond the signing of an agreement. By establishing robust communication protocols, ensuring strict compliance, and nurturing the relationship, licensors can maximize the benefits of their partnerships. Effective management not only sustains profitability but also preserves the integrity and value of the brand in the long term.

Avoiding Common Pitfalls in Licensing

Licensing can dramatically extend the reach and profitability of your brand, but it comes with its own set of risks and challenges. If not carefully managed, these pitfalls can lead to financial losses, brand dilution, or legal complications. This section explores common pitfalls in the licensing process and provides strategies to avoid them, ensuring your licensing agreements contribute positively to your brand's growth and reputation.

Overextending the Brand

1. **Dilution of Brand Identity**: One of the most significant risks in licensing is the dilution of your brand's identity. This can occur if the trademark is licensed too broadly, used in markets that do not align with the brand's core values, or associated with lower-quality products.

2. **Strategy to Avoid**: To prevent dilution, be selective in choosing licensing partners and market segments. Ensure that all licensed products and services meet your brand's standards for quality and consistency.

Regular audits and licensee evaluations can help maintain these standards.

Inadequate Partner Vetting

1. **Partner Misalignment**: Not all potential licensees will be suitable for your brand. Issues such as inadequate market knowledge, poor business practices, or a lack of alignment with your brand values can harm your brand's reputation and profitability.

2. **Strategy to Avoid**: Conduct thorough due diligence on all potential licensees. This includes reviewing their business history, reputation, financial stability, and compatibility with your brand ethos. Engaging in detailed negotiations and setting clear contractual terms can also safeguard against misalignment.

Lack of Clear Contractual Agreements

1. **Ambiguous Terms**: Vague or incomplete licensing agreements can lead to misunderstandings and disputes over rights and responsibilities. Such ambiguities may concern the scope of use, territory, duration, or financial arrangements.

2. **Strategy to Avoid**: Work with experienced legal professionals to draft clear, comprehensive licensing agreements. Ensure that all aspects of the partnership are explicitly defined, including rights, obligations, financial terms, dispute resolution mechanisms, and termination conditions.

Ineffective Management and Oversight

1. **Insufficient Oversight**: Failing to monitor the licensee's activities can lead to unauthorized uses of the trademark or substandard products and services being offered under your brand.

2. **Strategy to Avoid**: Implement a robust system for monitoring and enforcing the terms of the licensing agreement. Regular performance reviews, quality checks, and compliance audits are crucial. Technology solutions such as licensing management software can streamline this process.

Failing to Adapt to Market Changes

1. **Rigidity in Agreements**: Market conditions and consumer preferences can change rapidly. Licensing agreements that are too rigid can prevent your brand from adapting effectively, potentially missing out on new opportunities or continuing in declining markets.

2. **Strategy to Avoid**: Include flexible terms in licensing agreements that allow for periodic reassessment and adaptation to changing market conditions. This might involve renegotiation clauses or regular interval reviews that can trigger adjustments in strategy.

Successfully navigating the complex landscape of trademark licensing requires careful planning, thorough vetting, clear contractual agreements, and diligent management. By being aware of and actively working to avoid these common pitfalls, you can ensure that your licensing efforts enhance your brand's value and contribute to its long-term success.

Quick Tips and Recap

- **Select Partners Carefully**: Vet potential licensees thoroughly to ensure alignment with your brand values and market goals.

- **Draft Clear Agreements**: Utilize experienced legal counsel to draft comprehensive and clear licensing agreements that specify all terms including scope, territory, duration, and financial details.

- **Maintain Quality Control**: Regularly monitor the quality of products or services offered under your brand to prevent dilution of your trademark and ensure consistent customer experience.

- **Monitor Compliance**: Establish a robust system for monitoring licensee compliance with the licensing agreement to prevent unauthorized use and ensure adherence to contractual obligations.

- **Adapt to Market Changes**: Include flexible terms in your agreements that allow for adjustments based on shifting market conditions and consumer preferences.

- **Utilize Technology**: Implement licensing management software to help track performance, manage contracts, and ensure compliance more efficiently.

- **Regular Audits**: Conduct regular audits and performance reviews of licensing arrangements to assess their impact on your brand and make necessary adjustments.

- **Engage in Open Communication**: Maintain open lines of communication with licensees to foster a positive working relationship and address any issues promptly.

- **Protect Your Rights**: Be proactive in protecting your intellectual property rights through legal means when necessary to address infringements or breaches of contract.

- **Evaluate Financial Performance**: Regularly assess the financial performance of licensing arrangements to ensure they are meeting expected revenue goals and providing a good return on investment.

CHAPTER FIFTEEN

On the Horizon: Latest Trends

in Trademark Law

"As we look to the horizon, the latest trends in trademark law are shaping a landscape where intellectual property protection intersects with global commerce and digital innovation, challenging businesses to stay informed and agile." — RUTH BADER GINSBURG, ASSOCIATE JUSTICE OF THE U.S. SUPREME COURT

Just when you thought you had trademark law all figured out, the horizon shifts and new trends emerge like plot twists in a soap opera. Staying ahead in the game of trademarks means keeping an eye on these trends, which can be as unpredictable and influential as fashion in Hollywood.

First up, we have the rise of non-traditional trademarks. Think sounds, colors, and even smells. That's right, the scent of your favorite bakery or the unique jingle of an ad could soon be as defendable as the swoosh on a sneaker. This trend is turning the intangible into the invaluable, proving that sometimes, what you can't quite put your finger on can still be distinctly yours.

Next, there's the digital domain—where the virtual world becomes a playground for trademark titans. With the explosion of e-commerce, the need to protect digital assets has skyrocketed faster than you can click 'add to cart'. From hashtags to domain names, the digital landscape is the new frontier, and it's wilder than the Wild West.

And let's not overlook the impact of global markets. As businesses expand across borders, international trademark protection is becoming more of a chess game than a checkbox. This trend demands a strategy that's as globally minded as it is grounded in local nuances—a tall order, but a necessary one.

Finally, the legal battles themselves are evolving. The courts are seeing more action than a blockbuster movie premiere, with high-profile cases setting precedents that ripple across the industry. These decisions can reshape the landscape overnight, making it essential for anyone in the trademark trenches to stay informed and agile.

So, fasten your intellectual property seatbelts and prepare for a ride through the ever-changing world of trademark law. It's a journey that promises new challenges, unexpected allies, and plenty of opportunities to make your mark.

Non-Traditional Trademarks

The landscape of trademark law is expanding, allowing for the protection of more unconventional and non-traditional trademarks than ever before. These include sensory marks such as sounds, scents, and colors that are used distinctively in commerce. This section explores the evolution, challenges, and opportunities associated with non-traditional trademarks, demonstrating their growing importance in a diversified market environment.

Understanding Non-Traditional Trademarks

1. **Definition and Types**: Non-traditional trademarks go beyond the usual logos and words to include any mark that can be perceived by the senses. This category can encompass:

    o **Sounds**: Jingles or unique sounds associated with a brand, like the Intel bong or the MGM lion roar.

    o **Scents**: Distinctive smells linked to a product, such as the smell of Play-Doh or the floral scent used in Verizon stores.

    o **Colors**: Specific colors used consistently and exclusively by a brand, such as Tiffany blue or UPS brown.

    o **Textures**: A particular surface design or feel that identifies the source of a product, like the texture of a Burberry scarf.

    o **Motion Marks**: Moving images or animations that are consistently associated with a brand, such as the animated Google Doodle.

2. **Legal Recognition and Protection**: The protection of non-traditional trademarks varies by jurisdiction but generally requires that the mark be distinctive and identifiable by consumers as signifying the source of a product or service. Registration challenges often center on proving this distinctiveness and the non-functionality of the mark.

Challenges in Protecting Non-Traditional Trademarks

1. **Distinctiveness and Secondary Meaning**: Many non-traditional trademarks must acquire distinctiveness through use, as they are not inherently distinctive. Establishing a secondary meaning—that the public associates the sensory mark specifically with the brand—can be resource-intensive.

2. **Functionality Doctrine**: A significant challenge is the functionality doctrine, which states that a feature that is essential to the use or purpose of the article or affects the cost or quality of the article cannot be

protected as a trademark. This can apply particularly to colors and shapes.

3. **Subjectivity in Perception**: Non-traditional marks can be subjective in how they are perceived by different individuals, making it difficult to establish a consistent and recognizable identity across all consumer demographics.

Case Studies and Examples

1. **Successful Registrations**: Highlight cases where non-traditional trademarks have been successfully registered and enforced, such as the sound of the Harley-Davidson motorcycle engine (though later withdrawn) or the shape and color of the Toblerone chocolate bar.

2. **Controversial Cases**: Discuss more contentious instances, such as attempts to trademark common scents or colors used by multiple brands within the same industry, leading to legal battles over trademark rights.

Future Outlook

1. **Increasing Popularity**: As brands seek new ways to differentiate themselves, the use of non-traditional trademarks is likely to increase. This trend will require ongoing adaptation of legal standards and practices to accommodate these innovative identifiers.

2. **Technological Influence**: Advances in technology may bring new types of non-traditional trademarks, such as digital smells or holograms, challenging current legal frameworks to keep pace with innovation.

Non-traditional trademarks represent an exciting frontier in trademark law, offering businesses unique ways to strengthen their brand identity and consumer connections. As these types of marks become more common, the challenges of registering and enforcing them also evolve, highlighting the dynamic nature of intellectual property protection in the modern marketplace.

Digital and Virtual Trademarks

In the digital age, trademarks are not just confined to the physical world. The rise of e-commerce, social media, and virtual environments has created new opportunities—and challenges—for trademark protection. Digital and virtual trademarks include everything from domain names and social media handles to virtual goods and services in online platforms. This section explores the nuances of protecting trademarks in the digital realm and navigating the evolving landscape of virtual commerce.

Defining Digital and Virtual Trademarks

1. **Types of Digital Trademarks**: Digital trademarks encompass identifiers that are used in electronic commerce and online media, such as:

   o **Domain Names**: Internet addresses that align closely with a brand, such as Nike.com.

   o **Social Media Handles**: Unique identifiers on platforms like Twitter, Instagram, or TikTok, e.g., @Starbucks.

   o **Hashtags**: Often used for marketing campaigns, such as Coca-Cola's #ShareACoke.

2. **Virtual Trademarks**: As the line between virtual and physical realities blurs, trademarks in virtual environments, such as video games or virtual reality platforms, are becoming increasingly common. These can include:

   o **Virtual Goods**: Branded items sold within video games or virtual worlds, like fashion items in online games.

   o **Service Marks**: Used in the provision of online services, such as streaming platforms or cloud computing services.

Legal Challenges and Protection Strategies

1. **Registration and Enforcement**: Protecting digital and virtual trademarks involves ensuring they are registered correctly under relevant categories and jurisdictions. Challenges arise in proving distinctiveness

and managing cross-jurisdictional enforcement, given the global nature of the internet.

2. **Cybersquatting and Infringement**: Cybersquatting, where third parties register domain names reflecting known brands to exploit for profit, is a significant challenge. Trademark owners must be vigilant and may need to engage in domain name disputes under policies like the ICANN's Uniform Domain-Name Dispute-Resolution Policy (UDRP).

3. **Adapting to Platform Policies**: Social media platforms and virtual worlds have their own policies for handling trademark infringement. Navigating these requires understanding each platform's specific procedures and how they intersect with formal legal protections.

Strategies for Effective Management

1. **Proactive Registration**: Secure domain names and social media handles that align with your trademarks early on to prevent cybersquatting and unauthorized use by third parties.

2. **Monitoring Online Usage**: Regularly monitor the internet and social media for unauthorized use of your trademarks. Tools like brand monitoring software can automate this process and provide real-time alerts.

3. **Legal Action and Policy Engagement**: Be prepared to take swift legal action when infringement occurs. Engaging with online marketplaces and platforms to enforce trademark rights is crucial, as is staying updated with changes in digital commerce regulations and platform policies.

Future Trends in Digital Trademarking

1. **Evolving Technologies**: With the rise of blockchain technology, non-fungible tokens (NFTs), and advancements in AI, new types of digital and virtual trademarks are likely to emerge, requiring ongoing adaptation of trademark strategies.

2. **Increased Legal Recognition**: As digital and virtual environments continue to grow in commercial importance, legal systems worldwide

are likely to further recognize and refine the protection of digital and virtual trademarks.

Digital and virtual trademarks represent a critical frontier in trademark protection, reflecting the shift towards a more interconnected and technologically driven marketplace. Ensuring robust protection and strategic management of these trademarks is essential for maintaining brand integrity and capitalizing on the opportunities of digital expansion.

Globalization of Trademark Strategy

In today's interconnected world, expanding a brand internationally involves navigating complex trademark strategies across multiple jurisdictions. A globalization strategy for trademarks must address diverse legal systems, cultural differences, and varying consumer behaviors to effectively protect and leverage a brand's intellectual property on a global scale.

Understanding Global Trademark Protection

1. **Harmonization and Differences**: While international agreements such as the Madrid Protocol offer mechanisms to streamline the trademark registration process across countries, significant differences still exist in local trademark laws. Understanding these nuances is crucial for ensuring comprehensive protection.

2. **Strategic Registrations**: Deciding where to register a trademark should align with current business operations and future expansion plans. Prioritize markets that are key to your business growth, have high risks of infringement, or are known for rigorous intellectual property enforcement.

Developing a Global Trademark Strategy

1. **Centralized Management**: Manage your global trademarks centrally to maintain consistency and control over your brand's international presence. This approach helps in enforcing a unified branding strategy across all markets while accommodating local variations if needed.

2. **Use of International Treaties**: Utilize international treaties like the Madrid System for the international registration of trademarks. This system allows for a centralized application process to seek protection in up to 122 countries through a single application.

3. **Cultural Adaptation**: Adapt trademarks and branding strategies to fit cultural contexts without compromising the brand's core identity. This might involve modifying brand names, logos, or other elements to ensure cultural sensitivity and relevance.

Navigating Legal and Regulatory Environments

1. **Local Legal Expertise**: Engage with local legal experts who specialize in trademark law in each jurisdiction. These professionals can provide invaluable insights into local legal nuances, help navigate the registration process, and act swiftly in cases of infringement.

2. **Regular Legal Audits**: Conduct regular reviews of your trademark portfolio to ensure compliance with local laws and to address any potential legal challenges proactively. This includes keeping track of renewal deadlines, usage mandates, and changes in trademark laws.

3. **Monitoring and Enforcement**: Establish a robust monitoring system to detect trademark infringements across different regions. Utilize both traditional surveillance methods and modern digital tools to monitor online marketplaces, social media platforms, and other digital venues.

Mitigating Risks in International Markets

1. **Risk Assessment**: Perform thorough market and legal risk assessments before entering new territories. Assess the potential for trademark infringement and the strength of intellectual property rights enforcement in each market.

2. **Dispute Resolution**: Develop strategies for dispute resolution that consider the most effective and efficient means to handle conflicts in international jurisdictions. This may include litigation, arbitration, or alternative dispute resolution mechanisms depending on the legal landscape and business objectives.

Developing a robust globalization strategy for trademarks is essential for businesses looking to expand their reach across international borders. By understanding and navigating the complexities of global trademark protection, companies can safeguard their brands, capitalize on international market opportunities, and maintain a competitive edge in the global marketplace. Effective management, strategic planning, and proactive legal oversight are key to successfully implementing a global trademark strategy.

Legal Developments and Court Decisions

The field of trademark law is constantly evolving, influenced by landmark court decisions and significant legal developments. These changes can have profound impacts on how trademarks are registered, managed, and enforced globally. Staying abreast of these developments is crucial for businesses to protect their intellectual property effectively and leverage their trademarks strategically.

Overview of Recent Legal Changes

1. **Global Legal Trends**: Discuss recent global trends in trademark law, such as the increasing recognition of non-traditional trademarks, changes in the digital environment affecting online brands, and shifts in consumer protection laws that impact trademark strategies.

2. **Significant Court Decisions**: Analyze key court cases from major jurisdictions that have set important precedents in trademark law. Examples might include decisions on the scope of trademark protection, the treatment of generic terms, and the enforcement of intellectual property rights in digital marketplaces.

Impact of High-Profile Cases

1. **Case Studies**: Present detailed case studies of recent high-profile trademark disputes that highlight significant legal principles or shifts. For instance, discuss cases involving major brands that have battled over trademark infringement claims and the outcomes that have shaped industry practices.

2. **Precedent-Setting Decisions**: Explore how certain decisions have redefined the understanding of specific aspects of trademark law, such as fair use, the likelihood of confusion standard, or cross-border enforcement challenges.

Legal Adaptations and Strategies

1. **Adapting to Legal Changes**: Provide guidance on how businesses can adapt their trademark strategies in response to new legal rulings and legislative changes. This might involve altering trademark management practices, reevaluating risk assessment procedures, or revising enforcement strategies.

2. **Proactive Legal Planning**: Emphasize the importance of proactive legal planning in response to evolving trademark laws. Recommend regular legal audits, continuous monitoring of legislative changes, and consultations with intellectual property experts to stay compliant and competitive.

Leveraging Legal Developments

1. **Strategic Advantages**: Discuss how businesses can turn legal developments into strategic advantages. For example, by registering non-traditional trademarks that have gained legal recognition or by capitalizing on new laws that offer stronger protections for online brands.

2. **Global Coordination**: Highlight the necessity of coordinating trademark strategies across multiple jurisdictions in light of international legal developments. Address the complexities of managing a global trademark portfolio in an environment where legal landscapes can vary widely.

The dynamic nature of trademark law demands vigilant monitoring and agile responses to legal developments. By staying informed about significant court decisions and adapting strategies accordingly, businesses can not only protect their valuable trademarks but also position themselves favorably in a competitive global market. This section underscores the importance of legal awareness and strategic flexibility in navigating the ever-changing world of trademark law.

Future Projections and Adaptations

As we look forward, the landscape of trademark law is set to evolve in response to technological advancements, changing global trade dynamics, and shifts in consumer behavior. This section explores anticipated trends in trademark law and provides strategic recommendations for businesses to adapt and thrive in this changing environment.

Anticipated Trends in Trademark Protection

1. **Technological Influence**: With the rise of artificial intelligence, blockchain, and augmented reality, new types of trademarks are expected to emerge. This includes marks for digital products and services that may not yet fully exist, such as virtual reality environments or AI-generated content.

2. **Global Integration**: As businesses continue to expand globally, the need for a more integrated and harmonized approach to trademark protection will increase. This could lead to stronger international cooperation and possibly new global standards for trademark registration and enforcement.

3. **Consumer Interaction**: The way consumers interact with brands is evolving, especially with the increase in e-commerce and digital marketing. Trademark strategies will need to address these changes, focusing on online brand protection, digital advertising disputes, and the protection of virtual goods.

Legal and Regulatory Adaptations

1. **Adapting to New Technologies**: Laws and regulations will need to adapt to accommodate the registration and protection of non-traditional trademarks brought about by new technologies. This might include specific provisions for digital marks, virtual goods, and services that operate primarily in digital environments.

2. **Enhanced Online Enforcement**: As online infringements continue to rise, there will likely be an increase in the tools and legal mechanisms available to trademark owners for enforcing their rights online. This

could include more sophisticated online monitoring tools and stronger partnerships between legal authorities and digital platforms.

3. **Consumer Privacy and Trademarks**: With growing concerns over data privacy, future trademark strategies will need to carefully balance brand protection with consumer privacy rights. This may influence how trademarks are used in online marketing and data-driven advertising.

Strategic Business Considerations

1. **Proactive Intellectual Property Management**: Businesses will need to be proactive in managing their intellectual property by regularly updating their trademark strategies to incorporate new types of products and digital advancements. This includes staying informed about technological trends that may affect their industry and preparing to trademark new innovations.

2. **Cultural and Ethical Considerations**: As brands become more global, understanding cultural differences in trademark perception and the ethical use of trademarks will become more important. This includes being mindful of cultural sensitivities when registering and using trademarks in foreign markets.

3. **Sustainability and Trademarks**: The increasing focus on sustainability and corporate responsibility may lead to the use of trademarks that signify eco-friendliness or ethical business practices. Companies might consider developing trademarks that represent their commitment to sustainability.

The future of trademark law is dynamic and demands agility and foresight from businesses. By anticipating changes in technology, consumer behavior, and global market trends, companies can not only adapt to these changes but also use them to gain a competitive advantage. As trademark law continues to evolve, the most successful businesses will be those that view these changes as opportunities to innovate and strengthen their brand protection strategies globally.

Quick Tips and Recap

- **Stay Informed**: Regularly update your knowledge of global trademark laws and trends to ensure your brand protection strategies remain effective and compliant.

- **Embrace Technology**: Leverage new technologies such as blockchain and AI to monitor and protect your trademarks in digital spaces and virtual environments.

- **Think Globally**: Consider the implications of global market expansion on your trademark strategy and ensure you have protection in all relevant jurisdictions.

- **Adapt to Non-Traditional Marks**: Be prepared to embrace non-traditional trademarks, including sounds, scents, and virtual goods, as part of your intellectual property portfolio.

- **Monitor Online Activity**: Use advanced online monitoring tools to detect and act against trademark infringements quickly and effectively.

- **Engage Local Experts**: Utilize local legal expertise in foreign markets to navigate regional trademark laws and cultural nuances effectively.

- **Prioritize Consumer Engagement**: Adapt your trademark strategies to align with evolving consumer interactions and digital marketing trends.

- **Focus on Compliance**: Stay vigilant about regulatory compliance, especially in relation to digital marketing and consumer data privacy.

- **Plan for Sustainability**: Integrate sustainability into your trademark strategy to reflect your brand's commitment to ethical practices and appeal to eco-conscious consumers.

- **Use Strategic Partnerships**: Collaborate with digital platforms and international agencies to enhance the enforcement of your trademarks across different regions.

By following these tips, you can ensure that your trademark strategies are robust, adaptive, and aligned with the latest developments in trademark law and consumer behavior.

PART FOUR

Trademark Toolkit

Welcome to your Trademark Toolkit, the Swiss Army knife for navigating the wilds of brand protection. Inside this toolkit, you'll find everything from the robust hammer of registration strategies to the precision screwdriver of legal nuances, ensuring no screw is left loose in the construction of your brand fortress. Think of it as your intellectual property battle gear, equipped to tackle the sneaky pitfalls of infringement and the looming threats of trademark trolls. Whether you're a seasoned legal eagle or a fledgling entrepreneur, this toolkit is your trusty sidekick, ready to leap into action at the first sign of trademark trouble. Let's pop open this toolkit and show the world that when it comes to protecting your brand, you're well-armed and ready to roll!

CHAPTER SIXTEEN

Filing for Success: Sample Trademark Application

"Filing for a trademark isn't just a procedural step; it's a strategic move that protects your brand's core identity and paves the way for long-term success in the marketplace." — MICHAEL PORTER, PROFESSOR AND AUTHORITY ON CORPORATE STRATEGY AND THE COMPETITIVENESS OF NATIONS

Roll up your sleeves and sharpen your pencils—or, let's be real, just make sure your Wi-Fi is solid—because we're about to dive into the thrilling world of trademark applications. Consider this your step-by-step cookbook recipe for branding success, where missing a single ingredient could mean the difference between a trademark triumph and a legal letdown.

Imagine you're assembling a high-stakes IKEA furniture set, but instead of an Allen wrench, you're armed with your brand details, and instead of confusing

217

instructions, you have this clear, concise guide. We'll walk you through each part of the application like a GPS guiding a lost driver—clear, calm, and avoiding unnecessary detours.

First up, the goods or services description: this is where you shine a spotlight on what your mark will be gracing. Be as precise as a sushi chef's knife cuts—vague descriptions are the breadcrumbs that lead competitors to your door. Next, your specimen of use: think of this as your brand in action, a snapshot or screenshot that proves your mark isn't just a wallflower at the trademark party.

And don't forget the declaration! It's your solemn swear that everything you're claiming is as true as the calories listed on a chocolate bar (which, in this case, are actually accurate). Signing this might not feel as monumental as autographing your first book deal, but it has its own kind of celebrity moment.

By the time you hit 'submit', you'll feel the thrill of a racer at the starting line. And while the approval process might take longer than brewing a fine whiskey, remember: good things come to those who wait—and who fill out their applications meticulously. So, gear up for a journey into the heart of your brand's identity. It's filing time!

Preparing Your Application

Filing for a trademark registration marks a critical step in securing your brand's intellectual property. Effective preparation is analogous to laying the foundation for a building—vital for supporting all future endeavors. This section outlines the essential steps required to prepare a robust trademark application, ensuring a meticulous approach that lays the groundwork for success.

Detailed Steps for Gathering Essential Information

1. **Define Your Trademark**: Clearly identify the specific mark you intend to register. Determine if your application will cover a word mark, a logo, a slogan, or a combination thereof. For designs and logos, ensure you have clean, high-resolution images ready for submission.

2. **Conduct a Comprehensive Trademark Search**: Before you can proceed confidently, carry out an exhaustive search to check if your

desired trademark or a similar one is already in use for related goods or services. Utilize the USPTO's online search system, TESS (Trademark Electronic Search System), for initial guidance, and consider engaging a professional for a more thorough search.

3. **Understand and Select Appropriate Classes**: Familiarize yourself with the Nice Classification, which organizes trademarks into 45 standard classes (34 for products and 11 for services). Determining the correct class or classes is crucial as it defines the scope of protection your trademark will receive.

Legal Considerations and Filing Basis

1. **Choose Your Filing Basis**: You must specify the basis for your filing. This can be either "use in commerce" for marks already being used in business transactions, or "intent to use" if you plan to use the mark commercially in the future. Each basis has specific requirements and legal implications.

2. **Ownership and Applicant Details**: Accurately designate the trademark owner, whether an individual, a corporation, or another entity. The designated owner will hold the rights to the trademark and is responsible for its proper use in commerce.

Preparing Required Documentation and Legal Representation

1. **Prepare Supporting Documents**: Assemble all documents required for your application, which may include proofs of use (like advertisements and product packaging featuring the mark), any previous registrations, and, if applicable, consent agreements from individuals or entities referenced in the trademark.

2. **Consider Professional Representation**: While individuals can file trademarks on their own, the complexities of trademark law often necessitate hiring a trademark attorney. Legal experts can navigate the finer points of trademark law, handle the filing process, and respond to any USPTO actions or oppositions effectively.

Review and Fees

1. **Double-Check Application Details**: Meticulously review all parts of your application for accuracy. Errors in names, addresses, or descriptions can lead to delays or rejections of your application.

2. **Calculate and Prepare Fees**: Understand the fee structure, which varies based on the number of classes applied for and the filing basis. Ensure that you are prepared to cover all necessary fees to avoid processing delays.

Thorough preparation is paramount to a successful trademark application. By carefully defining your mark, conducting detailed market and legal research, and preparing all necessary documentation, you set a strong foundation for your trademark's registration. This proactive preparation minimizes the risk of objections or rejections, paving the way for a smooth path to securing your intellectual property rights.

Describing the Goods or Services

A critical component of the trademark application process is the accurate and clear description of the goods or services associated with the mark. This description not only defines the scope of protection but also determines the trademark's classification under the appropriate Nice categories. This section will guide you through crafting precise descriptions that meet legal requirements and support robust trademark protection.

Principles of Effective Description

1. **Specificity and Clarity**: The description should be specific enough to clearly define the nature of the goods or services without being overly broad or vague. Generic descriptions can lead to rejections or challenges later on, as they may not adequately delineate the trademark's use.

2. **Consistency with Use**: Ensure that the description accurately reflects how the trademark is used in commerce. This alignment is crucial for the enforcement of trademark rights, as any discrepancy between the description and actual use can weaken legal protections.

3. **Avoiding Legal Jargon**: While it's important to be precise, avoid overly technical or legalistic language that could obscure the meaning. The goal is to make the description accessible and understandable to those in the relevant industries.

Crafting Your Descriptions

1. **Identify the Nature of Goods or Services**: Start by categorizing your goods or services. Are they physical products, online services, educational programs, or something else? This categorization will help in aligning with the correct Nice classification.

2. **Detailing Features and Purposes**: Include details about the features, purposes, and potential uses of the goods or services. This level of detail helps to further clarify the scope of the trademark's use and distinguish it from similar marks.

3. **Using Acceptable Terminology**: Utilize terms and descriptions that are commonly understood in your industry. Refer to the USPTO's Acceptable Identification of Goods and Services Manual or corresponding guides in other jurisdictions to find standardized language that might be required for your application.

Examples and Templates

1. **Template for Goods**: For products, begin with the general category of goods and then describe specific items. Example: "Clothing, namely, t-shirts, sweaters, and jackets; footwear; headgear, namely, hats and caps."

2. **Template for Services**: For services, start with the broader service category followed by specific actions or operations. Example: "Educational services, namely, conducting classes, seminars, conferences in the field of business management; Providing online non-downloadable software for project management."

Legal Considerations

1. **Navigating Overlap and Ambiguity**: In cases where goods or services may overlap multiple categories or where descriptions could be interpreted in various ways, provide clarifying details that limit

221

ambiguity. This precision will aid in the defense of the trademark in potential disputes.

2. **Updating Descriptions**: If the nature of the goods or services evolves over time, consider updating your trademark registrations to reflect these changes accurately. This may require filing a new application or amending existing registrations.

Describing your goods or services with precision and clarity in a trademark application is crucial for securing the intended scope of protection. Detailed, accurate descriptions not only facilitate the registration process but also enhance the enforceability of your trademark rights. This careful articulation serves as a foundational element in defining and defending your brand in the marketplace.

Providing a Specimen of Use

In the trademark registration process, providing a specimen of use is a pivotal requirement that demonstrates how the trademark is actually used in commerce. A specimen of use supports your application by showing that the mark is actively associated with the goods or services listed in your application, solidifying the connection between the mark and its commercial presence.

Understanding Specimen of Use

1. **Definition and Purpose**: A specimen of use is a real-world example of how your trademark is used in the marketplace. It serves as proof that the trademark is not merely a theoretical concept but is actively used to identify and distinguish your goods or services from those of others.

2. **Requirements for Valid Specimens**: The specimen must clearly display the trademark as it is used in commerce. For goods, this typically means showing the mark on product packaging, labels, or tags. For services, it often involves showing the mark in advertising materials, brochures, or websites that directly relate to the services offered.

Preparing Your Specimen

1. **Selecting an Appropriate Specimen for Goods**: Choose specimens that clearly show the trademark on the actual goods or packaging. This can

include photographs of the product label, packaging showing the trademark, or other marketing materials that clearly associate the product with the trademark.

2. **Selecting an Appropriate Specimen for Services**: For services, provide examples of marketing materials, advertisements, business cards, or screenshots of websites where the services are offered under the trademark. Ensure that these specimens clearly link the trademark to the specific services being provided.

Best Practices for Specimen Submission

1. **Clarity and Legibility**: Ensure that the specimen is clear and the trademark is easily legible. If the trademark is part of a larger document, highlight or clearly point out where the trademark appears.

2. **Current and Relevant**: The specimen should reflect current use, so select materials that are up-to-date and relevant to the goods or services at the time of filing. Avoid outdated or obsolete examples, as they may not adequately represent the current use of the trademark.

3. **Compliance with USPTO Guidelines**: Familiarize yourself with the specific guidelines set by the United States Patent and Trademark Office (USPTO) or the corresponding agency in other jurisdictions. These guidelines outline what is acceptable as a specimen for different types of trademarks.

Common Mistakes to Avoid

1. **Mockups Are Not Acceptable**: Do not submit mockups or artist's renderings of the trademark as these do not prove actual use in commerce.

2. **Indirect Usage**: Avoid specimens that only indirectly imply use of the trademark or where the trademark is not clearly associated with the specific goods or services.

3. **Non-Public Use**: Ensure that the specimen reflects public use of the trademark. Internal documents or private communications are generally not acceptable.

Providing a proper specimen of use is a critical step in the trademark registration process, as it concretely demonstrates the trademark's use in commerce. By carefully selecting and preparing your specimens according to the guidelines, you can enhance the credibility of your application and facilitate a smoother registration process. This attention to detail in the presentation of your specimens ensures that the trademark office fully understands the context and scope of your trademark's use.

Completing the Declaration

The declaration is a fundamental part of the trademark application process, serving as a formal statement by the applicant attesting to the truthfulness and accuracy of the information provided. This legally binding document is crucial for affirming the applicant's rights and intentions regarding the trademark.

Understanding the Importance of the Declaration

1. **Legal Affirmation**: The declaration asserts that the applicant believes they are the rightful owner of the trademark and that there is no known reason why the trademark should not be registered. It's a commitment that the mark is being used in commerce according to U.S. trademark laws or that there is a bona fide intention to use the mark.

2. **Swearing to Accuracy**: It includes a statement that all information in the application is accurate to the best of the applicant's knowledge. This is important for maintaining the integrity of the trademark registration process and ensuring compliance with legal standards.

Key Elements of the Declaration

1. **Ownership and Authorization**: The declaration confirms that the applicant owns the trademark and is authorized to use it. This includes an assertion that the applicant is not infringing on another party's rights.

2. **Use in Commerce**: For applications based on use in commerce, the declaration must confirm that the trademark is already being used in commerce on or in connection with the goods/services listed in the application. It should align with the specimen of use provided.

3. **Intent to Use**: For intent-to-use applications, the declaration must state that the applicant has a bona fide intention to use the trademark in commerce. This is crucial for securing a filing date and maintaining the priority of the application.

Completing the Declaration Form

1. **Reviewing Instructions**: Carefully review the specific instructions provided by the trademark office, such as the USPTO, for completing the declaration. This ensures compliance with all procedural requirements and helps avoid common mistakes.

2. **Providing Accurate Information**: Double-check all details in the declaration for accuracy. Incorrect information can lead to delays, additional fees, or even the denial of the trademark application.

3. **Signature and Date**: The declaration must be signed by the applicant or an authorized representative. The signature legally binds the applicant to the statements made in the declaration. Ensure that the declaration is dated accurately.

Legal Implications of the Declaration

1. **Perjury Warning**: Be aware that false statements can have serious legal consequences, including charges of perjury. The declaration is not just a formality but a sworn statement that holds legal weight.

2. **Amendments and Corrections**: If errors are discovered after submission, it's important to correct them promptly. Amending a declaration can involve legal nuances, so consulting a trademark attorney might be necessary.

The declaration is more than just a procedural requirement; it is a critical legal document that validates the entire trademark application. Completing the declaration with careful attention to detail and full honesty ensures the strength and enforceability of the trademark application. It's essential to approach this step with the seriousness it demands, reflecting the applicant's commitment to ethical business practices and respect for intellectual property laws.

Submission and Follow-Up

After meticulous preparation, accurate completion of the application, and careful declaration, the final step in securing your trademark is the submission and subsequent follow-up. This phase is crucial as it ensures that your application is not only submitted correctly but also that you are prepared for any further requirements or responses from the trademark office.

Completing the Submission Process

1. **Online Submission**: Most trademark applications today are submitted online through the official portal of the respective trademark office, such as the USPTO's TEAS (Trademark Electronic Application System) in the United States. Ensure that all forms are filled out completely and all necessary documents, including specimens and the declaration, are attached.

2. **Double-Check for Accuracy**: Before submitting, review the entire application for any errors or omissions. A single mistake can delay the process or lead to a non-substantive office action, requiring further responses and potentially additional fees.

3. **Payment of Fees**: Confirm the payment of all required fees, which vary depending on the number of classes of goods or services and the specific processing options selected. Incomplete or incorrect payment can result in the rejection of your application.

Managing the Follow-Up

1. **Tracking the Application**: After submission, use the provided tracking number to monitor the status of your application through the trademark office's online system. This will show you the progress of your application and alert you to any actions or communications from the trademark office.

2. **Responding to Office Actions**: If the trademark office issues an office action, which could be either substantive (questioning the registrability of the mark) or non-substantive (requesting clarification or additional information), respond promptly and thoroughly. Engaging a trademark

attorney can be beneficial in addressing complex legal issues raised during this phase.

3. **Publication and Opposition**: Once preliminary approval is granted, your trademark will be published in an official gazette to allow the public an opportunity to oppose the registration. Monitor this phase closely and prepare to address any opposition filed, which may involve legal proceedings.

Preparing for Registration and Beyond

1. **Preparing for Registration**: If no opposition is filed, or if opposition is overcome, prepare for the final steps of registration. This may involve submitting additional documents or, in the case of an intent-to-use application, proving that the mark is now in use in commerce.

2. **Maintaining Your Registration**: Once registered, maintain your trademark by renewing it at the required intervals, monitoring for infringement, and using it correctly in commerce to avoid claims of abandonment. Regular audits of your trademark use and registration can ensure ongoing protection and compliance.

The submission of your trademark application and the follow-up process are as critical as the initial preparations. By carefully managing these final steps, you can secure the rights to your trademark and protect your brand's identity in the marketplace. Staying proactive during the follow-up phase, particularly in responding to office actions and managing opposition, will enhance your chances of successful registration and effective long-term trademark protection.

Quick Tips and Recap

- **Review Thoroughly Before Submission**: Double-check your application for accuracy and completeness before submitting to avoid delays and possible rejections.

- **Use Official Online Platforms for Submission**: Submit your trademark application through the official online system provided by the trademark office (e.g., USPTO's TEAS) for efficiency and tracking purposes.

- **Ensure Correct Fee Payment**: Verify that all necessary fees are paid in full at the time of application to prevent processing interruptions.

- **Monitor Application Status**: Regularly check the status of your application using the tracking number provided to stay informed of any updates or required actions.

- **Prepare for Office Actions**: Be ready to respond promptly and effectively to any office actions to address questions or requests from the trademark office.

- **Manage Publication and Opposition Phases**: Monitor the publication phase closely and be prepared to defend your trademark if opposition arises.

- **Engage Professional Help When Needed**: Consider consulting with a trademark attorney for complex legal issues, especially in response to substantive office actions or during opposition proceedings.

- **Maintain and Renew Your Registration**: Once registered, maintain your trademark by using it consistently in commerce and renewing it on time to ensure continued protection.

- **Stay Informed About Legal Changes**: Keep up-to-date with changes in trademark law and practice to ensure ongoing compliance and protection of your trademark rights.

- **Document All Correspondence and Actions**: Keep thorough records of all communications with the trademark office and any legal actions taken related to your trademark for future reference.

Following these tips can streamline the trademark registration process, enhance your ability to navigate potential challenges, and help maintain the strength and integrity of your trademark protection over time.

CHAPTER SEVENTEEN

Stay on Track: Trademark Management Checklists

"Maintaining your trademark involves consistent vigilance and strategic foresight. Utilizing detailed checklists ensures that no aspect of your brand's protection is overlooked, securing its integrity and value in a competitive market."— INDRA NOOYI, FORMER CEO OF PEPSICO AND INFLUENTIAL BUSINESS EXECUTIVE

Navigating the world of trademarks without a checklist is like trying to assemble a piece of furniture without instructions—you might end up with something vaguely resembling a chair, or you might just have a very artistic pile of wood and screws. That's why we've crafted the ultimate trademark management checklists; consider them your GPS through the trademark jungle, ensuring you don't miss any hidden turns or crucial stops along the way.

First on the list: Regular Audits. Just like checking your car's oil or confirming you haven't left your phone on the roof, regularly reviewing your trademark portfolio ensures everything's running smoothly and no sneaky issues are hiding under the hood.

Next, we have Renewal Deadlines. Mark these on your calendar with the urgency of a tax deadline or your anniversary. Forgetting either can be equally disastrous, but only one can result in losing legal protection for your brand.

Don't forget about Monitoring the Market. This is like setting up a neighborhood watch for your trademarks. Keep an eye on new applications and existing trademarks that might be too close for comfort. It's less about being nosy and more about being wisely cautious.

And finally, Enforcement Plans. This is your plan of action when you find someone encroaching on your trademark turf. It's like having a good fence and knowing exactly when to mend it—good fences, after all, make good, respectful neighbors.

With these checklists in hand, you're set to maintain your trademarks with the precision of a Swiss watchmaker. Stay vigilant, stay organized, and your trademarks will stay intact, continuing to mark your brand's territory in the vast marketplace.

Regular Audits Checklist

Regular audits of your trademark portfolio are essential for ensuring that your intellectual property remains protected and is utilized effectively. These audits help identify potential risks, opportunities for expansion, and ensure compliance with trademark laws. The following checklist will guide you through conducting a thorough audit of your trademark assets.

Steps for Conducting Trademark Audits

1. **Inventory of Trademarks**:
    - Compile a comprehensive list of all registered trademarks and pending applications.

o Include details such as registration numbers, filing dates, renewal dates, and the jurisdictions in which the marks are registered.

2. **Verify Status**:

   o Check the current status of each trademark in your portfolio to ensure they are active and in good standing.

   o Update any record that reflects changes in ownership, address, or representation.

3. **Review Specimen of Use**:

   o Examine the specimens of use filed with each trademark to ensure they are current and accurately reflect how the mark is being used in commerce.

   o Determine if new specimens are required due to changes in how the goods or services are marketed.

4. **Assess Scope of Protection**:

   o Evaluate whether the current scope of protection for each trademark adequately covers all relevant goods and services.

   o Consider filing for additional protection if new products, services, or markets have been developed since the original registration.

5. **Identify Conflicts and Potential Infringements**:

   o Monitor for unauthorized use of your trademarks within your industry and by competitors.

   o Check for potential conflicts with new trademarks filed by others that might be confusingly similar to your own.

6. **Evaluate Licensing and Agreement Compliance**:

   o Review current licensing agreements to ensure that licensees are in compliance with the terms, especially regarding the quality and scope of use of the trademark.

    o   Confirm that all contractual obligations related to trademarks (such as co-branding agreements) are being met.

7. **Consider International Protection Needs**:

    o   Analyze market expansion plans to determine if international trademark protection is needed.

    o   Review existing international registrations for compliance with local use requirements and renewal deadlines.

8. **Legal and Regulatory Compliance Check**:

    o   Stay updated on changes in trademark law that might affect your rights or strategy.

    o   Ensure compliance with new regulations, especially in international jurisdictions.

9. **Document and Report Findings**:

    o   Create a report summarizing the findings from the audit, highlighting any areas of concern or action items.

    o   Discuss the audit results with legal counsel or a trademark professional to decide on any necessary actions.

Regular Audit Scheduling

- **Set a Regular Schedule**: Establish a routine schedule for audits, typically annually or biannually, to ensure continuous protection and effective management of your trademark portfolio.

- **Trigger-based Audits**: In addition to regular audits, consider conducting an audit when major business changes occur, such as mergers, acquisitions, or entry into new markets.

Regular audits are a critical component of strategic trademark management, helping to safeguard your intellectual property assets and ensure their optimal use in supporting your business goals. By adhering to this checklist, you can maintain a robust defense against infringement, capitalize on market opportunities, and ensure compliance with evolving trademark laws.

Renewal Deadlines Checklist

Maintaining the validity of your trademarks requires attention to renewal deadlines. Trademarks are not protected indefinitely; they must be renewed at regular intervals as specified by the governing intellectual property office. This checklist ensures that you never miss a renewal deadline, helping to prevent unintentional lapses in protection which could be detrimental to your brand's legal security.

Steps for Managing Renewal Deadlines

1. **Maintain Accurate Records**:

   o Keep a detailed record of all trademarks within your portfolio, noting their registration dates and corresponding renewal deadlines.

   o Include the jurisdictions in which each trademark is registered, as renewal terms can vary significantly across different countries.

2. **Set Up Reminder Systems**:

   o Implement a reminder system to alert you well in advance of upcoming renewal deadlines. Consider using specialized IP management software that can automatically track these dates and send notifications.

   o Set multiple reminders leading up to the renewal date to allow ample time for preparing necessary documentation.

3. **Review Trademark Use**:

   o Before renewing, review how each trademark is being used in commerce. Ensure that all trademarks are still active and being used in a manner consistent with their registrations.

   o Determine if any modifications to the goods or services associated with the trademark are necessary, which might require additional filings or adjustments.

4. **Prepare Renewal Documentation**:

   o Collect and prepare all necessary documentation required for renewal submissions. This may include declarations of continued use, specimens showing current use of the mark, and, in some jurisdictions, proof of use affidavits.

   o Review each document for accuracy and completeness to ensure compliance with trademark office requirements.

5. **Budget for Renewal Fees**:

   o Plan and budget for renewal fees, which can vary depending on the jurisdiction and the number of classes under which the trademark is registered.

   o If managing a large portfolio, consider the financial impact of renewing multiple trademarks simultaneously and plan accordingly.

6. **Conduct a Legal Review**:

   o Have a trademark attorney or legal professional review the renewal application and supporting documents. A legal review can help identify potential issues that might affect the renewal process.

   o Use this opportunity to assess any legal changes in trademark law that could impact the renewal or protection of your trademarks.

7. **Submit Renewal Applications**:

   o Submit renewal applications according to the procedures of each specific trademark office. Ensure that all submissions are complete and that they meet all legal requirements to avoid rejection.

   o Keep copies of all submission receipts or confirmations as proof of renewal application.

8. **Confirm Renewal and Update Records**:

     o   Once the renewal is confirmed by the trademark office, update your records to reflect the new expiration date.

     o   Document all correspondence and official notices related to the renewal process for future reference.

Regular Review and Adjustment

- **Annual Portfolio Review**: Incorporate an annual review of your trademark portfolio to discuss and decide on the future of each mark. This helps in determining which trademarks continue to hold value and justify the renewal costs.

- **Adjustment to Business Changes**: Be agile in adjusting your renewal strategies to align with changes in business operations, market presence, or brand strategy.

Staying vigilant about renewal deadlines is crucial for continuous trademark protection. By systematically following this checklist, you ensure that none of your valuable trademarks inadvertently lapse, maintaining robust legal protection for your brand assets across all markets.

Monitoring the Market Checklist

Effective trademark management involves not just maintaining your registrations but also keeping a vigilant eye on the marketplace. Monitoring the market helps you spot potential infringements, observe emerging competitive trademarks, and understand overall trends that could impact your trademark strategy. This checklist provides a structured approach to ensuring your trademarks remain protected against unauthorized use and competition.

Steps for Effective Market Monitoring

1. **Set Up Monitoring Systems**:

     o   Utilize trademark monitoring services that can scan trademark databases, internet usage, and other public sources to identify potential infringements or similar marks being registered.

    o   Consider software solutions that automate the detection of logo use, domain name registrations, and social media mentions.

2. **Regular Search Routine**:

    o   Conduct regular searches on major search engines and social media platforms for unauthorized use of your trademarks.

    o   Check domain name registries to ensure no similar or potentially confusing domain names are registered.

3. **Review Industry Publications and Databases**:

    o   Subscribe to and review industry publications, trademark bulletins, and legal databases to stay informed about new trademark filings that could be similar to your own.

    o   Attend industry events and trade shows to gather intelligence on how competitors and new market entrants are using their trademarks.

4. **Engage in Competitive Analysis**:

    o   Regularly analyze competitors' use of trademarks to ensure they are not encroaching on your trademark rights or using marks that could cause confusion in the market.

    o   Monitor new product launches and marketing campaigns from competitors for potential trademark issues.

5. **Legal and Compliance Updates**:

    o   Stay updated with changes in trademark laws and enforcement practices in all jurisdictions where your trademarks are registered.

    o   Ensure compliance with new legal requirements that might affect how your trademarks should be monitored or enforced.

6. **Train Your Team**:

   o Educate your marketing and legal teams about the importance of market monitoring and the role it plays in protecting the company's intellectual property.

   o Provide training on how to identify potential trademark infringements and the steps to take when they are discovered.

Responding to Potential Infringements

1. **Establish Clear Procedures**:

   o Develop and document clear procedures for responding to potential infringements, including initial assessments, internal reporting, and escalation protocols.

   o Determine when legal action is necessary and what forms it should take (e.g., cease and desist letters, negotiations, or litigation).

2. **Legal Consultation**:

   o Consult with intellectual property attorneys to get professional advice on how to handle complex or high-stakes trademark infringements.

   o Use legal counsel to draft and send enforcement communications to ensure they are effective and legally sound.

Review and Adaptation

- **Periodic Review of Monitoring Strategies**: Regularly review and update your monitoring strategies to adapt to new technologies, market changes, and business needs.

- **Feedback Loop**: Implement a feedback mechanism to learn from past infringement cases and refine your monitoring and enforcement strategies.

Monitoring the market is a crucial aspect of proactive trademark management. By following this checklist, you ensure that your trademarks are not only registered but also respected in the market, reducing the risk of dilution or infringement. This vigilant approach supports the long-term strength and viability of your trademark assets.

Enforcement Plans Checklist

Effective enforcement of trademark rights is crucial for protecting your brand's integrity and market position. An organized and proactive approach to enforcement helps deter potential infringers and ensures that your trademarks continue to serve as strong identifiers of your goods or services. This checklist guides you through developing a comprehensive enforcement strategy tailored to your brand's needs.

Developing an Enforcement Strategy

1. **Establish Enforcement Objectives**:
   - Define clear objectives for your trademark enforcement efforts. Decide whether your primary goal is to prevent confusion, protect brand identity, or pursue monetary compensation for infringements.
   - Tailor your strategy based on the severity of the infringement and the potential impact on your business.

2. **Identify Key Trademarks**:
   - Prioritize which trademarks are most critical to your business and therefore require more stringent monitoring and quicker enforcement actions.
   - Consider factors such as market visibility, revenue generation, and geographical reach.

Creating an Enforcement Plan

1. **Document Standard Procedures**:

   o Develop standardized procedures for handling different types of trademark infringements, such as counterfeit products, unauthorized use online, or misuse by competitors.

   o Include steps for initial discovery, internal verification, legal assessment, and the decision-making process regarding escalation.

2. **Prepare Legal Documents**:

   o Draft templates for cease and desist letters, negotiation offers, and other legal documents commonly used in trademark enforcement.

   o Ensure that your legal team reviews and updates these documents regularly to comply with current laws and best practices.

3. **Determine Escalation Thresholds**:

   o Establish criteria for escalating an infringement case from a simple cease and desist letter to more serious legal actions such as litigation.

   o Consider factors like the infringer's response to initial contact, the scale of the infringement, and the potential damage to your brand.

Implementing the Enforcement Plan

1. **Training and Empowerment**:

   o Train relevant team members, especially those in legal, marketing, and customer service departments, on the enforcement plan and their specific roles within it.

   o Empower them to act swiftly and decisively when potential infringements are detected.

2. **Leverage External Resources**:

   o Collaborate with external legal counsel specialized in intellectual property law to handle complex cases or litigation.

   o Consider using external monitoring services to supplement your internal efforts, especially for detecting online infringements.

3. **Monitor and Adjust the Plan**:

   o Regularly review the effectiveness of your enforcement efforts. Monitor key metrics such as the number of infringements detected, actions taken, and resolutions achieved.

   o Adjust your strategy and procedures based on feedback and changes in the business environment or legal landscape.

Maintaining Communication and Documentation

1. **Record-Keeping**:

   o Maintain detailed records of all enforcement actions, including communications, legal documents, and outcomes. This documentation can be crucial for legal proceedings and future trademark disputes.

   o Use a secure and organized system to store these records for easy access and reference.

2. **Communication**:

   o Keep open lines of communication with all stakeholders involved in trademark enforcement, including senior management, legal teams, and external advisors.

   o Regularly report on enforcement activities and outcomes to ensure transparency and accountability within your organization.

A well-structured enforcement plan is essential for maintaining the integrity and value of your trademarks. By following this checklist, you can ensure that your brand is protected against infringement and that your business is positioned to respond effectively to threats against your intellectual property.

Legal Updates and Continuing Education Checklist

Staying informed about legal updates and engaging in continuous education are crucial for effective trademark management. Trademark laws can evolve rapidly, and understanding these changes is vital to maintaining the protection and enforcement of your trademark rights. This checklist outlines the key activities to keep you updated and knowledgeable about the latest developments in trademark law.

Establishing a Routine for Legal Updates

1. **Subscribe to Legal Newsletters**:

   o Subscribe to newsletters from reputable legal associations, law firms, and intellectual property organizations that provide updates on trademark law and court decisions.

   o Opt for sector-specific newsletters if available, to receive updates that are most relevant to your industry.

2. **Follow Legal Blogs and Journals**:

   o Identify and follow influential blogs and online journals dedicated to trademark law and intellectual property issues.

   o Engage with content that discusses recent case law, legislative changes, and expert opinions on emerging trademark issues.

3. **Monitor Government and Regulatory Announcements**:

   o Keep track of announcements from intellectual property offices such as the USPTO, EUIPO, or WIPO regarding changes in trademark registration processes, fees, or legal requirements.

   o Set alerts for press releases and updates from these organizations to receive immediate notifications.

Continuing Education Through Professional Development

1. **Attend Workshops and Seminars**:

   o Participate in workshops, seminars, and webinars focused on trademark law. These events are often hosted by legal associations or educational institutions and provide deep dives into specific areas of trademark law.

   o Look for events that offer Continuing Legal Education (CLE) credits if you are a legal professional.

2. **Engage in Online Courses**:

   o Enroll in online courses that cover broader aspects of intellectual property law or specific courses on trademarks. Many platforms offer courses taught by university professors or industry experts.

   o Choose courses that provide practical knowledge and up-to-date information on international trademark management.

3. **Join Professional Associations**:

   o Become a member of professional associations related to intellectual property, such as the International Trademark Association (INTA) or your national IP association.

   o Utilize association resources like forums, specialized groups, and annual conferences to network with peers and learn from experts.

Internal Training and Knowledge Sharing

1. **Conduct Internal Training Sessions**:

   o Organize regular training sessions for your team to disseminate new legal information and discuss how changes may impact your company's trademark strategy.

   o Use real-world scenarios and recent case studies to illustrate how legal changes could affect your business operations.

2. **Create a Resource Library**:

   o Develop an internal resource library that includes key legal texts, articles, case law summaries, and training materials on trademark law.

   o Ensure that all team members have access to this library and encourage them to use these resources to stay informed.

Regular Review and Update

- **Annual Legal Review**: Schedule an annual review of your legal update and education practices to evaluate their effectiveness and make necessary adjustments.

- **Feedback Mechanism**: Implement a feedback mechanism to gather insights from team members on the usefulness of the educational materials and sessions provided, using this information to improve future training and resources.

Maintaining legal vigilance through regular updates and continuous education is essential for navigating the complexities of trademark law effectively. By following this checklist, you ensure that your trademark management strategies are always aligned with the latest legal standards, protecting your intellectual property in a dynamic legal environment.

Quick Tips and Recap

- **Set Up Alerts**: Utilize legal update services or set up Google Alerts for keywords related to trademark law to stay informed about new developments.

- **Regular Audits**: Schedule periodic audits of your trademark portfolio to ensure continued compliance and effectiveness of your trademark strategy.

- **Renewal Reminders**: Use digital calendars and management software to set reminders for trademark renewal deadlines well in advance.

- **Active Market Monitoring**: Implement a routine for regularly monitoring the marketplace and online platforms to detect potential infringements or similar new trademarks.

- **Document Enforcement Actions**: Keep detailed records of all enforcement actions, including communications and outcomes, to support potential legal actions and maintain an organized strategy.

- **Continual Learning**: Engage in continuous education through workshops, online courses, and webinars to keep up-to-date with the latest trends and changes in trademark law.

- **Internal Training**: Organize regular training sessions for your team to ensure everyone understands current trademark laws and how to apply them effectively.

- **Professional Memberships**: Maintain memberships in relevant professional associations to gain access to specialized resources and networking opportunities.

- **Feedback on Training**: Regularly collect and analyze feedback on internal training and legal updates to continuously improve the information and support provided to your team.

By adhering to these tips, you can ensure that your trademark management practices are robust, up-to-date, and effective in protecting and enhancing the value of your intellectual property.

CHAPTER EIGHTEEN

Lessons Learned: Case Studies of Trademark Triumphs and Trials

"Each trademark success or setback teaches a critical lesson in brand protection. By studying these cases, we sharpen our strategies and strengthen our defenses."— WARREN BUFFETT, CHAIRMAN AND CEO OF BERKSHIRE HATHAWAY

S trap in for a rollercoaster ride through the annals of trademark history, where the highs are as exhilarating as a moon landing and the lows, well, they could sink the Titanic. This chapter is your front-row ticket to the blockbuster dramas and unexpected plot twists of trademark battles—complete with popcorn-worthy triumphs and teachable trials.

First, we'll spotlight the Triumphs—those savvy businesses that navigated the treacherous waters of trademark law with the precision of a Swiss watchmaker.

These are the Cinderella stories where a well-timed trademark application or a fiercely fought legal battle kept the brand's glass slipper intact and sparkling, even at midnight.

Then, brace yourself for the Trials—the cautionary tales where things went as pear-shaped as a bad haircut. These sagas serve up the kind of drama that's usually reserved for reality TV, featuring everything from tragic missteps in trademark filings to epic clashes over intellectual turf. It's like watching a slow-motion car crash; you can't look away, and you certainly can't forget the lessons they impart.

Through these narratives, we'll uncover the secrets to wielding trademarks like Excalibur and the pitfalls that can trap the unwary into a legal labyrinth worse than any Minotaur could guard. Each case study is a puzzle piece in the vast mosaic of trademark law, offering insights and strategies that can shield your brand from foes and elevate it to legendary status.

So, buckle up. Whether it's a tale of strategic genius or a cautionary fable, each story offers invaluable lessons that can help you write your own story of trademark triumph.

Triumphs: Strategic Wins in Trademark Registration

In the world of intellectual property, strategic trademark registration can pave the way for significant competitive advantages and long-term brand protection. This section highlights several triumphs where astute planning, timely actions, and keen foresight in trademark registration led to notable successes for businesses.

Case Study 1: Apple Inc. – The "iPhone" Trademark

Background: Apple's launch of the iPhone marked a significant turning point in mobile technology. However, the strategic moves began much earlier in trademark registration.

Strategy:

- **Early Registration**: Apple filed for the "iPhone" trademark in secret in various countries, including Singapore, under a shell company name. This move was to avoid drawing attention and potential speculative entries by competitors.

- **Comprehensive Filing**: The filings covered multiple classes, ensuring broad protection across various uses and products.

Outcome: When Apple finally announced the iPhone, they had secured a robust trademark position, allowing them to dominate the market and solidify the brand's identity globally without immediate legal challenges from competitors.

Case Study 2: Google – Securing "Google" for Diverse Applications

Background: Google, initially just a search engine, foresaw potential expansions into various tech sectors and took steps to protect its brand comprehensively.

Strategy:

- **Expansive Protection**: Google not only trademarked its name but also ensured it secured related trademarks for potential future expansions, such as Google Glass, Google Play, and Google Drive.

- **Diligent Monitoring and Enforcement**: Google maintains an aggressive stance in monitoring its trademarks and pursuing potential infringements, which helps in maintaining the exclusivity of its brand across various sectors.

Outcome: Google's preemptive and broad trademark strategy has allowed it to diversify without facing significant trademark hurdles, maintaining its brand integrity across different products and services.

Case Study 3: Burberry – Protecting the Check Pattern

Background: Burberry's iconic check pattern was at risk of becoming generic due to widespread counterfeiting and its extensive use by other brands.

Strategy:

- **Specific Design Trademark**: Burberry secured a trademark for its specific check pattern, not just in fashion but for a wide array of products, reinforcing its association with the brand.

- **Legal Enforcement**: Regular legal actions against counterfeiters and unauthorized users of the pattern helped reinforce the validity of the trademark and deterred misuse.

Outcome: Burberry successfully managed to reclaim its trademark's exclusivity, turning what could have been a generic pattern back into a luxury symbol directly associated with the Burberry brand.

Case Study 4: Starbucks – Global Trademark Strategy

Background: As Starbucks expanded globally, it faced challenges from existing similar trademarks in various markets.

Strategy:

- **Global Coordination**: Starbucks implemented a coordinated global trademark strategy, registering its name and logos well in advance of entering new markets.

- **Adaptation and Enforcement**: In regions where conflicts existed, Starbucks either negotiated for rights or adapted its trademarks while maintaining its core brand elements.

Outcome: Through effective planning and adaptability, Starbucks has managed to protect its brand in numerous global markets, supporting its worldwide expansion.

These case studies demonstrate the power of strategic trademark registration in protecting and enhancing the value of a brand. Each example provides valuable lessons in foresight, planning, and the execution of intellectual property strategies that can offer significant competitive advantages and market leadership.

Trials: Missteps in Trademark Protection

Navigating the realm of trademark protection can be fraught with pitfalls, and missteps can lead to significant setbacks for businesses. This section delves into notable cases where companies faced trials due to inadequate or erroneous approaches to trademark protection. Each example offers crucial lessons on what to avoid and how to better safeguard intellectual property.

Case Study 1: Xerox – The Battle Against Genericide

Background: Xerox, once a brand name, faced the threat of its trademark becoming generic due to its prevalent use as a verb for photocopying.

Strategy:

- **Extensive Public Campaigns**: Xerox launched campaigns to educate the public and discourage the use of "Xerox" as a verb, emphasizing that "to photocopy" was the correct term.

- **Legal Measures**: The company took legal steps to enforce its trademark rights, actively challenging misuse in publications and advertising.

Outcome: Despite these efforts, Xerox continues to fight against its brand name becoming generic. This case highlights the importance of proactive trademark use guidelines and the challenges in reversing genericide once it begins.

Case Study 2: Kodak – A Missed Digital Opportunity

Background: Kodak, a powerhouse in the photographic film industry, failed to adequately protect its trademarks in emerging digital photography technology.

Strategy:

- **Limited Scope of Protection**: Kodak focused its trademark protection efforts primarily on film photography, neglecting to extend protection into new digital realms adequately.

- **Slow Response to Market Changes**: The company was slow to recognize and adapt to the digital photography revolution, both in terms of technology and trademark strategy.

Outcome: Kodak's oversight allowed competitors to establish strong positions in the digital photography market, significantly diminishing Kodak's brand dominance and relevance in this sector.

Case Study 3: BlackBerry – Ignoring Market Evolution

Background: BlackBerry, once a leader in the smartphone industry, faced severe trials due to its rigid trademark and branding strategy, which did not evolve with consumer preferences and technological advancements.

Strategy:

- **Inflexible Brand Positioning**: BlackBerry continued to focus on its traditional business-oriented branding, failing to trademark or brand new innovations that appealed to a broader consumer market.

- **Neglect of Consumer Trends**: The company overlooked the importance of software and app-related trademarks, missing opportunities to secure its standing in these areas.

Outcome: BlackBerry's market share plummeted as it lost relevance among consumers who favored more versatile smartphones. The brand's failure to adapt its trademark and innovation strategy contributed to its decline.

Case Study 4: Sears – Trademark Dilution through Over-Expansion

Background: Sears, once a retail giant, experienced trademark dilution as it overextended its brand into too many unrelated product categories.

Strategy:

- **Over-Extension of Brand**: Sears applied its trademark to an overly broad range of products, from clothing to financial services, diluting the brand's identity and core value proposition.

- **Lack of Strategic Focus**: The indiscriminate use of the Sears trademark in various sectors led to consumer confusion and diminished brand equity.

Outcome: The dilution of the Sears brand contributed to its loss of market dominance and eventual financial troubles. This illustrates the risks of extending a trademark beyond its core association without a coherent strategic plan.

These case studies serve as cautionary tales, underscoring the critical need for strategic foresight in trademark protection. Companies must remain vigilant, adapt to changing markets, and enforce their trademarks judiciously to avoid the pitfalls that have ensnared even the most established brands. Each trial offers invaluable insights into the complexities of maintaining robust trademark protection in a dynamic business environment.

Litigation Landmarks: Major Trademark Battles

Trademark litigation often sets important legal precedents and can dramatically reshape the landscape of intellectual property law. This section explores landmark legal battles that have had profound impacts on how trademarks are understood, protected, and enforced globally. These cases not only offer a window into the complexities of legal disputes but also provide strategic insights for businesses on how to handle potential trademark conflicts.

Case Study 1: Apple vs. Samsung – The Battle of Designs

Background: One of the most high-profile trademark battles in recent history, Apple sued Samsung for trademark infringement, claiming that Samsung's smartphones and tablets infringed on Apple's designs and software.

Strategy:

- **Legal Claims**: Apple's strategy involved claiming both trademark and design patent infringements, emphasizing the distinctive look and feel of their products that they believed Samsung had copied.

- **Global Litigation**: The legal battle spanned numerous countries, each with its legal proceedings and outcomes, illustrating the challenges of international intellectual property enforcement.

Outcome: Apple initially won significant judgments, including a billion-dollar verdict in 2012. However, subsequent appeals and rulings reduced these damages and led to various settlements. The extensive litigation emphasized the importance of having a solid and defensible design and trademark strategy.

Case Study 2: Adidas vs. Payless – The Three Stripe Saga

Background: Adidas sued Payless Shoesource for trademark infringement, arguing that Payless was selling shoes with a stripe design that was confusingly similar to Adidas's iconic three stripes.

Strategy:

- **Asserting Distinctiveness**: Adidas focused on the distinctiveness of its three-stripe design, a key element of its brand identity, and its likelihood of causing consumer confusion.

- **Persistent Legal Enforcement**: The case demonstrated Adidas's commitment to aggressively enforcing its trademark rights against infringements by competitors, big and small.

Outcome: After nearly a decade of litigation, Adidas was awarded $305 million in damages, although this was later reduced. The case reinforced the strength of Adidas's trademark and the company's willingness to defend it extensively.

Case Study 3: Google vs. American Blind – The Keyword Advertising Dispute

Background: Google faced a trademark infringement lawsuit from American Blind & Wallpaper Factory, which claimed that Google's practice of selling trademarked terms as keywords to competitors for advertising purposes was a violation of its trademark rights.

Strategy:

- **Defense of Innovative Business Practices**: Google defended its AdWords program, arguing that the use of trademarked keywords by advertisers did not constitute trademark infringement as it was non-confusing and a legitimate use.

- **Promotion of Competition**: Google maintained that this practice promotes healthy competition and benefits consumers.

Outcome: The case settled out of court, with Google continuing its keyword advertising practices. This settlement helped pave the way for the continued use of trademarked terms in digital advertising, setting a precedent that this practice does not typically violate trademark laws.

Case Study 4: Tiffany & Co. vs. Costco – The Generic Use Defense

Background: Tiffany & Co. sued Costco for trademark infringement, claiming that Costco's use of the word "Tiffany" to describe certain ring settings misled consumers.

Strategy:

- **Protection of Brand Name**: Tiffany & Co. aimed to protect its brand name, asserting that "Tiffany" was not a generic term for a ring setting but a trademark that signifies the company's reputation and quality.

- **Asserting Consumer Confusion**: Tiffany argued that Costco's use of the name deceived consumers into thinking they were buying Tiffany & Co. branded rings.

Outcome: The court ruled in favor of Tiffany & Co., awarding them damages and reinforcing that the Tiffany trademark was not generic. This case underscored the importance of protecting brand names from becoming generic through misuse by others.

These landmark cases illustrate the critical importance of proactive trademark management and the complexities of litigation in protecting a brand's intellectual property. Each battle offers lessons on the strategic, financial, and reputational stakes involved in trademark disputes and highlights the need for robust legal strategies to navigate these challenges successfully.

Global Challenges: International Trademark Management

In today's globalized market, managing trademarks across multiple jurisdictions presents unique challenges and complexities. International trademark management requires navigating diverse legal systems, cultural nuances, and varied registration processes. This section delves into the complexities and strategies necessary for effective global trademark protection, illustrating through case studies the importance of a comprehensive international approach.

Case Study 1: Starbucks – Navigating Trademark Registration in China

Background: Starbucks, known globally for its coffee and related products, faced significant challenges when expanding into China, a market notorious for its complex intellectual property environment.

Strategy:

- **Early and Comprehensive Registration**: Starbucks proactively registered its trademarks in China before fully entering the market. They registered not just their name but also their distinctive logo and interior store design.

- **Aggressive Legal Action**: Starbucks vigorously enforced its trademark rights against infringers, which included a high-profile lawsuit against a local Chinese coffee chain using a similar name and branding.

Outcome: Starbucks won the lawsuit and secured a substantial settlement, reinforcing its brand presence in China. This case highlights the importance of early registration and readiness to engage in legal actions to protect intellectual property in a challenging market.

Case Study 2: Budweiser – Trademark Disputes in the European Market

Background: The name "Budweiser" has been the subject of a longstanding dispute between American brewer Anheuser-Busch and Czech brewery Budějovický Budvar. Both companies claimed rights to the trademark in various European markets based on historical and geographical claims.

Strategy:

- **Negotiation and Litigation**: Anheuser-Busch engaged in multiple legal battles across different European jurisdictions while also seeking to negotiate with Budvar to resolve the disputes amicably.

- **Adaptive Branding Strategies**: In some markets, Anheuser-Busch used the name "Bud" to avoid legal complications.

Outcome: The dispute has seen varied results, with decisions swinging between both breweries in different countries. The case underscores the complexity of managing a trademark globally, where historical and regional rights may impact standard branding strategies.

Case Study 3: IKEA – Trademark Issues in Indonesia

Background: IKEA lost its trademark in Indonesia after a local business registered it due to IKEA's inactivity in the market, based on Indonesia's use-it-or-lose-it trademark laws.

Strategy:

- **Legal Appeals**: IKEA sought to overturn the decision through the Indonesian legal system by arguing the global recognition of its brand and its intent to expand in the Indonesian market.

- **Public Relations and Branding**: IKEA continued to invest in building its brand in the Indonesian market despite the legal setback.

Outcome: IKEA's appeal was unsuccessful, highlighting the critical importance of understanding and actively managing trademarks according to local laws, especially in countries with stringent use requirements.

Case Study 4: Apple – Trademark Strategy for the iPhone in Brazil

Background: Apple faced a challenge in Brazil where the "iPhone" trademark was already owned by a local electronics company, IGB Eletrônica, which sold phones under the "G Gradiente iPhone" brand.

Strategy:

- **Negotiation and Settlement**: Apple entered into negotiations with IGB Eletrônica to resolve the trademark dispute amicably.

- **Strategic Coexistence**: Apple explored options to coexist with the local brand or potentially purchase the trademark rights.

Outcome: The dispute was resolved with a coexistence agreement, allowing both companies to use the "iPhone" name under specific conditions. This situation exemplifies the need for flexibility and strategic compromise in international trademark management.

Managing trademarks internationally requires a strategic, well-informed approach tailored to the legal and cultural realities of each market. The cases discussed demonstrate the necessity of proactive international planning, the potential for conflict in overlapping claims, and the importance of adapting to local legal environments to maintain trademark protection globally.

Emerging Trends: Adapting to New Trademark Realities

As technology and global commerce evolve, so do the challenges and opportunities in trademark management. This section explores the latest trends in the trademark landscape, including digital advancements, changes in consumer behavior, and global market dynamics. Understanding these trends is crucial for adapting trademark strategies to protect and leverage intellectual property effectively in the modern marketplace.

Case Study 1: Virtual and Augmented Reality Trademarks

Background: With the rise of virtual and augmented reality (VR/AR) technologies, companies are exploring new ways to engage consumers, creating immersive brand experiences that also raise new trademark questions.

Strategy:

- **Innovative Trademark Categories**: Companies are registering trademarks not only for software but also for virtual goods and services, extending their brand presence into virtual spaces.

- **Defensive Registrations**: Firms are preemptively registering trademarks in new categories to prevent misuse and prepare for future expansions.

Outcome: Companies that adapt early to these technological trends by securing trademarks in VR/AR are better positioned to capitalize on emerging markets and protect their intellectual property.

Case Study 2: Blockchain and Trademarks

Background: Blockchain technology is revolutionizing various industries, including how trademarks are registered and enforced. Blockchain can provide more transparent and tamper-proof systems for trademark registries.

Strategy:

- **Blockchain for Registration**: Some companies are exploring blockchain to create decentralized trademark registries that make the registration process more accessible and secure.

- **Smart Contracts for Enforcement**: Implementing smart contracts to automate the licensing and enforcement of trademarks, reducing the potential for disputes and unauthorized use.

Outcome: Early adopters of blockchain technology in trademark management are finding innovative ways to enhance the security and efficiency of their trademark processes, setting a precedent for others in the industry.

Case Study 3: Social Media Influencers and Brand Partnerships

Background: The rise of social media influencers has created new opportunities and challenges for trademark branding and enforcement.

Strategy:

- **Collaborative Trademark Strategies**: Brands are increasingly collaborating with influencers, co-creating products, and sometimes jointly registering trademarks for new ventures.

- **Monitoring and Enforcement**: With the expansive reach of influencers, companies are vigilant in monitoring the use of their trademarks on social media platforms to ensure compliance and consistency.

Outcome: Successful collaborations with influencers often hinge on clear contractual agreements that include trademark usage rights and enforcement responsibilities, safeguarding the brand while maximizing outreach.

Case Study 4: Geographic Indications and Traditional Knowledge

Background: There is growing recognition of geographic indications (GIs) and traditional knowledge as part of cultural heritage that needs legal protection, particularly in global markets.

Strategy:

- **International Registrations and Treaties**: Companies and governments are increasingly working together to register GIs and protect traditional knowledge through international treaties.

- **Cultural Branding**: Incorporating these elements into products while respecting and protecting the underlying intellectual property.

Outcome: By respecting and legally acknowledging geographic indications and traditional knowledge, companies not only protect cultural heritage but also enhance their brand authenticity and consumer trust.

Adapting to new trademark realities requires a proactive and forward-thinking approach. By embracing emerging trends and integrating them into comprehensive trademark strategies, companies can protect their intellectual assets and stay competitive in an increasingly digital and interconnected world. These case studies highlight the importance of agility and innovation in trademark management to meet the demands of the 21st century.

Quick Tips and Recap

- **Embrace Technology**: Stay ahead by embracing new technologies such as blockchain and VR/AR for trademark registration and protection. This approach not only secures your intellectual property but also positions your brand at the forefront of innovation.

- **Adapt to Digital Environments**: As digital landscapes evolve, ensure your trademark strategies cover new platforms and digital mediums. This includes social media, virtual marketplaces, and digital content where your trademarks need to be monitored and enforced.

- **Understand Global Implications**: Engage with international trademark laws and practices, especially if operating or planning to expand globally. Understanding these nuances is crucial for protecting your brand in different markets.

- **Leverage New Legal Tools**: Utilize emerging legal tools and resources, such as smart contracts for licensing and blockchain for registrations, to enhance the efficiency and security of your trademark management.

- **Monitor Trends and Competitors**: Regularly monitor industry trends and competitor activities to anticipate potential trademark conflicts and opportunities. Early identification can help you navigate challenges proactively.

- **Collaborate and Partner Wisely**: When entering into partnerships, especially with influencers or for co-branded products, ensure that trademark rights, responsibilities, and enforcement mechanisms are clearly outlined in the agreements.

- **Protect Cultural and Geographic Indications**: Recognize and protect geographic indications and traditional knowledge as part of your trademark strategy, enhancing brand value and respecting cultural heritage.

- **Educate Your Team**: Regularly educate and train your team on the latest trademark laws, digital trends, and enforcement practices to ensure everyone understands how to protect and promote your trademarks effectively.

- **Document and Update Policies**: Keep detailed records of your trademark strategies, enforcement actions, and any legal proceedings. Regularly update your policies to reflect current laws and best practices.

- **Stay Legally Compliant**: Always ensure compliance with local and international trademark laws to avoid legal challenges that can arise from non-compliance or infringement on others' rights.

By following these tips, you can effectively manage and protect your trademarks, adapting to changes and capitalizing on opportunities in the dynamic landscape of trademark law.

CHAPTER NINETEEN

Legal Labyrinths: Navigation Complex Trademark Challenges

"Navigating the complex legal labyrinths of trademark challenges requires not just knowledge of the law but strategic thinking to protect your brand's identity and leverage your intellectual property effectively." — ALAN DERSHOWITZ, LAWYER AND LEGAL SCHOLAR

Welcome to the labyrinthine world of complex trademark challenges, where every turn could lead to a new legal puzzle, and Minotaurs wear suits and carry briefcases. It's a world where the unwary can easily get lost among convoluted legal statutes and cunning competitive maneuvers. So, let's arm ourselves with a ball of thread and a good sense of humor to find our way through these intricate mazes.

First on our map is the Territory of International Regulations. Venturing here is like planning a world tour—exciting but fraught with logistical nightmares. You'll need to juggle the conflicting laws of multiple countries, where a trademark that's a hero at home might be a zero abroad. It's like trying to order a latte in six different languages, and each time getting something slightly unexpected.

Then, there's the Swamp of Online Infringement. Here, digital footprints are obscured by the murky waters of the internet. Tracking down infringers who hide behind screens and IP addresses can feel like playing the world's least fun game of whack-a-mole—one where the moles are hackers and the stakes are your brand's reputation.

Don't forget the Mountains of Litigation. Climbing these requires stamina and a team of sherpas (also known as your legal team). Each step upward can reveal breathtaking views or perilous drops, depending on the strength of your case and the skill of your guides.

Lastly, we navigate the Caves of Non-Traditional Marks. This is where you protect the unprotectable—from scents to sounds to the feel of your packaging. It's like convincing someone that the air in a bottle is worth its weight in gold. Quixotic? Perhaps. Essential? Absolutely.

Navigating these labyrinths requires more than just legal knowledge—it demands creativity, persistence, and strategic foresight. So tighten your laces, sharpen your wit, and prepare to delve into the complexities of trademark law. With the right map and a keen eye, even the most daunting legal labyrinth can be navigated successfully.

Navigating International Trademark Regulations

In the global marketplace, managing trademarks internationally is akin to navigating a complex labyrinth of varied legal frameworks across different countries. Each jurisdiction has its own rules, procedures, and nuances, making international trademark registration a challenging but crucial task for global brand protection.

Understanding Diverse Legal Systems

1. **Harmonization vs. National Differences**:

    o While international agreements like the Madrid Protocol attempt to harmonize some aspects of trademark law, significant differences still exist between countries. Understanding these variations is crucial for developing an effective global trademark strategy.

    o Key areas of difference often include the scope of protection, the criteria for trademark registration, and the processes for handling disputes.

2. **First-to-File vs. First-to-Use Systems**:

    o Different countries follow different rules regarding who has rights to a trademark. In first-to-file jurisdictions, such as China, the first person to register a trademark holds the rights to it, regardless of who first used it. In contrast, first-to-use countries, like the United States, grant rights based on who first used the trademark in commerce.

    o Businesses need to be strategic about where and when they file their trademarks, especially in first-to-file countries, to prevent others from securing trademark rights to their brands.

Strategic Registration Approaches

1. **Utilizing the Madrid System**:

    o The Madrid Protocol allows for the international registration of trademarks by filing a single application that can extend protection to over 120 countries. This system can significantly simplify the process of obtaining and managing international trademarks.

    o However, companies should be aware that not all countries are members of the Madrid system, and even within the system, local laws still apply, requiring careful attention to the specifics of national regulations.

2. **Regional Systems and Local Filings**:

   o   In addition to or instead of using the Madrid System, companies might consider regional systems like the European Union Intellectual Property Office (EUIPO), which offers a unitary trademark registration effective throughout the EU.

   o   In some cases, direct national filings may be necessary either because a country is not part of a regional system or because specific local legal peculiarities require a tailored approach.

Overcoming Common Pitfalls

1. **Language and Cultural Barriers**:

   o   Trademarks that work well in one language or culture might be inappropriate or unregistrable in another. Conducting cultural and linguistic checks before filing can prevent costly mistakes and ensure that the brand is perceived positively across different markets.

2. **Monitoring and Enforcement**:

   o   Active monitoring of trademark use internationally is crucial to detect and act against infringements. Due to the territorial nature of trademarks, enforcement must often be carried out under local laws, necessitating the assistance of local counsel.

Case Example: The Starbucks Brand in Asia

- **Challenge**: Starbucks faced challenges when entering Asian markets, where local variations in trademark law and existing similar trademarks posed risks to brand integrity.

- **Strategy**: By employing a combination of Madrid Protocol filings and direct applications in countries not covered by the protocol, Starbucks managed to secure its trademarks efficiently.

- **Outcome**: Effective registration and vigilant enforcement supported Starbucks' successful expansion into these markets, maintaining the brand's strong global presence.

Navigating international trademark regulations requires a well-planned and informed approach. By understanding the complexities of different legal systems and strategically using international registration systems, companies can effectively manage their trademark portfolios across multiple jurisdictions. This proactive approach ensures that brands are not only protected but also poised for successful global growth.

Confronting Online Infringement

The digital age has expanded the reach of brands but also increased the complexity of protecting trademarks online. Online infringement can occur across various platforms, including e-commerce websites, social media, and digital marketplaces. Navigating these issues requires a comprehensive approach to monitoring, identifying, and acting against violations in the digital space.

Key Areas of Online Infringement

1. **Cybersquatting**:

   o This involves registering, selling, or using a domain name with the intent of profiting from the goodwill of someone else's trademark. Brands must be vigilant in monitoring domain registrations that closely resemble their trademarks to prevent consumer confusion and potential revenue loss.

2. **Counterfeit Goods**:

   o Online marketplaces have made it easier for counterfeit products to reach consumers. Brands must work closely with these platforms to enforce their intellectual property rights and utilize available tools such as Amazon's Brand Registry or eBay's Verified Rights Owner (VeRO) program.

3. **Misuse on Social Media**:

   o Trademarks can be misused in social media handles, posts, and unauthorized advertisements. Companies need to establish a strong presence on major platforms and actively monitor for misuse or misrepresentation of their brand.

Strategies for Addressing Online Infringement

1. **Proactive Registration and Monitoring**:

   o Register trademarks and domains preemptively, including common misspellings or variations, to prevent cybersquatting.

   o Implement regular monitoring routines using specialized software that scans for trademark misuse across the internet, including social media and domain registrations.

2. **Engagement with Online Platforms**:

   o Establish relationships with online marketplaces and social media platforms to facilitate faster responses to infringement issues. Utilize legal and technological tools provided by these platforms to protect intellectual property.

   o Participate in programs specifically designed for brand protection, such as Google's AdWords trademark policy or Facebook's intellectual property protection tools.

3. **Legal Actions and Takedowns**:

   o Utilize the Digital Millennium Copyright Act (DMCA) in the U.S. and similar regulations worldwide to request the removal of infringing content from websites and online platforms.

   o When necessary, pursue legal action to enforce trademark rights, which may involve sending cease and desist letters or filing lawsuits against egregious infringers.

Leveraging Technology for Enforcement

1. **Automated Monitoring Tools**:

   o Employ automated systems that track the use of trademarks online and alert the brand to potential infringements.

   o These tools can scan a vast array of online sources, from marketplaces to personal blogs, ensuring comprehensive coverage and quick detection.

2. **Data Analytics**:

   o Use data analytics to understand the scope and impact of online infringement on brand reputation and sales.

   o Analyze trends to predict where infringements are most likely to occur and tailor monitoring efforts accordingly.

Case Study: Nike's Fight Against Online Counterfeits

- **Challenge**: Nike identified a surge in counterfeit versions of its products being sold through online marketplaces.

- **Strategy**: Nike employed a combination of automated monitoring tools to detect counterfeit listings and collaborated with online platforms to remove infringing products quickly.

- **Outcome**: Through continuous monitoring and cooperation with online marketplaces, Nike has significantly reduced the availability of counterfeit goods, protecting its brand integrity and customer trust.

Confronting online infringement requires a blend of proactive strategies, technological solutions, and legal enforcement. By staying vigilant and utilizing advanced tools and platforms, brands can effectively safeguard their trademarks in the increasingly complex digital landscape.

The Dynamics of Trademark Litigation

Trademark litigation involves navigating complex legal battles to enforce trademark rights. It can be a lengthy and costly process but is often necessary to protect a brand's integrity and market position. This section explores the key phases of trademark litigation, strategies for managing disputes, and the implications of legal outcomes for businesses.

Phases of Trademark Litigation

1. **Pre-Litigation Strategy**:

   o Before entering the courtroom, it is crucial to conduct a thorough investigation to assess the strength of the trademark claim, the potential for settlement, and the risks involved in litigation.

   o Engage in pre-litigation correspondence, such as cease and desist letters, which may resolve the issue without needing to go to court.

2. **Filing the Lawsuit**:

   o Trademark litigation formally begins with the filing of a complaint, which outlines the basis of the claim, the relief sought, and the legal arguments supporting the trademark owner's position.

   o The defendant will have an opportunity to respond, typically with an answer that may include counterclaims challenging the validity of the plaintiff's trademark.

3. **Discovery Process**:

   o This phase involves the exchange of information between the parties through depositions, interrogatories, and document requests. Discovery aims to gather evidence that will support each party's case.

o Effective management of the discovery process is vital, as it often uncovers critical evidence that can determine the outcome of the case.

4. **Summary Judgment and Pre-Trial Motions**:

   o Parties may file motions for summary judgment, asking the court to make a ruling based on the facts that are not in dispute. If successful, this can lead to a quicker resolution without a full trial.

   o Pre-trial motions can also address procedural issues, such as the admissibility of evidence, that will shape how the trial proceeds.

5. **Trial**:

   o If the case goes to trial, each side presents its evidence and arguments to a judge or jury. The trial phase includes opening statements, witness testimony, cross-examinations, and closing arguments.

   o Effective presentation and argumentation are crucial during the trial, as this is where legal and factual issues are finally resolved.

6. **Post-Trial Motions and Appeals**:

   o Following a trial, either party may file post-trial motions, including motions for a new trial or motions to alter or amend the judgment.

   o Unfavorable decisions can be appealed to a higher court, which can review the trial court's application of the law and its procedural rulings.

Key Considerations in Trademark Litigation

- **Cost vs. Benefit Analysis**:

   o Litigation can be expensive and time-consuming. It is essential to perform a cost-benefit analysis to determine if the potential outcomes justify the resources invested in the lawsuit.

- **Impact on Brand Reputation**:

  o Consider the potential impact of litigation on public perception of the brand. Sometimes, even if legally justified, aggressive litigation can harm a brand's image.

- **Alternative Dispute Resolution (ADR)**:

  o Explore options like mediation or arbitration, which can be less adversarial and more cost-effective than court litigation. ADR can provide a more private forum for resolving disputes and is often faster than traditional litigation.

Navigating the dynamics of trademark litigation requires careful planning, strategic decision-making, and adept legal maneuvering. Understanding the various phases and preparing adequately can help ensure that businesses not only survive the legal labyrinth but emerge with their trademark rights firmly intact and enforceable.

Protecting Non-Traditional Trademark

Non-traditional trademarks include a variety of mark types such as sounds, colors, scents, and shapes that do not fall into the conventional categories of words or logos. Protecting these types of trademarks poses unique challenges due to their intangible nature and the difficulty in demonstrating distinctiveness to consumers. This section explores strategies for registering and defending non-traditional trademarks, using notable examples to illustrate successful protection efforts.

Understanding Non-Traditional Trademarks

1. **Categories of Non-Traditional Trademarks**:

   o **Sounds**: Jingles or distinctive sounds associated with a brand, like the MGM lion's roar.

   o **Scents**: Unique smells linked to a product, such as perfumes or scented markers.

   o **Colors**: Specific shades used consistently and exclusively by a brand, like Tiffany blue.

o **Shapes**: The distinctive shape of a product or its packaging, such as the Coca-Cola bottle.

o **Motion Marks**: Animations or moving images that identify the source of goods or services, often used in digital contexts.

2. **Challenges in Protection**:

o **Proving Distinctiveness**: Non-traditional trademarks must be shown to perform the essential trademark function of uniquely identifying the commercial origin of products or services.

o **Functional Features**: If a feature is deemed functional (essential to the use or purpose of the article or affects the cost or quality of the article), it cannot be protected as a trademark.

o **Consumer Perception**: Demonstrating that consumers recognize a non-traditional mark as an indicator of source can be difficult without extensive use or marketing.

Strategies for Registration and Defense

1. **Documenting Distinctiveness**:

o Compile evidence of consistent and exclusive use of the mark in commerce. This may include marketing materials, consumer surveys, and affidavits to establish that the mark serves as a source identifier.

o For marks that are not inherently distinctive, accumulate evidence to support acquired distinctiveness or secondary meaning due to long-term use.

2. **Legal Framework and Precedents**:

o Review relevant legal standards and precedents within the jurisdiction where protection is sought. Understanding how similar marks have been treated can guide the preparation of your application.

o Engage with intellectual property lawyers who specialize in non-traditional trademarks to navigate the complexities of registration effectively.

3. **Monitoring and Enforcement**:

o Implement monitoring systems to detect unauthorized use of non-traditional trademarks. Given their unique nature, specialized monitoring tools may be required.

o Develop a swift and decisive enforcement strategy. Given the difficulty in establishing rights in non-traditional marks, prompt action against infringers is crucial to maintaining the strength of the mark.

Notable Case Examples

- **Christian Louboutin's Red Sole**: Louboutin successfully registered and defended the specific shade of red used on the soles of its shoes, demonstrating distinctive character through consistent and exclusive use.

- **Harley-Davidson's Sound Mark**: Harley-Davidson filed for trademark protection for the distinctive sound of its motorcycle engines, though it later withdrew the application, illustrating the challenges of protecting sound marks.

Protecting non-traditional trademarks requires a nuanced understanding of intellectual property law and a strategic approach to demonstrating distinctiveness and source identification. With the right preparation and evidence, non-traditional marks can be powerful tools in distinguishing a brand's products and services in the marketplace, offering unique branding opportunities that resonate deeply with consumers.

Emerging Trends in Trademark Law

As markets evolve and technology advances, trademark law faces continuous shifts that require brands to adapt quickly. Emerging trends in trademark law are shaping how companies protect their intellectual assets and enforce their rights both locally and globally. This section outlines some of the most significant recent trends in trademark practices and their implications for trademark strategy.

Key Trends in Trademark Law

1. **Technology's Impact on Trademarks**:

    o   **Artificial Intelligence (AI)**: AI is playing a significant role in trademark creation, registration, and enforcement. AI algorithms can now generate logos and even suggest brand names, raising questions about authorship and originality in trademarks.

    o   **Blockchain**: This technology is becoming increasingly relevant in managing trademark registrations and combating counterfeits more efficiently. Blockchain provides a transparent and immutable ledger, ideal for proving the provenance and use of a trademark over time.

2. **Globalization and International Enforcement**:

    o   As companies expand globally, there is a growing need for international cooperation in trademark enforcement. Efforts to streamline cross-border enforcement and dispute resolution are on the rise, including harmonization of trademark laws and shared databases among international trademark offices.

3. **Non-Traditional Trademarks**:

    o   There is an increasing acceptance and registration of non-traditional trademarks such as holograms, motion marks, and multimedia marks. These types of trademarks cater to digital products and online services, reflecting the changing ways that consumers interact with brands.

4. **Social Media and Online Branding**:

    o   Social media platforms have become battlegrounds for trademark disputes due to user-generated content and the global reach of online advertisements. Trademark law is adapting to address issues of infringement and misuse that occur in these digital environments, emphasizing the need for clear policies and proactive brand protection strategies.

5. **Sustainability and Ethical Branding**:

   o Consumers' growing interest in sustainability has led to an increase in trademarks related to environmental friendliness and ethical practices. This trend is seeing brands trademarking terms related to sustainability to capitalize on this market shift, but also facing scrutiny over the genuineness of such claims (often referred to as "greenwashing").

Adapting to These Trends

1. **Enhanced Monitoring Tools**:

   o Utilize advanced software and AI tools to monitor the use of trademarks across various platforms globally, especially important for digital and non-traditional marks.

2. **Collaborative Legal Strategies**:

   o Engage in international partnerships and networks to facilitate easier enforcement and protection of trademarks across different jurisdictions.

3. **Legal Education and Training**:

   o Continuously educate legal teams and brand managers on the latest developments in trademark law to ensure that brand protection strategies remain effective and compliant with current laws.

4. **Public Engagement**:

   o Actively engage with consumers to educate them about genuine brand marks and the importance of ethical consumption, particularly in the context of sustainability claims.

The landscape of trademark law is rapidly evolving with advances in technology and changes in consumer behavior. Companies must stay informed about these trends and be agile in adapting their trademark strategies to maintain robust protection and leverage their intellectual property effectively. Understanding and anticipating these shifts will enable brands to navigate the complexities of modern trademark law and secure their competitive edge in the marketplace.

Quick Tips and Recap

- **Stay Informed on AI Developments**: Keep abreast of how artificial intelligence is influencing trademark creation and enforcement to ensure your practices remain current and legally sound.

- **Utilize Blockchain Technology**: Consider adopting blockchain for trademark registrations and to combat counterfeit activities, enhancing transparency and security in your trademark management.

- **Adapt to Global Standards**: Engage with international trademark law developments and consider how global trends can impact your domestic and international trademark strategies.

- **Embrace Non-Traditional Marks**: Stay updated on the evolving acceptance of non-traditional trademarks, and consider how these could be utilized to protect new forms of branding, especially in digital and multimedia formats.

- **Monitor Social Media Closely**: Implement robust monitoring strategies for social media platforms to quickly identify and address potential trademark infringements or misuse.

- **Educate About Sustainability Marks**: If your brand uses sustainability-related trademarks, ensure claims are substantiated to avoid accusations of greenwashing and to maintain consumer trust.

- **Proactive Online Enforcement**: Develop a proactive approach to online trademark enforcement, utilizing technological tools for monitoring and rapidly responding to infringements.

- **Regular Legal Training**: Regularly train your legal and brand teams on the latest trademark laws and technological tools to ensure they are equipped to handle new challenges effectively.

- **Public Engagement on Trademarks**: Educate the public about the importance of recognizing genuine trademarks, particularly for brands emphasizing ethical practices and sustainability.

- **Review and Update Trademark Strategies**: Regularly review and update your trademark strategies to reflect new legal developments, market conditions, and technological advancements.

By following these tips, you can ensure that your approach to trademark management remains dynamic, responsive, and aligned with the latest trends and challenges in trademark law.

CHAPTER TWENTY

Future-Proof Your Trademark: Strategic Planning for Longevity

"Future-proofing your trademark isn't just about securing rights today; it's about strategic planning and continuous vigilance to protect and enhance your brand's value for years to come." — SIMON SINEK, LEADERSHIP EXPERT AND AUTHOR

Ready to make your trademark timeless? Think of it as crafting a vintage wine that only gets better with age, not an old soda that loses its fizz. Future-proofing your trademark isn't just about securing it now; it's about ensuring it stays relevant, vibrant, and legally enforceable as decades roll by—because who doesn't want their brand to be the next Levi's or Coca-Cola?

First, keep a keen eye on the shifting sands of consumer trends and technological advances. Your trademark needs to ride the waves of change like a seasoned surfer, not sink under them like a stone. Imagine trying to sell floppy disks in an era of cloud storage—don't let your trademark get stuck in the past!

Next up, embrace the art of adaptation. This isn't about changing your core identity but evolving it to meet new market landscapes. It's like updating your wardrobe: you keep the classics, but maybe you ditch the bell-bottoms. Whether it's tweaking your logo to keep it fresh or expanding your services, staying relevant is key.

Then there's the vigilance of monitoring and enforcement. Think of your trademark as a garden—it needs regular tending to fend off the weeds of infringement and the pests of piracy. No one wants their prize roses (or their brand reputation) nibbled away by invaders!

Lastly, don't forget to keep your legal arsenal updated. The world of trademark law can shift as quickly as fashion trends. Regularly consulting with your trademark attorney is like having a yearly check-up; it ensures your trademark's health and catches potential issues before they become real headaches.

With these strategies, your trademark can achieve legendary status, becoming a beacon of both innovation and tradition. So let's get planning, and turn your trademark into a legacy that future generations will admire and respect!

Monitoring Market Trends and Consumer Behavior

In the dynamic landscape of commerce, understanding and adapting to market trends and consumer behaviors are crucial for keeping trademarks relevant and effective. This section explores the importance of proactive market monitoring and its role in ensuring that trademarks continue to resonate with target audiences over time.

Importance of Staying Current

1. **Evolving Consumer Preferences**:

   o   Consumer tastes and preferences can shift rapidly due to changes in technology, cultural trends, or socio-economic factors. Trademarks that once appealed strongly to consumers may become outdated or lose their relevance.

    o   Regularly assessing consumer feedback and market research data helps brands understand evolving preferences and adjust their marketing strategies accordingly.

2. **Technological Advancements**:

    o   New technologies can transform industries overnight, creating new products, services, and marketing channels. Brands must ensure their trademarks are associated with current and emerging technologies to stay relevant.

    o   Example: The shift from print to digital media required many publishers to reassess their trademarks' visibility and relevance in digital formats.

Strategies for Effective Monitoring

1. **Consumer Surveys and Feedback Loops**:

    o   Implement regular consumer surveys to gather insights into how brand perceptions and expectations are changing. This direct feedback can guide how a trademark should evolve.

    o   Establish feedback loops through social media and customer service channels to capture real-time consumer sentiments and reactions.

2. **Market Research and Analysis**:

    o   Utilize market research firms to conduct in-depth analyses of trends affecting your industry. This can include competitive analysis, brand health tracking, and identification of emerging market opportunities.

    o   Stay informed about global market trends that could impact your trademark strategy, especially if you operate in multiple regions.

3. **Engaging with Trend Analysts**:

   o Collaborate with trend analysts and industry experts who can provide insights into future trends and potential market shifts. This can help predict changes before they fully materialize, allowing for strategic trademark adjustments.

Adapting to Market Changes

1. **Dynamic Branding Strategies**:

   o Develop a dynamic branding strategy that allows for flexibility in how your trademark is used and marketed. This could involve variations of your trademark for different products or advertising campaigns that highlight different aspects of your brand.

   o Example: A fashion brand might adapt its logo's color scheme to align with changing fashion trends without altering the fundamental design.

2. **Innovative Product Development**:

   o Align product development strategies with current trends and consumer demands. Ensuring that new products and services reflect modern values and technologies can reinforce the relevance of your trademark.

   o Launch limited-edition products or variations that capitalize on current trends to keep the trademark active and engaging for consumers.

Monitoring market trends and consumer behavior is not just about safeguarding a trademark; it's about strategically steering it through the ever-changing market landscape to maintain its strength and relevance. By staying informed and adaptable, businesses can ensure their trademarks continue to resonate with consumers and withstand the test of time.

Adapting and Refreshing the Trademark

A key aspect of future-proofing your trademark involves its ability to evolve alongside the brand it represents. This section focuses on strategies for refreshing and adapting trademarks to maintain relevance in changing markets without losing the essence of the original brand identity.

Reasons for Trademark Adaptation

1. **Brand Evolution**:

   o As companies grow and diversify, their brands often evolve to encompass new products, services, or values. A trademark may need updating to reflect these changes accurately.

   o Example: A technology company expanding from hardware to software solutions might adapt its trademark to reflect its broader focus.

2. **Market Expansion**:

   o Entering new geographical or demographic markets may require adjustments to a trademark to ensure cultural relevance and sensitivity, especially in global markets.

   o Example: A Western brand entering Asian markets might adapt its logo or tagline to better resonate with local consumers.

3. **Modernization**:

   o Brands need to stay modern and appealing to new generations of consumers who may have different expectations and values. Refreshing a trademark can help a brand maintain its appeal among younger demographics.

   o Example: Refreshing color schemes, fonts, or iconography to align with contemporary design trends.

Strategies for Effective Trademark Adaptation

1. **Incremental Changes**:

   o   Implement gradual changes to a trademark to maintain brand continuity and recognition. Sudden or radical changes can confuse customers and dilute brand equity.

   o   Plan a phased approach that allows customers to acclimate to the new trademark design gradually.

2. **Consumer Testing**:

   o   Before finalizing any changes to a trademark, conduct extensive consumer testing to gauge public reaction and acceptance. This can include focus groups, A/B testing, or online surveys.

   o   Feedback from these tests can guide the final design decisions, ensuring the updated trademark resonates with the target audience.

3. **Maintaining Core Elements**:

   o   Preserve key elements of the original trademark that are most associated with the brand. This might include specific shapes, colors, or motifs that have strong brand recognition.

   o   Adjust less critical elements to enhance relevance or appeal without losing the trademark's original essence.

4. **Legal Considerations**:

   o   Consult with trademark attorneys to ensure that any modifications to the trademark do not infringe on other trademarks and are still protectable under trademark law.

   o   Register any significant changes to the trademark to secure legal protection for the new design.

Case Study: Apple's Logo Evolution

- **Background**: Apple's logo has evolved from a detailed illustration of Isaac Newton to a much simpler bitten apple. This evolution reflects a shift towards minimalism and modern design.

- **Strategy**: Each iteration maintained core elements such as the apple shape while simplifying the design to keep the brand modern and relevant.

- **Outcome**: The gradual and thoughtful evolution of the logo helped maintain Apple's brand recognition and customer loyalty while keeping the brand's visual identity fresh and contemporary.

Refreshing and adapting your trademark is a strategic approach to ensure that your brand remains competitive and relevant. By carefully planning and executing these changes, you can enhance your trademark's appeal and longevity, ensuring it continues to effectively represent your brand's values and offerings in an ever-evolving marketplace.

Vigilant Monitoring and Enforcement

Effective trademark protection is not only about registration but also about vigilant monitoring and enforcement. This section highlights the importance of these activities in maintaining the integrity and value of your trademark. Constant vigilance ensures that your trademark remains a unique identifier of your brand and is not diluted or infringed upon by unauthorized use.

Key Aspects of Monitoring

1. **Comprehensive Surveillance**:

   o Implement a systematic approach to monitor the use of your trademark across various platforms, including digital media, physical marketplaces, and international borders.

   o Use advanced technology solutions, such as AI-powered tools, to scan the internet and social media for unauthorized use of your trademark.

2. **Partner with Watch Services**:

   o Engage professional watch services that specialize in tracking trademark usage globally. These services can alert you to potential infringements based on predefined criteria.

   o Regular reports from these services can help you stay updated on how your trademark is being used worldwide.

3. **Monitor Competitive Activity**:

   o Keep an eye on competitors and new market entrants to ensure they are not using trademarks that are confusingly similar to yours.

   o This includes attending industry events, monitoring trade publications, and subscribing to competitor updates.

Enforcement Strategies

1. **Cease and Desist Letters**:

   o A first line of action upon detecting infringement should be sending a cease and desist letter. This formal request urges the infringer to stop unauthorized use of the trademark.

   o The tone and content of these letters can vary depending on the severity of the infringement and the jurisdiction involved.

2. **Negotiation and Settlement**:

   o Before escalating to legal action, consider resolving the issue through negotiation. This can often be a quicker and less costly way to address trademark disputes.

   o Settlements might involve licensing agreements if the infringement was not malicious and the infringer is cooperative.

3. **Legal Action**:

   o If informal resolution methods fail, pursuing legal action may be necessary. This involves filing a lawsuit against the infringer to seek remedies such as injunctions, damages, and legal costs.

    o   Choose experienced intellectual property attorneys who can navigate the complexities of trademark law to ensure the best possible outcome.

4. **International Enforcement**:

    o   For brands operating globally, enforce trademarks in each country where they are registered. This may involve working with local legal experts familiar with the specific trademark laws of those countries.

    o   Utilize international agreements and local government mechanisms to aid in cross-border enforcement.

Case Study: Nike's Vigilant Brand Protection

- **Background**: Nike is known for vigorously protecting its trademarks, especially the iconic Swoosh logo.

- **Strategy**: Nike employs a combination of in-house and external legal teams to monitor trademark usage globally. They utilize cease and desist letters and, if necessary, legal proceedings to handle infringements.

- **Outcome**: Nike's aggressive enforcement strategy has successfully deterred many potential infringers and maintained the brand's strong presence in the market.

Vigilant monitoring and enforcement are crucial to maintaining the strength and integrity of your trademark. By being proactive in these areas, you can prevent unauthorized use of your trademark, preserve your brand's reputation, and ensure that your trademark remains a valuable asset to your business.

Legal Updates and Compliance

In the rapidly evolving landscape of trademark law, staying informed about legal updates and ensuring compliance are crucial for the longevity and effectiveness of your trademark. This section examines the importance of keeping abreast of legal changes and adapting your trademark strategy to remain compliant with current laws.

Importance of Legal Updates

1. **Changing Legal Standards**:

   o Trademark laws can change due to legislative updates, court decisions, or international agreements. These changes can impact the scope of trademark protection, enforcement mechanisms, and registration processes.

   o Regularly updating your legal knowledge ensures that your trademark rights are not compromised and that your enforcement strategies are effective.

2. **Adapting to New Regulations**:

   o New regulations may introduce additional requirements or procedures for trademark registration and renewal. Staying informed helps in making necessary adjustments to comply with these new rules.

   o Compliance with the latest regulations not only protects you from legal pitfalls but also strengthens the overall protection of your trademark.

Strategies for Staying Updated

1. **Legal Subscriptions and Continuing Education**:

   o Subscribe to legal newsletters, journals, and databases that focus on trademark law. These resources provide timely updates on legal changes and insightful analyses.

   o Attend seminars, webinars, and continuing legal education courses offered by legal associations or intellectual property organizations.

2. **Engage with Legal Professionals**:

   o Maintain a relationship with a qualified trademark attorney who specializes in intellectual property law. Regular consultations can help navigate complex legal scenarios and ensure compliance.

o Consider having in-house legal counsel or a dedicated legal team if your organization is large enough, to focus on trademark issues and other intellectual property matters.

3. **Utilize Technology**:

   o Implement legal technology tools that offer real-time updates on law changes and automated compliance checks. These tools can help track the status of your trademarks and alert you to necessary legal actions.

   o Advanced software can also assist in managing deadlines for trademark renewals and ensuring timely responses to legal challenges.

Legal Compliance in Practice

1. **Documentation and Record-Keeping**:

   o Keep meticulous records of all trademark registrations, renewals, enforcement actions, and related legal correspondence. Good record-keeping not only aids in legal compliance but also supports your case in any legal disputes.

   o Ensure that your trademark usage guidelines are documented and regularly updated to reflect the latest legal standards and best practices.

2. **Risk Management**:

   o Conduct regular audits of your trademark portfolio to assess risks associated with non-compliance or potential legal challenges. This proactive approach helps identify issues before they escalate into more significant problems.

   o Develop a compliance checklist tailored to your business's specific needs and the jurisdictions in which you operate.

Case Study: Global Tech Corporation's Compliance Overhaul

- **Background**: A multinational technology company faced multiple trademark disputes due to non-compliance with new trademark laws in several countries.

- **Strategy**: The company overhauled its trademark management processes, instituted regular legal training for its marketing and legal teams, and engaged more frequently with external trademark counsel.

- **Outcome**: These proactive measures significantly reduced legal risks, ensured compliance across all operating countries, and stabilized the company's trademark portfolio.

Active engagement with legal updates and a strong compliance strategy are vital to future-proofing your trademark. By staying informed and ready to adapt to legal changes, you can protect your intellectual property from becoming obsolete or legally vulnerable, ensuring that your trademark continues to support your brand's success and growth.

Building a Legacy with Your Trademark

A trademark transcends being merely a legal identifier; it can embody the ethos and heritage of a brand, creating a legacy that resonates through generations. This section explores strategies for leveraging your trademark not just as a symbol of identification but as a cornerstone of your brand's enduring legacy.

The Importance of a Timeless Trademark

1. **Symbolic Value**:

   o A trademark can encapsulate the history, culture, and values of a brand, becoming symbolic of quality and trustworthiness in the eyes of consumers.

   o By consistently delivering on its brand promise, a company can transform its trademark into a symbol of excellence and reliability.

2. **Brand Storytelling**:

   o Effective storytelling that integrates the history and significance of the trademark can deepen emotional connections with consumers. This narrative adds a layer of depth to the brand, enhancing consumer loyalty.

   o Stories about the origin of the trademark, major milestones, and how it has evolved can be powerful tools in marketing campaigns.

Strategies for Enhancing Trademark Value

1. **Consistent Quality and Innovation**:

   o Maintain high standards of quality and continuously innovate to ensure that the products or services associated with your trademark are best-in-class.

   o Consistency in quality assures customers that any offering under the trademark meets a certain standard, reinforcing the brand's value.

2. **Cultural Resonance and Social Responsibility**:

   o Align the trademark with cultural trends and social responsibility initiatives. This alignment can enhance brand perception, particularly among younger demographics who value ethical and socially responsible brands.

   o For example, adopting environmentally friendly practices can be reflected in the trademark's branding strategy, thereby connecting with broader societal values.

3. **Strategic Collaborations and Licensing**:

   o Engage in strategic collaborations that can elevate the trademark by associating it with other prestigious brands or influencers. This not only broadens the trademark's appeal but also introduces it to new audiences.

o Licensing the trademark for use in different sectors or products can extend its reach and reinforce its presence in the market.

Leveraging Digital Platforms

1. **Digital Footprint**:

    o Establish a strong online presence for the trademark through an official website, social media, and digital marketing. This digital footprint helps in telling the brand's story and reaching a global audience.

    o Utilize SEO and content marketing strategies to ensure that the trademark and its legacy are prominently featured and easily discoverable online.

2. **Engagement and Community Building**:

    o Build a community around the trademark by engaging with consumers through social media platforms, forums, and brand-sponsored events.

    o This engagement should foster a sense of belonging and loyalty among consumers, making them advocates for the trademark and its associated brand.

Case Study: The Legacy of Rolex

- **Background**: Rolex has built a legacy around its trademark by combining exceptional product quality with a strong brand narrative that speaks of prestige, innovation, and craftsmanship.

- **Strategy**: Rolex has carefully managed its trademark by maintaining product excellence, engaging in high-profile sponsorships, and leveraging its history in its marketing.

- **Outcome**: The Rolex trademark is universally recognized and revered, symbolizing more than just luxury watches but a legacy of enduring quality and timeless style.

Building a legacy with your trademark involves more than legal protection; it requires a strategic, multifaceted approach that encompasses maintaining quality, engaging storytelling, and effective brand management. By elevating your trademark to a symbol of heritage and trust, you can ensure it leaves a lasting impression on the market and endures as a valuable asset for future generations.

Quick Tips and Recap

- **Embrace Consistency**: Maintain consistent quality and innovation in your products and services to reinforce the trust and recognition associated with your trademark.

- **Tell Your Story**: Use brand storytelling to connect emotionally with consumers, integrating the history and values behind your trademark into your marketing strategies.

- **Monitor Trends**: Stay attuned to consumer trends and technological advancements to keep your trademark relevant and appealing.

- **Adapt and Evolve**: Periodically refresh your trademark to align with current market landscapes and consumer preferences while preserving its core identity.

- **Vigilant Protection**: Regularly monitor for trademark infringements and enforce your rights through legal actions when necessary to protect your brand's integrity.

- **Legal Compliance**: Keep updated with changes in trademark law and ensure compliance to avoid potential legal challenges.

- **Utilize Digital Tools**: Establish a strong online presence for your trademark, using digital platforms for marketing and community engagement.

- **Build Community**: Foster a community around your trademark through social media engagement, customer interaction, and brand loyalty programs.

- **Seek Professional Advice**: Regularly consult with trademark attorneys to navigate complex legal landscapes and refine your trademark strategy.

- **Document Everything**: Keep detailed records of all trademark registrations, renewals, and enforcement actions to maintain a well-managed and protected trademark portfolio.

By following these tips, you can ensure that your trademark not only survives but thrives through changing times, cementing its place as a valuable asset and a legacy of your brand.

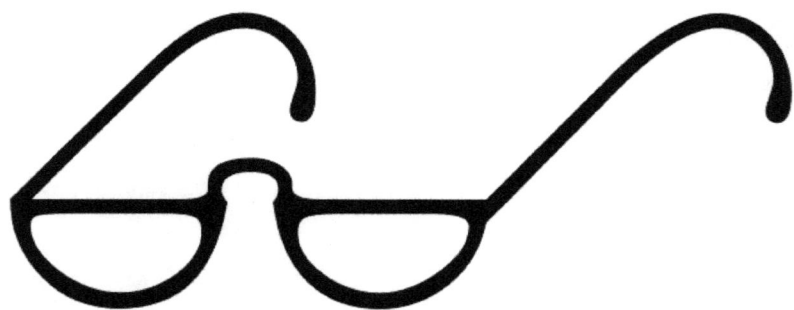

Conclusion

Wrap-Up: Where Do We Go from Here?

As we conclude this exploration into the multifaceted world of trademarks, we reflect on the enduring importance of these unique symbols in defining, protecting, and elevating a brand in the marketplace. From the initial steps of crafting a distinctive mark to navigating the complexities of global trademark management, the journey of a trademark is both challenging and rewarding. Each chapter of this book has provided strategic insights and practical guidance to help you secure and manage your trademarks effectively.

Key Takeaways

1. **Foundation of Trademarks**:

   o   Trademarks are not merely legal tools but essential assets that communicate the identity and quality of your brand to the world. The careful selection and registration of trademarks set the foundation for a brand's recognition and protection.

2. **Strategic Management**:

   o   Effective trademark management involves continuous monitoring and enforcement to guard against infringement and maintain the trademark's distinctiveness. The dynamic landscape of global commerce and digital technology demands vigilant oversight and agile responses.

3. **Legal Challenges and Compliance**:

   o   Navigating the legal intricacies of trademark law requires a proactive approach. Regular updates on legal developments and compliance with international regulations are crucial for protecting trademarks across diverse markets.

4. **Adaptation and Evolution**:

   o   As markets evolve and new trends emerge, trademarks must also adapt. Refreshing and evolving trademarks while maintaining their core identity helps keep the brand relevant and competitive.

5. **Building a Legacy**:

   o   Beyond protection, trademarks are about building a lasting legacy. They are symbols of trust and quality that can transcend generations, embodying the spirit and values of the brand.

The Path Forward

The journey of a trademark is a continual process of adaptation and vigilance. As we look to the future, the successful management of trademarks will increasingly rely on innovative strategies that embrace technological advancements and reflect global cultural shifts. Brands that can skillfully navigate these waters will not only protect their intellectual property but also build a legacy that endures.

Final Thoughts

In closing, remember that trademarks are the beating heart of your brand's identity. They encapsulate your brand's past achievements and future aspirations. Whether you are a budding entrepreneur or a seasoned business leader, the strategic insights provided in this book are designed to equip you with the knowledge and tools necessary to harness the full potential of your trademarks. By future-proofing your trademarks, you are setting the stage for sustained success and leaving a mark on the industry that will last for generations to come. Embrace the journey, commit to continuous learning and adaptation, and let your trademarks pave the way to a legacy of excellence and innovation.

Where Do We Go From Here?

As we conclude "Mark Your Territory: Navigating Trademarks in the Modern Marketplace," we reflect not only on the complexities and strategies discussed but also on the broader journey of building and protecting your business empire. This book represents just one part of a comprehensive suite designed to equip you with the expertise needed to excel in today's competitive business environment.

Introducing the Next Step

The next book in our Empire Builders Series: Masterclasses in Business and Law is titled "From Idea to Empire: Mastering the Art of Business Planning." Building upon the foundational knowledge provided in "Mark Your Territory," this next installment shifts focus from trademark protection to the essential strategies of business planning.

What to Expect in the Next Book

1. **Comprehensive Business Planning**:

    o   Dive into the art of transforming a simple idea into a robust business plan. Learn to outline your business objectives, market strategies, and financial forecasts in a detailed and executable manner.

2. **Risk Management and Strategy Development**:

    o   Explore sophisticated techniques for identifying potential risks and developing mitigation strategies that safeguard your business while promoting sustainable growth.

3. **Resource Allocation and Management**:

   o Gain insights into efficient resource management, ensuring that every aspect of your business, from capital to human resources, is optimized for maximum productivity and efficiency.

4. **Innovation and Market Trends**:

   o Stay ahead of the curve by learning how to incorporate innovation into your business model and adapt to changing market trends, ensuring long-term success.

5. **Legal and Ethical Foundations**:

   o Understand the legal considerations that underpin a successful business strategy, ensuring compliance and ethical integrity in all your business dealings.

Building on What You've Learned

"From Idea to Empire" is designed not only to build on the legal insights from "Mark Your Territory" but also to expand your capabilities in orchestrating and executing a successful business strategy. This book aims to guide you through the intricate process of business planning, turning your visions into actionable, profitable strategies.

Conclusion and Call to Action

We invite you to continue this journey with us, moving from the specifics of trademark management to the broader aspects of business planning. Each book in the Empire Builders Series is crafted to bring you closer to realizing your dream of building a lasting business empire. Equip yourself with the knowledge to move confidently forward, turning your innovative ideas into reality, and laying down the strategic foundations that will support your business's future growth and success.

READ ON for a bonus chapter!

The Role of Artificial Intelligence in Trademark Management

"Artificial Intelligence is revolutionizing trademark management by automating complex processes, enhancing accuracy, and providing predictive insights that allow for proactive brand protection strategies."
— JACK MA, FOUNDER OF ALIBABA GROUP

Welcome to the futuristic realm of trademark management, where artificial intelligence (AI) is more than just your coffee-fetching assistant—it's your secret weapon in the battle for brand protection. Integrating AI into your trademark strategy is like having a supercomputer in your corner, equipped with the brainpower of a thousand lawyers and the processing speed of a high-speed train.

Imagine an AI system that can scan the global marketplace with the precision of a hawk, spotting potential infringements faster than you can say "cease and desist." This isn't just efficient; it's transformative. AI can analyze patterns, predict trends, and even suggest the optimal times to file for renewals or new registrations. It's like having a crystal ball, but instead of murky predictions, you get data-driven insights.

But wait—there's more! AI isn't just good for defense; it's an offensive powerhouse too. It can help craft your brand's identity by sifting through vast amounts of data to determine what resonates with consumers, identifying untapped markets, and suggesting new areas for trademark expansion. Think of it as your very own brand strategist, only without the need for coffee breaks.

And for those worried about the soullessness of technology, fear not. AI in trademark management isn't about replacing the human touch; it's about enhancing it. It frees up human minds from the drudgery of repetitive tasks, allowing lawyers, marketers, and brand managers to focus on creative and strategic activities—like planning the next big advertising campaign or negotiating a complex licensing deal.

So, embrace the AI revolution in trademark management. With this powerful ally, your brand isn't just protected; it's poised to conquer new frontiers. Just remember to keep it on a tight digital leash—you wouldn't want your AI going rogue and starting its own brand!

AI in Trademark Searches and Monitoring

In the realm of trademark management, artificial intelligence (AI) is revolutionizing how businesses conduct searches and monitor their trademarks. AI's ability to process large volumes of data rapidly and with precision greatly enhances the efficiency and effectiveness of these crucial tasks.

AI-Driven Trademark Searches

1. **Automated Searches**:
   - AI systems can automate the process of searching trademark databases, reducing the time and labor traditionally required.

These systems use algorithms to scan through vast amounts of data, identifying potential conflicts and similar trademarks across multiple jurisdictions.

o This automation ensures that trademark searches are thorough and more cost-effective, enabling businesses to conduct them more frequently and proactively.

2. **Accuracy and Precision**:

o AI enhances the accuracy of trademark searches by analyzing the phonetic, visual, and semantic similarities between trademarks. Advanced algorithms can detect subtle similarities that might be overlooked during manual reviews.

o This precision helps in assessing the risk of trademark infringement more reliably, thus informing better strategic decisions regarding trademark applications and usage.

AI in Trademark Monitoring

1. **Continuous Surveillance**:

o Traditionally, monitoring trademarks for potential infringement involved periodic manual checks, which could miss short-lived but significant violations. AI systems offer continuous surveillance, constantly scanning the internet, social media, and databases for unauthorized use of trademarks.

o This ongoing monitoring ensures that infringements are detected in real-time, allowing for swift actions to mitigate potential damages.

2. **Global Scope**:

o AI systems are not confined by geographical boundaries. They can monitor trademarks globally, providing a significant advantage for businesses with international presence or aspirations.

- o This global monitoring capability is crucial in today's interconnected market, where infringements can arise in any part of the world and spread rapidly online.

Enhancing Monitoring with AI Tools

1. **Integration with Other Technologies**:

   - o AI can be integrated with other technologies such as blockchain to further secure and streamline trademark monitoring processes. For instance, blockchain can provide an immutable record of trademark use and registrations, while AI analyzes and flags potential conflicts or misuses.

2. **Customizable Alerts**:

   - o AI systems can be programmed to alert businesses to specific types of trademark use that may be of particular concern. This customization allows companies to focus on potential infringements that pose the greatest risk to their brand.

3. **Predictive Capabilities**:

   - o Beyond reactive monitoring, AI can predict potential areas of concern by analyzing trends in trademark infringements. These predictive capabilities enable businesses to take preventive measures before actual infringements occur.

AI is transforming the landscape of trademark searches and monitoring by making these processes more thorough, efficient, and globally encompassing. By adopting AI technologies, businesses can enhance their ability to protect their trademarks effectively, ensuring that their brand identity is maintained and their intellectual property rights are upheld.

Predictive Analytics in Trademark Strategy

Predictive analytics is transforming how companies strategize their trademark management by using historical data, trend analysis, and machine learning to forecast future outcomes. This proactive approach allows businesses to anticipate market changes, potential legal conflicts, and strategic opportunities, making predictive analytics a powerful tool in trademark strategy.

The Role of Predictive Analytics

1. **Forecasting Market Trends**:

    o   AI-driven predictive analytics can analyze vast amounts of market data to identify emerging trends in consumer behavior, industry shifts, and technological advancements. This information helps companies to predict which types of trademarks (words, logos, or non-traditional marks) are likely to gain popularity.

    o   Understanding these trends enables businesses to register trademarks that are likely to resonate with future markets, ensuring long-term relevance and protection.

2. **Anticipating Legal Conflicts**:

    o   Predictive models can assess the likelihood of trademark disputes by analyzing patterns in trademark filings, oppositions, and litigations. These models take into account factors such as industry-specific risks, commonalities in disputed trademarks, and historical outcomes of similar cases.

    o   By predicting potential legal challenges, companies can take preemptive actions such as modifying a trademark, enhancing its distinctiveness, or preparing for possible legal defenses.

Implementing Predictive Analytics

1. **Data Collection and Analysis**:

   o   Gather comprehensive data from internal records, trademark databases, legal filings, and market research reports. The accuracy of predictive analytics relies heavily on the quality and breadth of the data collected.

   o   Use sophisticated AI algorithms to process and analyze this data, uncovering patterns and insights that may not be apparent through traditional analysis.

2. **Integration with Trademark Strategy**:

   o   Integrate predictive insights into the broader trademark strategy by using them to guide decisions on where and when to file trademarks, how to design them, and identifying which trademarks to prioritize for renewals or enforcement.

   o   Use predictive analytics to tailor marketing strategies that align with anticipated changes in consumer preferences and market conditions.

Case Studies

1. **Global Tech Company**:

   o   A multinational technology firm used predictive analytics to understand emerging tech trends and successfully registered trademarks related to artificial intelligence and machine learning before these fields became highly competitive.

   o   The proactive trademark strategy not only secured robust legal protection but also positioned the company as a leader in these technological sectors.

2. **Fashion Retailer**:

   o   By analyzing trends in fashion and consumer goods, a retailer predicted a resurgence in vintage styles and accordingly revived several of its older trademarks. These trademarks were reintegrated into marketing campaigns, resonating with both nostalgic older consumers and trend-following younger demographics.

Challenges and Considerations

- **Data Privacy and Accuracy**:
  - ○ Ensure that data used in predictive analytics complies with all relevant data protection laws. Additionally, the data must be accurate and current to produce reliable predictions.

- **Dynamic Market Adaptation**:
  - ○ The effectiveness of predictive analytics depends on its ability to adapt to rapidly changing markets. Regular updates and recalibrations of predictive models are necessary to maintain their accuracy and relevance.

Predictive analytics represents a significant advancement in the field of trademark management, offering businesses the tools to not just react to the market and legal challenges but to anticipate and strategically plan for them. By effectively integrating predictive analytics into their trademark strategies, companies can secure a competitive edge, adapt to future market changes, and manage their trademarks more effectively.

AI-Driven Brand Development

In the ever-evolving landscape of brand management, artificial intelligence (AI) is revolutionizing how brands develop and refine their identities. AI-driven brand development leverages vast data sets and advanced analytics to enhance decision-making processes, from identifying market opportunities to tailoring brand messaging.

Leveraging AI for Strategic Branding

1. **Consumer Insights and Personalization**:
   - ○ AI excels in analyzing consumer data, extracting patterns and preferences that are not immediately obvious. By processing

customer interactions, purchase histories, and social media behavior, AI can provide a deep understanding of consumer segments.

o These insights enable brands to craft highly personalized marketing strategies and product offerings that resonate more effectively with targeted demographics, increasing brand loyalty and engagement.

2. **Brand Identity Development**:

   o AI tools can help identify gaps in the market where a new brand or sub-brand could succeed. By analyzing current trends, competitor strengths, and consumer needs, AI suggests characteristics that the new brand identity should embody.

   o This process includes recommending brand names, logos, and other trademark elements that are unique, relevant, and likely to appeal to the intended audience.

AI in Creative Processes

1. **Automated Content Creation**:

   o AI algorithms are increasingly capable of generating creative content, including visual designs, textual content for ads, and even video scripts. These tools can produce numerous variations quickly, allowing brands to test and select the most effective options.

   o While AI-generated content may require human refinement, it significantly speeds up the creative process and introduces new, data-driven ideas that might not have been considered otherwise.

2. **Dynamic Branding**:

   o AI can assist in developing dynamic branding strategies where brand elements are adapted based on real-time data. For instance, logo colors or advertising themes might change based on seasonal trends, geographic factors, or current events, keeping the brand relevant and engaging.

Implementing AI in Brand Strategy

1. **Integration with Marketing Teams**:

   o Ensure that AI tools are integrated seamlessly with marketing teams by providing training and setting clear guidelines on how and when to use AI outputs. This collaboration maximizes the effectiveness of both human creativity and AI efficiency.

   o Regular feedback loops should be established to assess the performance of AI-driven initiatives and adjust strategies as needed.

2. **Ethical and Consistent Brand Representation**:

   o While AI can offer innovative branding solutions, it's crucial to maintain a consistent and ethically sound brand image. Oversight is necessary to ensure that AI-generated branding elements align with the company's values and public image.

   o Address potential biases in AI algorithms to prevent any inadvertent negative impact on brand perception.

Case Study: Innovative Beverage Company

- **Background**: An innovative beverage company utilized AI to analyze emerging beverage preferences and social media trends, identifying a growing demand for health-centric, eco-friendly drinks among young adults.

- **Strategy**: Leveraging AI insights, the company developed a new line of beverages under a sub-brand that emphasized sustainability and wellness. AI suggested the brand name, designed the logo, and generated initial ad campaigns.

- **Outcome**: The sub-brand successfully captured the targeted market segment, and the AI-driven approach allowed for rapid adaptation and scaling based on consumer feedback and evolving trends.

305

AI-driven brand development offers a transformative approach to how brands are created and maintained, providing a competitive edge in today's fast-paced market. By harnessing AI for both strategic decision-making and creative processes, brands can achieve a higher level of personalization and market responsiveness, leading to stronger consumer connections and sustained growth.

Enhancing Legal and Compliance Operations

In the complex world of trademark law, compliance and legal operations are paramount. Artificial Intelligence (AI) significantly enhances these aspects by automating routine tasks, increasing accuracy in compliance monitoring, and providing predictive insights into potential legal issues. This section explores how AI can be integrated into legal and compliance operations to streamline processes and ensure that trademarks are maintained efficiently and effectively.

AI Applications in Legal Compliance

1. **Automated Document Analysis**:

    o   AI-powered tools can quickly analyze large volumes of legal documents, including trademark registration applications, renewal filings, and litigation materials. These tools identify critical information, flag inconsistencies, and ensure that all documentation complies with current laws and regulations.

    o   This automation reduces human error and frees up legal teams to focus on more strategic tasks, such as case preparation and negotiation.

2. **Compliance Monitoring**:

    o   AI systems continuously monitor regulatory changes that could affect trademark strategies. They can automatically update compliance frameworks and alert teams to necessary adjustments in real-time.

    o   This proactive monitoring is crucial in jurisdictions with frequently changing laws, ensuring that a company's trademarks always adhere to the latest legal standards.

Enhancing Trademark Management with AI

1. **Risk Assessment and Management**:

   o Predictive AI models assess the risk associated with potential trademark infringements and the legal vulnerability of trademark portfolios. By analyzing historical data and current market conditions, AI can forecast areas of concern and suggest preemptive actions.

   o These insights help businesses to prioritize their legal resources effectively, focusing on protecting trademarks that are most at risk or hold the highest value.

2. **Streamlining Legal Processes**:

   o AI can automate routine legal processes such as the drafting of standard legal documents, filing forms, and managing correspondence. This streamlining leads to more efficient operations and faster response times in dynamic market conditions.

   o For instance, AI can auto-generate cease and desist letters in response to detected infringements, allowing for rapid enforcement of trademark rights.

Integrating AI with Legal Teams

1. **Training and Adaptation**:

   o For AI tools to be effective, legal teams need appropriate training to understand how to use these technologies and interpret their outputs. Ongoing training ensures that staff remain proficient as AI technologies evolve.

   o Establishing protocols for when and how to use AI support effectively integrates these tools into daily legal practices without undermining the expertise of seasoned attorneys.

2. **Ethical Considerations**:

    o   Implement AI solutions responsibly, ensuring they adhere to ethical guidelines, especially regarding data privacy and the transparency of AI decision-making processes.

    o   Regular audits of AI tools are necessary to identify any biases or errors that could affect compliance or legal outcomes.

Case Study: Multinational Corporation Streamlines Trademark Registrations

*   **Background**: A multinational corporation faced challenges managing its extensive trademark portfolio across multiple jurisdictions with varying legal requirements.

*   **Strategy**: The corporation implemented an AI system that automated the analysis and filing of trademark registrations, monitored compliance changes globally, and prioritized legal actions based on risk assessments.

*   **Outcome**: This integration of AI significantly reduced administrative overhead, improved compliance rates, and enhanced the strategic management of the corporation's intellectual property assets.

Integrating AI into legal and compliance operations offers substantial benefits for trademark management, including increased efficiency, enhanced accuracy, and proactive legal positioning. As AI technology continues to advance, it promises to further revolutionize how legal teams support and protect business trademarks in a rapidly evolving global marketplace.

Ethical Considerations and Human Oversight

As artificial intelligence (AI) becomes increasingly integrated into trademark management, it is crucial to address the ethical considerations and maintain rigorous human oversight. This section explores the ethical challenges posed by AI and the importance of human intervention in ensuring that AI systems are used responsibly and effectively.

Ethical Challenges in AI Implementation

1. **Data Privacy**:

   o AI systems often require access to vast amounts of data, including potentially sensitive corporate and personal information. Ensuring the privacy and security of this data is paramount to comply with global data protection regulations such as GDPR.

   o Companies must implement robust data governance policies to manage how data is collected, used, and stored, preventing misuse and maintaining confidentiality.

2. **Bias and Fairness**:

   o AI algorithms can inadvertently perpetuate or amplify biases present in the data they are trained on. In the context of trademark management, this could lead to unfair practices, such as discriminatory enforcement actions or biased trademark approval processes.

   o Regularly auditing AI models for bias and training AI systems with diverse, representative data sets are critical steps in mitigating these issues.

Human Oversight in AI Systems

1. **Maintaining Human Decision-Making**:

   o While AI can automate many aspects of trademark management, critical decisions should remain under human control, especially those involving complex legal and ethical considerations.

   o Legal professionals should oversee AI outputs, applying human judgment to areas like enforcement decisions and conflict resolution where nuanced understanding and empathy are required.

2. **Training and Awareness**:

   o Organizations must train their legal and compliance teams not only in how to use AI tools effectively but also in understanding the limitations and potential risks associated with AI.

   o Ongoing education about the ethical use of AI, including understanding potential biases and the importance of data security, is essential for maintaining ethical standards.

Integrating AI Ethically

1. **Transparent AI Processes**:

   o Transparency in how AI systems operate and make decisions is crucial for building trust among stakeholders and maintaining accountability. This includes clear documentation of AI methodologies and decision-making processes.

   o Companies should be prepared to disclose and explain the role of AI in their trademark management processes, particularly when AI decisions affect third parties.

2. **Collaboration and Stakeholder Engagement**:

   o Engage with stakeholders, including legal experts, data scientists, and ethicists, to review and guide the development and implementation of AI systems in trademark management.

   o Collaboration can help identify potential ethical risks early and ensure that AI applications align with broader societal values and legal standards.

Case Study: Ethical AI Deployment in a Global Retail Brand

- **Background**: A global retail brand implemented an AI system to monitor and enforce its trademarks globally. The brand faced challenges regarding data privacy and the fairness of AI-driven enforcement actions.

- **Strategy**: The company established a multidisciplinary ethics committee to oversee the AI's deployment, focusing on data privacy, bias mitigation, and maintaining human oversight in key decision-making processes.

- **Outcome**: By prioritizing ethical considerations and human oversight, the brand successfully navigated potential pitfalls, maintaining public trust and upholding high ethical standards in its trademark management.

The integration of AI into trademark management offers tremendous potential but also presents significant ethical challenges. Addressing these challenges through rigorous human oversight, ethical AI practices, and stakeholder engagement ensures that AI tools enhance trademark management without compromising ethical standards or legal integrity. This balanced approach is essential for leveraging AI's benefits while safeguarding the interests and rights of all stakeholders.

Quick Tips and Recap

- **Prioritize Data Privacy**: Implement strict data governance practices to protect sensitive information used by AI systems in trademark management.

- **Audit for Bias**: Regularly review and audit AI models to identify and mitigate any biases, ensuring fairness and accuracy in AI-driven processes.

- **Maintain Human Oversight**: Keep critical decision-making under human control, particularly for complex legal and ethical issues that require nuanced judgment.

- **Ensure Transparency**: Maintain transparency in AI operations to build trust and accountability, making methodologies and decision-making processes clear to all stakeholders.

- **Educate and Train**: Provide ongoing education and training for teams on the ethical use of AI, including understanding AI limitations and data security.

- **Engage Stakeholders**: Collaborate with a diverse group of stakeholders, including ethicists, legal experts, and technologists, to guide the ethical implementation of AI.

- **Document AI Processes**: Keep detailed documentation of AI procedures and decisions to facilitate reviews and provide accountability.

- **Implement Ethical Standards**: Develop and enforce ethical standards for AI use that align with organizational values and legal requirements.

- **Review Legal Compliance**: Regularly review AI tools and processes for compliance with current trademark laws and international regulations.

- **Monitor and Adjust**: Continuously monitor AI systems for performance and ethical integrity, making adjustments as needed to align with best practices and stakeholder expectations.

By following these tips, businesses can effectively integrate AI into their trademark management strategies while adhering to ethical practices and maintaining the necessary human oversight.

Appendix

Essential Agreements and Documents

The Appendix of this book is designed to provide readers with practical tools and templates that can be directly applied in the management and protection of intellectual property. This section includes a series of critical documents that are essential for navigating the complex landscape of trademark law. Each document serves a specific function, ranging from enforcement to the assignment of rights, offering readers a comprehensive toolkit for effective trademark management.

1. **Trade Name License Agreement**: This agreement permits one party to use another party's trade name under specified conditions, helping to expand brand presence without transferring ownership.

2. **Infringement Demand Letter**: This template provides a standard format for addressing potential infringements and formally requesting cessation of unauthorized use of a trademark. It's a first step in legal action to protect a trademark from being diluted or misused.

3. **Domain Name Infringement Demand Letter**: Specifically tailored for issues in the digital realm, this letter is used when a domain name too

313

closely resembles a trademark, potentially leading to confusion or deception.

4. **Complaint**: This is a formal legal document that initiates a lawsuit against a party that is suspected of trademark infringement. It outlines the basis of the claim, the facts supporting the infringement, and the relief sought.

5. **Assignment of Service Marks and Trademarks**: This form is used to legally transfer ownership of a trademark or service mark from one party to another, including all associated rights and goodwill.

6. **Trademark Ownership and License Agreement**: This comprehensive agreement outlines the terms under which a trademark is licensed, including rights, responsibilities, and royalties, ensuring that trademark use benefits both the licensor and licensee while protecting the brand's integrity.

Together, these documents form a robust foundation for safeguarding intellectual property rights in various scenarios, from straightforward licensing to complex litigation. By incorporating these templates into their operations, businesses can preemptively address potential legal issues and streamline their intellectual property management processes.

Disclaimer: Please note that all agreements are provided for informational purposes only and should not be construed as legal advice. We recommend consulting with a qualified attorney to ensure that any legal documents or decisions are tailored to your specific circumstances.

> ▶ If you are interested in receiving an electronic copy of any of the following documents, please email us at documents@AuthorsDoor.com with the subject line "Request for [fill in the blank]." Upon receiving your email, we will promptly send you a Microsoft Word copy of the document. **Disclaimer:** Please note that all agreements are provided for informational purposes only and should not be construed as legal advice. We recommend consulting with a qualified attorney to ensure that any legal documents or decisions are tailored to your specific circumstances.

1. Trade Name License Agreement

TRADE NAME LICENSE AGREEMENT

This Trade Name License Agreement ("Agreement") is made and effective the [Date]

BETWEEN: [LICENSOR NAME] (the "Licensor"), a corporation organized and existing under the laws of the [STATE/PROVINCE], with its headquarters located at _____.

AND: [LICENSEE NAME] (the "Licensee"), a corporation organized and existing under the laws of the [STATE/PROVINCE], with its headquarters located at _____.

WHEREAS, Licensee acknowledges that Licensor is the owner of the name "[BRAND NAME]" and any variation thereof (the "Name"); and

WHEREAS, Licensee is desirous of using the Name in connection with [DESCRIBE].

NOW, THEREFORE, in consideration of the mutual promises herein contained, the parties hereto agree as follows:

1.   Grant of License. Licensor hereby grants to Licensee and Licensee hereby accepts the right, privilege and nonexclusive license to use the Name solely in connection with [DESCRIBE] (the "Business"). Licensee shall use the Name at all times for the Business and no other purposes. Licensor represents and warrants that, to the best of its knowledge, it owns the rights to the Name.

2.   Term. The term of the license hereby granted shall be effective upon the date of execution of this Agreement and shall continue for [number] years, unless sooner terminated in accordance with the provisions hereof.

3.   License Fee. Licensee shall pay to Licensor, as a license fee for the use of the Name, [amount], payable [on the date hereof] [set forth payment date or dates].

4.   Nonexclusivity. Nothing in this Agreement shall be construed to prevent Licensor from granting any other licenses for the use of the Name or from utilizing the Name in any manner whatsoever.

5.   Good Will. Licensee recognizes that there exists great value and good will associated with the Name, and acknowledges that the Name and all rights therein and good will pertaining thereto belong exclusively to Licensor, and that the Name has a secondary meaning in the mind of the public.

6.   Licensor's Title and Protection of Licensor's Rights

a.   Licensee agrees that it will not during the term of this Agreement, or thereafter, attack the title or any rights of Licensor in and to the Name or attack the validity of the license granted herein.

b.   Licensee agrees to assist Licensor to the extent necessary in the procurement of any protection or to protect any of Licensor's right to the Name, and Licensor, if it so desires, may commence or prosecute any claims or suits in its own name or in the name of Licensee or join Licensee as a party thereto. Licensee shall notify Licensor in writing of any infringements or imitations by others of the Name which may come to Licensee's attention, and Licensor shall have the sole right to determine whether or not any action shall be taken on account of any such infringements or imitations. Licensee shall not institute any suit or take any action on account of any such infringements or imitation without first obtaining the written consent of the Licensor so to do.

     c.   Licensee agrees to cooperate fully and in good faith with Licensor for the purpose of securing and preserving Licensor's rights in and to the Name, and Licensor shall reimburse Licensee its reasonable costs for such cooperation (unless Licensee is in breach of this Agreement). It is agreed that nothing contained in this Agreement shall be construed as an assignment or grant to the Licensee of any right, title or interest in or to the Name, it being understood that all rights relating thereto are reserved by Licensor, expect for the license hereunder to Licensee of the right to use and utilize the Name only as specifically and expressly provided in this Agreement. Licensee hereby agrees that at the termination or expiration of this Agreement, Licensee will be deemed to have assigned, transferred and conveyed to Licensor any trade rights, equities, good will, titles or other rights in and to the Name which may have been obtained by Licensee or which may have vested in Licensee in pursuance of any endeavors covered hereby, and that Licensee will execute any instruments requested by Licensor to accomplish or conform the foregoing. Any such assignment, transfer or conveyance shall be without other consideration than the mutual covenants and considerations of this Agreement.

7.   Inspection. Licensor, or its nominee, shall have access to the Business during normal business hours and to books and records of Licensee for the purpose of ensuring compliance with this Agreement.

8.   Use of Name. Licensee shall have no right to affix the Name to any building, sign, merchandise or other item without first obtaining Licensor's express written consent, which consent shall be within the reasonable discretion of Licensor.

9.   Termination

     a.   Licensee may not terminate this Agreement.

     b.   The license rights granted hereunder may be terminated by Licensor upon immediate notice without the opportunity to cure should any of the following events occur:

     i.   If Licensee shall: (A) admit in writing its inability to pay its debts generally as they become due; (B) file a petition in bankruptcy or a petition to take advantage of any insolvency act; (C) make an assignment for the benefit of its creditors; (D) consent to the appointment of a receiver of itself or of the whole or any substantial part of its property; (E) on a petition in bankruptcy filed against it, be adjudicated as bankrupt; (F) file a petition or answer seeking reorganization or arrangement under the bankruptcy laws or any other applicable law or statute; (G) become subject to a final order, judgment or decree entered by a court of competent jurisdiction appointing, without the consent of Licensee, a receiver of Licensee or of the whole or any substantial part of its property or approving a petition filed against Licensee seeking reorganization or arrangement of Licensee under the bankruptcy laws or any other applicable law or statute; or

     ii.   Licensee shall fail or refuse to perform any other obligation created by this Agreement of Licensee breaches any term or condition of this Agreement or any other agreement between Licensee and Licensor or its affiliates; or

     iii.   Licensee has made any misrepresentations relating to the acquisition of the license granted herein, or Licensee or any of Licensee's shareholders, officers, directors, or managing personnel engages in conduct which reflects unfavorable on the Name or upon the operation and reputation of the Licensor's business; or

     iv.   Licensee or any of Licensee's shareholders, officers, directors, or managing personnel is convicted of a felony or any other criminal misconduct which is relevant to the operation of the business of Licensee.

In the event of termination of this License for any reason, Licensee shall immediately cease all use of the Name and shall not thereafter use any name, mark or trade name similar thereto. Termination of the license under the provisions of this Section 9 shall be without prejudice to any rights, which Licensor may otherwise have against Licensee.

10. Compliance with Laws and Regulations. Licensee shall, and shall cause its shareholders, officers, directors, and managing personnel to, comply with all laws, rules and government regulations pertaining to its business and shall not violate any laws, which would create an adverse effect on the Name.

11. Relationship of Parties. Licensee shall not in any manner or respect be the legal representative or agent of Licensor and shall not enter into or create any contracts, agreements, or obligations on the part of Licensor, either expressed or implied, nor bind Licensor in any manner or respect whatsoever; it being understood that this Agreement is only a contract for the license of the Name.

12. Name Ownership. Licensee agrees that the Name is the sole property of Licensor and that Licensee has no interest whatsoever in such Name, and Licensee shall use the Name only for so long as the license granted hereby remains in full force and effect. Licensee shall not take any actions, or aid or assist any other party to take any actions that would infringe upon, harm or contest the proprietary rights of Licensor in and to the Name.

13. Other Licensees. Licensee agrees not to interfere in any manner with, or attempt to prohibit the use of the Name by, any other Licensee duly licensed by Licensor. Licensee further agrees to execute any and all documents and assurances reasonably requested by Licensor to effectuate the licensing of the Name to any other party and agrees to cooperate fully with Licensor or any other Licensees of Licensor to protect Licensor's lawful authority to use the Name.

14. Indemnification and Insurance

     a.   Licensee agrees to defend, indemnify and hold harmless Licensor, its officers, affiliates, directors, agents, and employees from and against any and all property damage, personal injuries or death and other liability, loss, cost, expense, or damage, including, without limitation, court costs and reasonable attorney's fees arising out of operations of the Business and from Licensee's breach of any of the terms contained herein.

     b.   Licensee agrees that it will obtain, at its own expense, liability insurance from a recognized insurance company which is qualified to do business in the State of [state/province], providing protection which is standard in the industry for businesses similar to the Business for the benefit of Licensor and its affiliates and their officers, directors, agents, and employees (as well for Licensee) against any claims, suits, loss or damage arising out of or in connection with the Business. As proof of such insurance, a fully paid certificate of insurance naming Licensor as an insured party will be submitted to Licensor by Licensee for Licensor's approval within thirty (30) days after the date of execution of this Agreement. Any proposed change in certificates of insurance shall be submitted to Licensor for its prior approval.

15. Notices. All notices and statements and all payments to be made hereunder, shall be given or made at the respective addresses of the parties as set forth below such party's name unless notification of a change of address is given in writing, and the date of mailing shall be deemed the date the notice or statement is given.

16. No Joint Venture. Nothing herein contained shall be construed to place the parties in the relationship of partners or joint venturers or of franchisor/franchisee.

17. No Assignment or Sublicense by Licensee. This Agreement and all rights an duties hereunder are personal to Licensee and Licensee shall not, without the written consent of Licensor, which consent shall be granted or denied in the sole and absolute discretion of Licensor, be assigned, mortgaged, sublicensed or otherwise encumbered by Licensee or by operation of law.

18. No Waiver, Etc. This Agreement may not be waived or modified except by an express agreement in writing signed by both parties. There are no representations, promises, warranties, covenants or undertakings other than those contained in this Agreement with respect to its subject matter, which represents the entire understanding of the parties. The failure of either party hereto to enforce, or the delay by either party in enforcing, any of its rights under this Agreement shall not be deemed a continuing waiver or a modification thereof and either party may, within the time provided by applicable law, commence appropriate legal proceedings to enforce any or all of such rights.

19. Governing Law. This Agreement shall be construed under the laws of the State of [state/province].

20. Severability. Whenever possible each provision of this Agreement shall be interpreted in such a manner as to be effective and valid under applicable law, but if any provision of this Agreement shall be prohibited, void, invalid, or unenforceable under applicable law, such provision shall be ineffective to the extent of such prohibition, invalidity, voidability, or enforceability without invalidating the remainder of such provision or the remaining provisions of this Agreement.

21. Survival. All obligations of the Licensee shall survive the termination of this Agreement.

22. Attorneys' Fees. Should any litigation be commenced between the parties to this Agreement concerning this Agreement, or the rights and duties of either in relation thereto, the party prevailing in such litigation shall be entitled, in addition to such relief as may be granted, to its attorneys' fees and costs in the litigation.

IN WITNESS WHEREOF, the parties have executed this Agreement as of the date first above written.

LICENSOR   LICENSEE

_____   _____

Authorized Signature   Authorized Signature

_____   _____

Print Name and Title   Print Name and Title

2. Infringement Demand Letter

Date

Mr. _____

Title

Company Name

Street Address

City, State and Zip code

Re: <u>XYZ Registered Trademark "XXX" in classes 9 and 10</u>

Dear Mr. _____,

Attached are copies of XYZ's U.S. registrations for the trademark XXX®. The mark was registered in the U.S. on 28 January 2010 in classes 9 and 10. The mark is also registered in the European Community, Switzerland, Norway and other countries.

Also attached is a copy of marketing information published in the United States by your ABC division for your AAA™ product. We have highlighted your use of our registered trademark.

As your AAA™ product is in the same market and performs the same functions as XYZ's YYY® infant hearing testing product, your use of our registered trademark XXX® with reference to your AAA™ product will inevitably create confusion in the marketplace.

XYZ therefore respectfully requests that your company and all of its affiliates and subsidiaries immediately cease all usage of our XXX® trademark in at least all referenced jurisdictions.

If you have any questions, we are certainly available to discuss this matter with you. However, given the requirements of trademark law, we cannot wait very long for your compliance with our request to cease all use of this registered trademark.

We look forward to hearing from you no later than [one month from date of mailing].

Sincerely,

Your Name

Your Title

Your Company Name

3. Domain Name Infringement Demand Letter

Date

Mr. _____

Title

Company Name

Street Address

City, State and Zip code

Re: XYZ Registered Trademark "XXX" in classes 9 and 10

Dear Mr. _____,

It has recently come to the attention of XYZ, Inc. that you are operating a website at the address www.XYZ.com. It appears that you are offering on this website Internet search services aimed at individuals who use medical software for hand-held computers.

Since at least as early as October 2010, XYZ has advertised, promoted and sold computer software for medical professionals under the mark XYZ. For more details about XYZ's current product line, go to www.XYZ.com. As a result, the XYZ trademark has become well known to consumers and the industry as identifying our client's products. On September 15, 2010, XYZ filed an application for registration of the XYZ trademark with the United States Patent & Trademark Office ("USPTO"), which has since issued. XYZ's use and registration of the XYZ trademark predates by several years your registration of the www.XYZ.com domain name.

Given the above facts, we strongly believe that you wrongfully represented that the www.XYZ.com domain name did not infringe upon or otherwise violate the rights of any third party when you registered the www.XYZ.com domain name and, thus, that registration was made in bad faith. This conclusion is further supported by several UDRP decisions which demonstrate that you have a history of making such bad faith registrations of domain names.

XYZ therefore requests that you immediately transfer the www.XYZ.com domain name to XYZ. If you refuse to do so, XYZ will take swift and appropriate action in response to your infringement of its valuable trademark rights.

Sincerely,

Your Name

Your Title

Your Company Name

4. Complaint

COMPLAINT TRANSMITTAL COVERSHEET

Attached is a Complaint that has been filed against you with the World Intellectual Property Organization (***WIPO***) Arbitration and Mediation Center (the ***Center***) pursuant to the Uniform Domain Name Dispute Resolution Policy (the ***Policy***) adopted by the Internet Corporation for Assigned Names and Numbers (***ICANN***) on October 24, 1999, the Rules for Uniform Domain Name Dispute Resolution Policy (the ***Rules***), and the WIPO Supplemental Rules for Uniform Domain Name Dispute Resolution Policy (the ***Supplemental Rules***).

The Policy is incorporated by reference into your Registration Agreement with the Registrar(s) of your domain name(s), in accordance with which you are required to submit to and participate in a mandatory administrative proceeding in the event that a third party (a ***Complainant***) submits a complaint to a dispute resolution service provider, such as the Center, concerning a domain name that you have registered. You will find the name and contact details of the Complainant, as well as the domain name(s) that is/are the subject of the Complaint in the document that accompanies this Coversheet.

You have no duty to act at this time. Once the Center has checked the Complaint to determine that it satisfies the formal requirements of the Policy, the Rules and the Supplemental Rules, it will forward an official copy of the Complaint to you. You will then have 20 calendar days within which to submit a Response to the Complaint in accordance with the Rules and Supplemental Rules to the Center and the Complainant. Should you so desire, you may wish to seek the assistance of legal counsel to represent you in the administrative proceeding.

- The **Policy** can be found at http://arbiter.wipo.int/domains/rules/

- The **Rules** can be found at http://arbiter.wipo.int/domains/rules/

- The **Supplemental Rules**, as well as other information concerning the resolution of domain name disputes can be found at http://arbiter.wipo.int/domains/rules/

- A **model Response** can be found at
  http://arbiter.wipo.int/domains/respondent/index.html

Alternatively, you may contact the Center to obtain any of the above documents. The Center can be contacted in Geneva, Switzerland by telephone at +41 22 338 8247, by fax at +41 22 740 3700 or by e-mail at domain.disputes@wipo.int.

You are kindly requested to contact the Center to provide the contact details to which you would like (a) the official version of the Complaint and (b) other communications in the administrative proceeding to be sent.

A copy of this Complaint has also been sent to the Registrar(s) with which the domain name(s) that is/are the subject of the Complaint is/are registered.

By submitting this Complaint to the Center the Complainant hereby agrees to abide and be bound by the provisions of the Policy, Rules and Supplemental Rules. ***Before the:***

WORLD INTELLECTUAL PROPERTY ORGANIZATION
ARBITRATION AND MEDIATION CENTER

XYZ, Inc.	
Street Address	
City, State and Zip code	
Complainant	**Disputed Domain Name:**
-v-	xyz.com
	xyzs.com
ABC, Inc.	
Street Address	
City, State and Zip code	
Respondent	

COMPLAINT
(Rules, Para. 3(b))

I.   Introduction

1.   This Complaint is hereby submitted for decision in accordance with the Uniform Policy for Domain Name Dispute Resolution, adopted by the Internet Corporation for Assigned Names and Numbers (**ICANN**) on August 26, 1999 (the **Policy**), the Rules for Uniform Domain Name Dispute Resolution Policy, approved by ICANN on October 24, 1999 (the **Rules**) and the WIPO Supplemental Rules for Uniform Domain Name Dispute Resolution Policy (the **Supplemental Rules**).

II.   The Parties

A.   The Complainant
(Rules, para. 3(b)(ii) and (iii))

2.   The Complainant in this administrative proceeding is XYZ Inc., a California corporation, with its principal place of business at [street address and city], California, United States of America [zip code].

Appendix

3.   The Complainant's contact details are as follows:

Address: Your Name
                XYZ, Inc.
                Street Address
                City, State and Zip code
                United States of America

Telephone: _____

Fax: _____

E-mail: _____

4.   The Complainant's preferred method of communications directed to the Complainant in the administrative proceeding is as follows:

<u>Electronic-only material</u>

Method: e-mail

Address: _____

Contact: _____

<u>Material including hardcopy</u>

Method: Post/courier

Address: XYZ, Inc.

      Street Address

      City, State and Zip code
      United States of America

Contact: _____

B.   The Respondent

(Rules, para. 3(b)(v))

5.   According to the concerned registrar's Whois database, the Respondent in this administrative proceeding is ABC, Inc., [street address, city and state], United States of America [zip code]. Copies of the printouts of the WHOIS database searches for the two domain names at issues, conducted on December 30, 2010 and January 12, 2011 respectively, are provided as Annex 1.

6.   All information known to the Complainant regarding how to contact the Respondent is as follows:

ABC, Inc.

Street Address

City, State and Zip code

United States of America

Telephone: _____

Email: _____

III. The Domain Names and Registrar

(Rules, para, 3(b)(vi) and (vii))

7. This dispute concerns the domain names identified below:

xyz.com

xyzs.com

8. The registrar with which the domain names are registered is:

Company Name

Street Address

City, State and Zip code

Telephone: _____

Email: _____ ; _____

IV. Jurisdictional Basis for the Administrative Proceeding

(Rules, paras. 3(a), 3(b)(xv))

9. This dispute is properly within the scope of the Policy and the Administrative Panel has jurisdiction to decide the dispute. The registration agreement, pursuant to which the domain names that are the subject of this Complaint are registered, incorporates the Policy. The domain name xyz.com was registered on December 15, 2009 and the Uniform Dispute Resolution Policy was incorporated in the registrar's services agreement at that time. The domain name xyzs.com was registered on September 15, 2010 and the Uniform Dispute Resolution Policy was incorporated in the registrar's services agreement at that time. A true and correct copy of the domain name dispute policy that applies to the domain names in question is provided as Annex 2 to this Complaint.

10. In addition, in accordance with Policy, Paragraph 4(a), the Respondent is required to submit to a mandatory administrative proceeding because:

(1) The domain names are identical or confusingly similar to a trademark or service mark in which the Complainant has rights; and

(2) The Respondent has no rights or legitimate interests in respect of the domain names; and

(3) The domain names were registered and are being used in bad faith.

V. Factual and Legal Grounds

(Policy, paras. 4(a), (b), (c); Rules, para. 3)

11. This Complaint is based on the following grounds:

A. COMPLAINANT'S TRADEMARK XYZ

- Complainant XYZ, Inc. ("XYZ" or "Complainant") was founded in 2010 and now is a leading provider of computer software databases related to drug information, drug formularies, infectious diseases, diagnostics and other health-care related topics. XYZ' databases are used by physicians and other health care professionals in the course of rendering care to their patients and can be easily downloaded onto handheld computers or personal digital assistants, or can be accessed through an Internet account.

- XYZ has a network of more than 470,000 subscribers, including more than one in four U.S. physicians, students at every U.S. medical school, and hundreds of thousands of other allied healthcare professionals, who use XYZ mobile and online clinical reference and support solutions daily.

- XYZ has been widely acknowledged for its accomplishments and successes, and copies of exemplary articles from such publications as *Medical Economics, PC Magazine, Forbes, Newsday, Wall Street Journal* and *The New York Times* recognizing high regard for XYZ and its products are attached hereto as Annex 3.

- The high quality and value of XYZ's products is widely recognized by individuals and entities in the health care field, as demonstrated in part by the commitment of Harvard Medical School, the University of Pennsylvania School of Medicine and Duke University Health System, the nation's leading medical schools, to provide their students with access to XYZ databases. XYZ's products have also received positive reviews, appearing in the Journal of the American Journal of Medicine, Advance News Magazines for Nurse Practitioners, and the Indiana University School of Medicine Scope Newsletter, as well as other publications. See Annex 4.

- In addition, XYZ has also received awards and accolades from the computer industry, recognizing the excellence of its products. For example, in 2011, XYZ was recognized as one of the best healthcare solutions for Windows Mobile devices by the editors of PC Magazine; in 2011, XYZ received the "eHealth Impact Award" at the eHealth Institute's annual Developers' Summit for making the greatest positive impact on health and/or health care; and in 2010, XYZ received two PalmSource "Powered Up" awards -- Best Enterprise Solution and Best Overall Solution -- for its innovative software applications. See Annex 5.

- XYZ has a considerable presence on the Internet as evidenced by its primary website, <www.XYZ.com>. In particular, the XYZ website contains information about the company, its products, industry solutions, technology, services, press room, events, and so on. The XYZ website is also the primary distribution channel for the company's software and databases. Copies of exemplary pages from the <www.XYZ.com> website are attached hereto as Annex 6.

- The XYZ trademark is coined and therefore is an arbitrary and strong trademark.

- XYZ is the owner of numerous registrations for trademarks incorporating the word XYZ in connection with computer software and related services:

Country/ Registration No.	Mark	Registration Date
United States 1,234,567	XYZ	August 13, 2009
United States 1,234,568	XYZ DX	November 15, 2009
United States 1,234,569	XYZ HONORS	April 20, 2010
United States 2,896,170	XYZ MEDTOOLS	October 19, 2011
European Union 1234567	XYZ	August 20, 2010
European Union 2234567	XYZ MEDTOOLS	November 26, 2011
Israel 123456	XYZ	June 7, 2010
Japan 1234567	XYZ	December 2, 2010

Copies of the above-listed registration certificates are attached hereto as Annex 7.

- Complainant has used and continues to use the mark XYZ extensively. The mark XYZ is distinctive, and is understood and associated by consumers throughout the world as Complainant's mark, denoting its products, services, and business.

B. **The Three Elements of Paragraph 4(a) of the Policy Are Clearly Present Here.**

1. **The <XYZ.COM> and <XYZS.COM> Domain Names Are Confusingly Similar to the XYZ Trademark.**

- XYZ believes that Respondent registered the <XYZ.com> domain name at issue on November 13, 2009. Sometime thereafter, Respondent introduced its <www.XYZ.com> website which references medical software and resources, including drug and prescription information, as well as software and hardware products related to personal digital assistants. A copy of a printout from this website is attached hereto as Annex 8.

- The <XYZ.com> domain name is virtually identical to Complainant's mark XYZ, with the only difference being the deletion of the letter "s." Thus, the two terms are confusingly similar.

- XYZ believes that Respondent registered the <XYZS.com> domain name at issue on September 1, 2010. Sometime thereafter, Respondent introduced its <www.XYZS.com> website which references medical software and resources, including drug and prescription information, as well as software and hardware products related to personal digital assistants. A copy of a printout from this website is attached hereto as Annex 9.

- The <XYZS.com> domain name is virtually identical to Complainant's mark XYZ, with the only difference being the addition of the letter "s." Thus, the two terms are confusingly similar.

- In this regard, numerous decisions under the ICANN policy recognize that this conduct, commonly referred to as "typo squatting," creates a virtually identical and/or confusingly similar mark to the Complainant's trademark under paragraph 4(a)(i) of the Policy. *See, e.g., Bang & Olufsen a/s v. Unasi Inc.*, WIPO Case No. D2005-0728 (September 7, 2005) § 6A (finding that <bag-olufsen.com>, <bagolufsen.com>, <bang-olusen.com> and <bangolusen.com> are confusingly similar to Bang & Olufsen's mark); *Autosales Inc., dba Summit Racing Equip. v, Domain Active Pty. Ltd.*, WIPO Case No. D2004-0459 (September 3, 2004) § 6A (finding the domain names <summitracin.com> and <wwwsummitracing.com> confusingly similar to Complainant's marks); *CareerBuilder, LLC v. Azra Khan*, WIPO Case No. D2003-0493 (August 5, 2003) § 6A (finding the domain name <careeerbuilder.com> confusingly similar to CareerBuilder's trademarks and service marks); *Wachovia Corp. v. Carrington*, WIPO Case No. D2002-0775 (October 2, 2002) § 6A (finding that <wochovia.com>, <wachvia.com> and <wachovai.com> are confusingly similar to the trademark WACHOVIA); *America Online, Inc. v. Johuanthan Invs., Inc.*, WIPO Case No. D2001-0918 (September 14, 2001) § 6 (finding the domain name <aollnews.com> confusingly similar to trade and service marks in which AOL has rights, namely <aolnews.com>); *Backstreet Prods., Inc. v. Zuccarini*, WIPO Case No. D2001-0654 (August 24, 2001) § 8A (finding, *inter alia*, the domain names <backsreetboys.com> and <backstreetboyz.com> virtually identical and confusingly similar to the Backstreet Boys' mark); *AltaVista Co. v. Yomtobian*, WIPO Case No. D2000-0937 (October 13, 2000) § 6 (finding the domain names <altabista.com> and <altaista.com> confusingly similar to the trademark Alta Vista); *Encyclopaedia Britannica, Inc. v. Zuccarini*, WIPO Case No. D2000-0330 (June 7, 2000), § 3 (finding the domain name <encyclopediabrittanica.com> virtually identical and confusingly similar to Encyclopedia Britannica's mark). Copies of these and all cases cited in this Complaint are attached hereto as Annex 10.

2.   **RESPONDENT HAS NO RIGHTS OR LEGITIMATE INTERESTS IN THE <XYZ.COM> AND < XYZS.COM> DOMAIN NAMES.**

- Respondent is not a distributor or licensee of Complainant. Indeed, Respondent has no relationship with Complainant whatsoever. Complainant has never given its permission or consent to Respondent to use Complainant's well-known trademark XYZ or any other of Complainant's intellectual property.

- Complainant is informed and believes and thereon alleges that Respondent does not own any trademark registrations for or applications to register the marks XYZ or XYZS and that Respondent has not been commonly or otherwise known by the names, "XYZ" or "XYZS."

- Thus, Respondent has no rights or legitimate interest in either the "XYZ" or "XYZS" name.

3. **RESPONDENT HAS REGISTERED AND IS USING THE <XYZ.COM> AND <XYZS.COM> DOMAIN NAMES IN BAD FAITH.**

- Respondent deliberately uses both the www.XYZ.com and www.XYZS.com domain names in an attempt to attract, for commercial gain, Internet users to its websites, by creating a likelihood of confusion with the Complainant's mark as to the source, sponsorship, affiliation, or endorsement of its websites. Respondent registered the domain names at issue to improperly suggest sponsorship by Complainant of Respondent's website.

- In particular, the type of content which Respondent displays on both the www.XYZ.com and www.XYZS.com websites demonstrates that Respondent is aware of the uses connected with the XYZ trademark. Respondent has listed links to what it describes as "popular categories," each of which relate to Complainant's business of providing downloadable software concerning information regarding medications and insurance coverage but which are not associated with Complainant. Those searches include: XYZ Rx, Palm Software, Medical, Drug Information, Pharmacy, Rxfree, Drugs, XYZS, Medical Software, Palm, and the like, as well as links to other categories. See Annexes 8 and 9.

- Misspellings alone, such as that used by Respondent, "are sufficient to prove bad faith under paragraph 4(b)(iv) of the Policy because Respondent has used these names intentionally to attract, for commercial gain, Internet users to his website by creating a likelihood of confusion with the Complainant's mark." *AltaVista Co. v. Yomtobian*, WIPO Case No. D2000-0937 (October 13, 2000).

- Furthermore, Respondent's bad faith is evident by its pattern of conduct in repeatedly using other's misspelled trademarks to attract traffic to its websites. *See, e.g., Mimran Group, Inc. v. LaPorte Holdings,* WIPO Case No. D2005-1016 (December 22, 2005); *NBTY, Inc. v. LaPorte Holdings,* WIPO Case No. D2005-0835 (September 30, 2005); *Sodexho Alliance v. LaPorte Holdings,* WIPO Case No. D2005-0287 (July 2, 2005); *Adorama, Inc. v. LaPorte Holdings, Inc.,* WIPO Case No. D2005-0240 (June 1, 2005); *DaimlerChrysler Corp. et al. v. LaPorte Holdings, Inc.,* WIPO Case No. D2005-0143 (April 1, 2005); *DaimlerChrysler Corp. et al. v. LaPorte Holdings, Inc.,* WIPO Case No. D2005-070 (April 13, 2005); *Matrix Group Ltd., Inc. v. LaPorte Holdings, Inc.,* WIPO Case No. D2005-0059 (April 7, 2005); *Medco Health Solutions, Inc. v. LaPorte Holdings, Inc.,* WIPO Case No. D2004-0800

(December 22, 2004); *Credit Industriel et al. v. LaPorte Holdings, Inc.,* WIPO Case No. D2004-1110 (March 31, 2005); and *Questar Corp. v. LaPorte Holdings, Inc.,* National Arbitration Forum Claim Number: FA0510000573940 (November 28, 2005). Copies of these cases are included in Annex 10.

- Based on the foregoing, it is clear that Respondent has no rights or legitimate interests in the domain names. It is clear that Respondent uses Complainant's well-known trademark to attract Internet users to Respondent's websites and, by so doing, creates a likelihood of confusion with the complainant's mark as to the source, sponsorship, affiliation, or endorsement of the registrant's websites. As such, Respondent registered and uses the domain names in bad faith.

VI. Remedies Requested

(Rules, para. 3(b)(x))

12. In accordance with Paragraph 4(i) of the Policy, for the reasons described in Section V above, the Complainant requests the Administrative Panel appointed in this administrative proceeding issue a decision that the contested domain names be transferred to the Complainant.

VII. Administrative Panel

(Rules, para. 3(b)(iv))

13.   The Complainant elects to have the dispute decided by a single-member Administrative Panel.

VIII. Mutual Jurisdiction

(Rules, para. 3(b)(xiii))

14. In accordance with Paragraph 3(b)(xiii), the Complainant agrees to submit, only with respect to any challenge that may be made by the Respondent to a decision by the Administrative Panel to transfer or cancel the domain names that are the subject of this Complaint, to the jurisdiction of the courts where the principal office of the concerned registrar is located.

IX. Other Legal Proceedings

(Rules, para. 3(b)(xi))

15. No other legal proceedings have been commenced or terminated in connection with or relating to the domain names which are the subject of this Complaint.

X. Communications

(Rules, para. 3(b)(xii); Supplemental Rules, para. 4(b))

16. A copy of this Complaint and Annexes, together with the cover sheet as prescribed by the Supplemental Rules, has been sent or transmitted to the Respondent on February __, 2012 by U.S. Postal Service, to [company name, street address, city and state], United States of America [zip code].

17.   A copy of this Complaint, has been sent or transmitted to the concerned registrar on February __, 2012 by U.S. Postal Service to [company name, street address, city and state], United States of America [zip code].

XI.   **Payment**

18.   As required by the Rules and Supplemental Rules, payment in the amount of USD $1500.00 by check made payable to World Intellectual Property Organization accompanies the paper copy of this complaint.

XII.   **Certification**

(Rules, para. 3(b)(xiv))

19.   The Complainant agrees that its claim and remedies concerning the registration of the domain names, the dispute, or the dispute's resolution shall be solely against the holder of the domain names and waives all such claims and remedies against (a) the WIPO Arbitration and Mediation Center and Panelists, except in the case of deliberate wrongdoing, (b) the concerned registrar(s), (c) the registry administrator, (d) the Internet Corporation for Assigned Names and Numbers, as well as their directors, officers, employees, and agents.

20.   The Complainant certifies that the information contained in this Complaint is to the best of the Complainant's knowledge complete and accurate, that this Complaint is not being presented for any improper purpose, such as to harass, and that the assertions in this Complaint are warranted under the Rules and under applicable law, as it now exists or as it may be extended by a good-faith and reasonable argument.

Respectfully submitted,

_____

Your Name

Your Company Name

Date: February __, 20__

5. Assignment of Service Marks and Trademarks

ASSIGNMENT OF SERVICE MARKS AND TRADEMARKS made as of _____, 20__, by and among XYZ Inc., a _____ corporation with its principal place of business at _____ ("XYZ"), and ABC Corporation, a _____ corporation with its principal place of business at _____ ("ABC") (XYZ and ABC are referred to as "Assignor"), to NYC Corporation, a _____ corporation with its principal place of business _____ ("Assignee").

RECITAL

Assignee and Assignor are parties to an Asset Purchase Agreement dated as of _____, 20__ (the "Agreement"), pursuant to which Assignor has agreed to sell to Assignee and Assignee has agreed to buy from Assignor the Assets (as defined in the Agreement), including without limitation the service marks, trademarks and trade names of Assignor. Pursuant to the Agreement, Assignor has agreed to execute such instruments as the Assignee may reasonably request in order to more effectively assign, transfer, grant, convey, assure and confirm to Assignee and its successors and assigns, or to aid and assist in the collection of or reducing to possession by the Assignee of, all of such assets.

In accordance therewith, Assignor desires to transfer and assign to Assignee, and Assignee desires to accept the transfer and assignment of, all of Assignor's worldwide right, title and interest in, to and under Assignor's registered and unregistered domestic and foreign service marks, trademarks, trademark applications and trade names, including without limitation the service marks, trademarks, service mark and trademark applications and trade names listed on Schedule A annexed hereto and incorporated herein by reference (all of the foregoing being referred to herein as the "Marks").

NOW, THEREFORE, Assignor, for and in exchange for the payment of the purchase price set forth in the Agreement, the receipt of which is hereby acknowledged, does hereby transfer and assign to Assignee, and Assignee hereby accepts the transfer and assignment of, all of Assignor's worldwide right, title and interest in, to and under the Marks, together with the goodwill of the business associated therewith and which is symbolized thereby, all rights to sue for infringement of any Mark, whether arising prior to or subsequent to the date of this Assignment of Service Marks and Trademarks, and any and all renewals and extensions thereof that may hereafter be secured under the laws now or hereafter in effect in the United States, Canada and in any other jurisdiction, the same to be held and enjoyed by the said Assignee, its successors and assigns from and after the date hereof as fully and entirely as the same would have been held and enjoyed by the said Assignor had this Assignment of Service Marks and Trademarks not been made.

Except to the extent that federal law preempts state law with respect to the matters covered hereby, this Assignment of Service Marks and Trademarks shall be governed by and construed in accordance with the laws of the State of _____ without giving effect to the principles of conflicts of laws thereof.

IN WITNESS WHEREOF, Assignor has caused its duly authorized officer to execute this Assignment of Service Marks and Trademarks as of the date first above written.

NYC CORPORATION   ABC CORPORATION

(Assignee):   (Assignor):

Mark Your Territory

By: _____   By: _____

Name: _____   Name: _____

Title: _____   Title: _____

XYZ INC. (Assignor):

By: _____

Name: _____

Title: _____

[SEAL]

State of   )

County of   )

On this _____ day of _____, 20__, before me, _____, personally appeared _____ of _____, personally known to me (or proved to me on the basis of satisfactory evidence) to be the person whose name is subscribed to the within instrument and acknowledged to me that he executed the same in his authorized capacity and that by his signature on the instrument the person, or the entity upon behalf of which the person acted, executed the instrument.

Witness my hand and official seal.

_____

Notary Public

6. Trademark Ownership and License Agreement

TRADEMARK OWNERSHIP AND LICENSE AGREEMENT

This Trademark Ownership and License Agreement (the "Agreement") is effective as of _____ (the "Effective Date"), between XYZ Corporation, a _____ corporation ("XYZ"), having an office at _____, and ABC, Inc., a _____ corporation ("ABC"), having an office at _____.

WHEREAS, the Board of Directors of XYZ has determined that it is in the best interest of XYZ and its stockholders to separate XYZ's existing businesses into two independent businesses;

WHEREAS, as part of the foregoing, XYZ and ABC have entered into a Separation Agreement (as defined below) which provides, among other things, for the separation of certain ABC assets and ABC liabilities, the initial public offering of ABC stock, the distribution of such stock and the execution and delivery of certain other agreements in order to facilitate and provide for the foregoing;

WHEREAS, the parties desire that XYZ assign and transfer to ABC the ABC Business Marks (as defined below); and

WHEREAS, the parties further desire that XYZ license the Licensed Marks (as defined below) to ABC after the separation of the ABC businesses.

NOW, THEREFORE, in consideration of the mutual promises of the parties, and of good and valuable consideration, it is agreed by and between the parties as follows:

ARTICLE I

DEFINITIONS

For the purpose of this Agreement, the following capitalized terms are defined in this Article I and shall have the meaning specified herein:

1.1   ABC BUSINESS. "ABC Business" means (a) the business and operations of the following business entities of XYZ, as described in the IPO Registration Statement (as defined in the Separation Agreement):

1.2   ABC BUSINESS MARKS. **[Need to determine if there are ABC trademarks owned by XYZ that need to be assigned to ABC.]** "ABC Business Marks" means the Marks listed in the ABC Business Marks Database.

1.3   ABC BUSINESS MARKS DATABASE. "ABC Business Marks Database" means the ABC Business Marks Database, as it may be updated by the parties upon mutual agreement to add additional Marks as of the Separation Date.

1.4   ABC BUSINESS PRODUCTS means **[Need to determine what products and new versions may keep the XYZ mark after termination]**

1.5   AFFILIATED COMPANY. "Affiliated Company" means, with respect to XYZ, any entity in which XYZ holds a 50% or less ownership interest and that is listed on Exhibit A hereto and, with respect to ABC, any entity in which ABC holds a 50% or less ownership interest and that is listed on Exhibit A hereto; provided, however, that any such entity listed in Exhibit A shall be considered to be an Affiliated Company under this Agreement only if it agrees in writing to be bound by the terms and conditions of this Agreement. Exhibit A may be amended from time to time after the date hereof upon mutual consent of the parties. **[Need to determine if there are any non-controlled subsidiaries (i.e. joint ventures) that should be under this Agreement.]**

1.6   AUTHORIZED DEALERS. "Authorized Dealers" means any distributor, dealer, OEM customer, VAR customer, VAD customer, systems integrator or other agent that on or after the Separation Date is authorized to market, advertise, sell, lease, rent, service or otherwise offer ABC Business Products. ABC will provide XYZ a list of the then current Authorized Dealers within a reasonable period after XYZ's request.

1.7   COLLATERAL MATERIALS. "Collateral Materials" means all packaging, tags, labels, advertising, promotions, display fixtures, instructions, warranties and other materials of any and all types associated with the ABC Business Products that are marked with at least one of the Licensed Marks.

1.8   CORPORATE IDENTITY MATERIALS. "Corporate Identity Materials" means materials that are not products or product-related and that ABC may now or hereafter use to communicate its identity, including, by way of example and without limitation, business cards, letterhead, stationery, paper stock and other supplies, signage on real property, buildings, fleet and uniforms.

1.9   DISTRIBUTION DATE. "Distribution Date" has the meaning set forth in the Separation Agreement.

1.10   LICENSED MARKS. **[Does ABC need a transitional license to XYZ trademarks?]** "Licensed Marks" means the Marks set forth on Exhibit A hereto.

1.11   MAINTENANCE CONTRACTS. "Maintenance Contracts" means agreements pursuant to which ABC, its Subsidiaries or Affiliated Companies or its or their Authorized Dealers or their designees provide repair and maintenance services (whether preventive, diagnostic, remedial, warranty or non-warranty) in connection with ABC Business Products, including without limitation agreements entered into by XYZ prior to the Separation Date and assigned to ABC pursuant to the Separation Agreement or the Ancillary Agreements (as such term is defined in the Separation Agreement).

1.12   MARK. "Mark" means any trademark, service mark, trade name, domain name, and the like, or other word, name, symbol or device, or any combination thereof, used or intended to be used by a Person to identify and distinguish the products or services of that Person from the products or services of others and to indicate the source of such goods or services, including without limitation all registrations and applications therefor throughout the world and all common law and other rights therein throughout the world.

1.13   PERSON. "Person" means an individual, a partnership, a corporation, a limited liability company, an association, a joint stock company, a trust, a joint venture, an unincorporated organization, and a governmental entity or any department, agency or political subdivision thereof.

1.14   QUALITY STANDARDS. "Quality Standards" means standards of quality applicable to the ABC Business Products, as in use immediately prior to the Separation Date, unless otherwise communicated in writing by XYZ from time to time.

1.15   SELL. To "Sell" a product means to sell, transfer, lease or otherwise dispose of a product. "Sale" and "Sold" have the corollary meanings ascribed thereto.

1.16   SEPARATION AGREEMENT. "Separation Agreement" means the Separation and Distribution Agreement between the parties.

1.17   SEPARATION DATE. "Separation Date" means _____ or such other date as may be fixed by the Board of Directors of XYZ.

1.18   SUBSIDIARY. "Subsidiary" means with respect to any specified Person, any corporation, any limited liability company, any partnership or other legal entity of which such Person owns, directly or indirectly, more than 50% of the stock or other equity interest entitled to vote on the election of the members of the board of directors or similar governing body. Unless the context otherwise requires, reference to XYZ and its Subsidiaries shall not include the subsidiaries of XYZ that will be transferred to ABC after giving effect to the Separation (as defined in the Separation Agreement), including the actions taken pursuant to the Non-US Plan (as defined in the Separation Agreement). For example, if XYZ owns 70% of the stock of another corporation, and that corporation owns 60% of the equity interest of a limited liability company, then that corporation is a Subsidiary of XYZ but that limited liability company is not. However, if such corporation owns 90% of the equity interest of a limited liability company, then that limited liability company is a Subsidiary of XYZ. For the avoidance of doubt, this definition of Subsidiary is different from the definition of Subsidiary in the Separation Agreement.

1.19   THIRD PARTY. "Third Party" means a Person other than XYZ and its Subsidiaries and Affiliated Companies and ABC and its Subsidiaries and Affiliated Companies.

1.20   TRADEMARK USAGE GUIDELINES. "Trademark Usage Guidelines" means the guidelines for proper usage of the Licensed Marks, as in use immediately prior to the Separation Date, as such guidelines may be revised and updated in writing by XYZ from time to time.

ARTICLE II

ASSIGNMENT

2.1   ASSIGNMENT OF ABC BUSINESS MARKS. **[Need to determine if there are ABC trademarks owned by XYZ that need to be assigned to ABC.]** Subject to Sections 2.2 and 2.3 below, XYZ hereby grants, conveys and assigns (and agrees to cause its appropriate Subsidiaries to grant, convey and assign) to ABC, by execution hereof (or, where appropriate or required, by execution of separate instruments of assignment), all its (and their) right, title and interest in and to the ABC Business Marks, including all goodwill of the ABC Business appurtenant thereto, to be held and enjoyed by ABC, its successors and assigns. XYZ further grants, conveys and assigns (and agrees to cause its appropriate Subsidiaries to grant, convey and assign) to ABC all its (and their) right, title and interest in and to any and all causes of action and rights of recovery for past infringement of the ABC Business Marks. XYZ will, without demanding any further consideration therefor, at the request and expense of ABC (except for the value of the time of XYZ employees), do (and to cause its Subsidiaries to do) all lawful and just acts that may be or become necessary for evidencing, maintaining, recording and perfecting ABC's rights to such ABC Business Marks consistent with XYZ's general business practice as of the Separation Date, including but not limited to execution and acknowledgement of (and causing its Subsidiaries to execute and acknowledge) assignments and other instruments in a form reasonably required by ABC or the relevant governmental or other authorities for each Mark in all jurisdictions in which XYZ owns rights thereto.

2.2   PRIOR GRANTS.   ABC acknowledges and agrees that the foregoing assignment is subject to any and all licenses or other rights that may have been granted by XYZ or its Subsidiaries with respect to the ABC Business Marks prior to the Separation Date. XYZ shall respond to reasonable inquiries from ABC regarding any such prior grants.

2.3   ASSIGNMENT DISCLAIMER.   ABC ACKNOWLEDGES AND AGREES THAT THE FOREGOING ASSIGNMENTS ARE MADE ON AN "AS-IS," QUITCLAIM BASIS AND THAT NEITHER XYZ NOR ANY SUBSIDIARY OR AFFILIATED COMPANY OF XYZ HAS MADE OR WILL MAKE ANY WARRANTY WHATSOEVER, EXPRESS, IMPLIED OR STATUTORY, INCLUDING, WITHOUT LIMITATION, ANY IMPLIED WARRANTIES OF TITLE, ENFORCEABILITY OR NON-INFRINGEMENT.

ARTICLE III

LICENSE

3.1   LICENSE GRANT.   **[Does ABC need a transitional license to XYZ trademarks? Need to determine if license should be perpetual or limited and tax implications of such choice.]** XYZ grants (and agrees to cause its appropriate Subsidiaries to grant) to ABC a personal, irrevocable, nonexclusive, perpetual, worldwide, fully-paid and non-transferable (except as set forth in Section 14.9) license to use the Licensed Marks on the ABC Business Products and in connection with the Sale and offer for Sale of ABC Business Products (or, in the case of ABC Business Products in the form of software, in connection with licensing of ABC Business Products) and to use the Licensed Marks in the advertisement and promotion of such ABC Business Products.

3.2   LICENSE RESTRICTIONS.   As a condition to the licenses granted hereunder, ABC undertakes to XYZ that:

3.2.1   Once ABC abandons the use of all of the Licensed Marks on a particular ABC Business Product, then ABC agrees that its license granted hereunder with respect to that ABC Business Product shall thereupon terminate.

3.2.2   ABC may not make any use whatsoever, in whole or in part, of the Licensed Marks, or any other Mark owned by XYZ, in connection with ABC's corporate, doing business as, or fictitious name, or on Corporate Identity Materials without the prior written consent of XYZ, except as expressly set forth in this Section 3.2(b) or in Section 3.4 below. Notwithstanding the foregoing, ABC may use any business cards, letterhead, stationery, paper stock and other supplies, uniforms and the like throughout their useful life in connection with the conduct of the ABC Business, to the extent that, as of the Separation Date, they are in use, in inventory or on order.

3.2.3   ABC may not use any Licensed Mark in direct association with another Mark such that the two Marks appear to be a single Mark or in any other composite manner with any Marks of ABC or any Third Party (other than the ABC Business Marks as permitted herein).

Appendix

3.2.4 In all respects, ABC's usage of the Licensed Marks pursuant to the license granted hereunder shall be in a manner consistent with the high standards, reputation and prestige represented by the Licensed Marks, and any usage by ABC that is inconsistent with the foregoing shall be deemed to be outside the scope of the license granted hereunder. As a condition to the license granted hereunder, ABC shall at all times present, position and promote the ABC Business Products marked with one or more of the Licensed Marks in a manner consistent with the high standards and prestige represented by the Licensed Marks.

3.3 LICENSEE UNDERTAKINGS. As a condition to the licenses granted hereunder, ABC undertakes to XYZ that:

3.3.1 ABC shall not use the Licensed Marks (or any other Mark of XYZ) in any manner contrary to public morals, in any manner which is deceptive or misleading, which ridicules or is derogatory to the Licensed Marks, or which compromises or reflects unfavorably upon the goodwill, good name, reputation or image of XYZ or the Licensed Marks, or which might jeopardize or limit XYZ's proprietary interest therein.

3.3.2 ABC shall not use the Licensed Marks in connection with any products or services other than the ABC Business Products, including, without limitation, any other products of the ABC Business.

3.3.3 ABC shall not (i) misrepresent to any Person the scope of its authority under this Agreement, (ii) incur or authorize any expenses or liabilities chargeable to XYZ, or (iii) take any actions that would impose upon XYZ any obligation or liability to a Third Party other than obligations under this Agreement, or other obligations which XYZ expressly approves in writing for ABC to incur on its behalf.

3.3.4 All press releases and corporate advertising and promotions that embody the Licensed Marks and messages conveyed thereby shall be consistent with the high standards and prestige represented by the Licensed Marks.

3.4 NON-TRADEMARK USE. Each party may make appropriate and truthful references to the other party and the other party's products and technology.

3.5 RESERVATION OF RIGHTS. Except as otherwise expressly provided in this Agreement, XYZ shall retain all rights in and to the Licensed Marks, including without limitation:

3.5.1 All rights of ownership in and to the Licensed Marks;

3.5.2 The right to use (including the right of XYZ's Subsidiaries and Affiliated Companies to use) the Licensed Marks, either alone or in combination with other Marks, in connection with the marketing, offer or provision of any product or service, including any product or service which competes with ABC Business products; and

3.5.3 The right to license Third Parties to use the Licensed Marks.

3.6 THIRD PARTY LICENSES. **[Need to determine if this restriction is appropriate.]** XYZ agrees that it and its Subsidiaries and Affiliated Companies will not license or transfer the Licensed Marks to Third Parties (other than to and among Subsidiaries of XYZ) for use in connection with products or services which compete with ABC Business Products that are listed on an ABC corporate price list as of the Distribution Date until three (3) years after the Separation Date. Such restriction shall be binding on any successors and assigns of the Licensed Marks.

ARTICLE IV

PERMITTED SUBLICENSES

a. SUBLICENSES

i. SUBLICENSES TO SUBSIDIARIES AND AFFILIATED COMPANIES. Subject to the terms and conditions of this Agreement, including all applicable Quality Standards and Trademark Usage Guidelines and other restrictions in this Agreement, ABC may grant sublicenses to its Subsidiaries and Affiliated Companies to use the Licensed Marks in accordance with the license grant in Section 3.1 above; provided, that (i) ABC enters into a written sublicense agreement with each such Subsidiary and Affiliated Company sublicensee, and (ii) such agreement does not include the right to grant further sublicenses other than, in the case of a sublicensed Subsidiary of ABC, to another Subsidiary of ABC. ABC shall provide copies of such written sublicense agreements to XYZ upon request. If ABC grants any sublicense rights pursuant to this Section 4.1(a) and any such sublicensed Subsidiary ceases to be a Subsidiary or ABC ceases to hold at least a thirty percent (30%) ownership interest in such sublicensed Affiliated Company, then the sublicense granted to such Subsidiary or Affiliated Company pursuant to this Section 4.1(a) shall terminate _____ (__) days from the date of such cessation.

ii. SUBLICENSES TO TRANSFEREES. In addition, if ABC, within _____ (__) years after the Separation Date, transfers a going business (but not all or substantially all of its business or assets), and such transfer includes at least one marketable product and tangible assets having a net value of at least _____ U.S. dollars ($____) then, subject to the terms and conditions of this Agreement, including all applicable Quality Standards and Trademark Usage Guidelines and other restrictions in this Agreement, ABC may grant sublicenses to the transferee of such business to use the Licensed Marks on the ABC Business Products that are in the transferred business as of the effective date of the transfer in accordance with the license grant in Section 3.1 above; provided, that (i) ABC enters into a written sublicense agreement with the sublicensee, (ii) such agreement does not include the right to grant further sublicenses and (iii) in any event, such sublicense shall terminate one hundred eighty (180) days after the effective date of the transfer. ABC shall provide copies of such written sublicense agreements to XYZ upon request.

b. AUTHORIZED DEALERS' USE OF MARKS. Subject to the terms and conditions of this Agreement, including all applicable Quality Standards and Trademark Usage Guidelines and other restrictions in this Agreement, ABC (and those Subsidiaries and Affiliated Companies sublicensed to use the Licensed Marks pursuant to Section 4.1) may allow Authorized Dealers to, and may allow such Authorized Dealers to allow other Authorized Dealers to, use the Licensed Marks in the advertisement and promotion of ABC Business Products Sold by such Authorized Dealers.

c. ENFORCEMENT OF AGREEMENTS. ABC shall take all appropriate measures at ABC's expense promptly and diligently to enforce the terms of any sublicense agreement or other agreement with any Subsidiary, Affiliated Company or Authorized Dealer, or of any existing agreement with any Authorized Dealer, and shall restrain any such Subsidiary, Affiliated Company or Authorized Dealer from violating such terms, including without limitation (i) monitoring the Subsidiaries', Affiliated Companies' and Authorized Dealers' compliance with the relevant Trademark Usage Guidelines and Quality Standards and causing any noncomplying Subsidiary, Affiliated Company or Authorized Dealer promptly to remedy any failure, (ii) terminating such agreement and/or

338

(iii) commencing legal action, in each case, using a standard of care consistent with XYZ's practices as of the Separation Date. In the event that XYZ determines that ABC has failed promptly and diligently to enforce the terms of any such agreement using such standard of care, XYZ reserves the right to enforce such terms, and ABC shall reimburse XYZ for its fully allocated direct costs and expenses incurred in enforcing such agreement, plus all out-of-pocket costs and expenses, plus five percent (5%) (or, if such costs and expenses are incurred more than two (2) years after the Separation Date, ten percent (10%)). **[Need to determine what appropriate remedy should be for failing to enforce a trademark agreement.]**

ARTICLE V

ROYALTIES

5.1   ROYALTIES **[Will there be any royalties? Tax concerns may drive this section.]** Upon (i) any Sale occurring more than five (5) years after the Separation Date by ABC, its Subsidiaries or Affiliated Companies of tangible ABC Business Products that are marked with one or more of the Licensed Marks (other than repaired, refurbished or reconstructed ABC Business Products or repair parts and other than Sales to XYZ, its Subsidiaries and its Affiliated Companies), and (ii) the use by ABC, its Subsidiaries or Affiliated Companies of one or more of the Licensed Marks as a service mark in connection with the sale of services associated with ABC Business Products (other than repair, maintenance and calibration services and other than sales to XYZ, its Subsidiaries and its Affiliated Companies), ABC shall pay to XYZ a royalty on the Net Sales earned by ABC in each ABC fiscal quarter as a result of such sale. The royalty rate shall be the standard royalty rate that is charged by XYZ to the ABC Business as of the Separation Date for use of the Licensed Marks.

5.1.1   As used in this Article V, "Net Sales" means the gross invoice price from (i) royalty-bearing Sales under Section 5.1(a)(i) above and (ii) royalty-bearing sales of services under Section 5.1(a)(ii) above, in any case less (A) charges for handling, freight, sales taxes, insurance costs and import duties where such items are included in the invoiced price, (B) point-of-sale credits (or other similar adjustments to price) granted to independent distributors and (C) credits actually granted or refunds actually given for returns during such ABC fiscal quarter. In the event that the foregoing ABC Business Products are Sold for no or nominal consideration or to a Subsidiary or Affiliated Company or in any other circumstances in which the selling price is established on other than an arms-length basis, the Net Sales on such Sales shall be determined on the average selling price earned by ABC during the preceding ABC fiscal quarter on Sales of like volumes of the applicable ABC Business Products to unaffiliated customers in arms-length sales. However, in the event that the foregoing ABC Business Products are Sold to ABC's Subsidiaries or Affiliated Companies for resale to Third Parties, then the royalties will be based on Net Sales from the Subsidiaries or Affiliated Companies to the Third Parties and no royalties will be due on the Sales to the Subsidiaries and Affiliated Companies.

5.1.2   For the purposes of clarification, no royalty is due under this Article V for uses of the Licensed Marks that are covered by Section 3.4.

5.2   PAYMENTS AND ACCOUNTING. With respect to the royalties set forth herein, ABC shall keep full, clear and accurate records until otherwise provided in Section 5.2(b). These records shall be retained for a period of three (3) years from the date of payment notwithstanding the expiration or other termination of this Agreement. XYZ shall have the right, through a mutually agreed upon independent certified public accountant (consent to which shall not be unreasonably withheld or delayed by ABC), and at XYZ's expense, to examine and audit, not more than once a year, and during normal business hours, all such records and such other records and accounts as may under recognized accounting practices contain information bearing upon the amount of royalty payable to XYZ under this Agreement. Prompt adjustment shall be made by either party to compensate for any errors and/or omissions disclosed by such examination or audit. Should any such error and/or omission result in an underpayment of more than five percent (5%) of the total royalties due for the period under audit, ABC shall upon XYZ's request pay for the cost of the audit and pay XYZ an additional fee equal to a compound annual interest rate of ten percent (10%) of such error and/or omission.

        5.2.1   Within forty-five (45) days after the end of each ABC fiscal quarter, ABC shall furnish to XYZ a statement in suitable form showing all ABC Business Products and related services subject to royalties that were sold, during such quarter, and the amount of royalty payable thereon. If no products or services subject to royalty have been sold, that fact shall be shown on such statement. Also, within such forty-five (45) days, ABC shall pay to XYZ the royalties payable hereunder for such quarter. XYZ and ABC will determine the form of the statement prior to submission of the first such statement. All royalty and other payments to XYZ hereunder shall be in United States dollars. Royalties based on sales in other currencies shall be converted to United States dollars according to the official rate of exchange for that currency, as published in the Wall Street Journal on the last day of the calendar month in which the royalty accrued (or, if not published on that day, the last publication day for the Wall Street Journal during that month). If two consecutive ABC fiscal quarters pass in which no royalties are due under this Agreement and ABC reasonably believes no royalties will be due, the obligations pursuant to this Article V shall terminate. If ABC resumes sale of ABC Business Products or related services that are subject to royalties, the obligations of this Article V shall automatically resume.

ARTICLE VI

TRADEMARK USAGE GUIDELINES

        6.1   TRADEMARK USAGE GUIDELINES.   ABC and its Subsidiaries, Affiliated Companies and Authorized Dealers shall use the Licensed Marks only in a manner that is consistent with the Trademark Usage Guidelines.

        6.2   TRADEMARK REVIEWS. At XYZ's request, ABC agrees to furnish or make available for inspection to XYZ samples of all ABC Business Products and Collateral Materials of ABC, its Subsidiaries, Affiliated Companies and Authorized Dealers that are marked with one or more of the Licensed Marks (to the extent that ABC has the right to obtain such samples). If ABC is notified or determines that it or any of its Subsidiaries, Affiliated Companies or Authorized Dealers is not complying with any Trademark Usage Guidelines, it shall notify XYZ and the provisions of Article VII and Section 4.3 shall apply to such noncompliance.

ARTICLE VII

TRADEMARK USAGE GUIDELINE ENFORCEMENT

        7.1   INITIAL CURE PERIOD. If XYZ becomes aware that ABC or any Subsidiary, Affiliated Company or Authorized Dealer is not complying with any Trademark Usage Guidelines, XYZ shall notify ABC in writing, setting forth in reasonable detail a written description of the noncompliance and any requested action for curing such noncompliance. ABC shall then have sixty (60) days with regard to noncompliance by Authorized Dealers and thirty (30) days with regard to noncompliance by ABC or any Subsidiary or Affiliated Company after receipt of such notice ("Guideline Initial Cure

Appendix

Period") to correct such noncompliance or submit to XYZ a written plan to correct such noncompliance which written plan is reasonably acceptable to XYZ.

7.2 SECOND CURE PERIOD. If noncompliance with the Trademark Usage Guidelines continues beyond the Guideline Initial Cure Period, ABC and XYZ shall each promptly appoint a representative to negotiate in good faith actions that may be necessary to correct such noncompliance. The parties shall have thirty (30) days following the expiration of the Guideline Initial Cure Period to agree on corrective actions, and ABC shall have thirty (30) days from the date of an agreement of corrective actions to implement such corrective actions and cure or cause the cure of such noncompliance ("Second Guideline Cure Period").

7.3 FINAL CURE PERIOD. If the noncompliance with the Trademark Usage Guidelines remains uncured after the expiration of the Second Guideline Cure Period, then at XYZ's election, ABC, or the noncomplying Subsidiary, Affiliated Company or Authorized Dealer, whichever is applicable, promptly shall cease using the noncomplying Collateral Materials until XYZ determines that ABC, or the noncomplying Subsidiary, Affiliated Company or Authorized Dealer, whichever is applicable, has demonstrated its ability and commitment to comply with the Trademark Usage Guidelines. Nothing in this Article VII shall be deemed to limit ABC's obligations under Section 4.3 above or to preclude XYZ from exercising any rights or remedies under Section 4.3 above.

ARTICLE VIII

QUALITY STANDARDS

8.1 GENERAL. ABC acknowledges that the ABC Business Products permitted by this Agreement to be marked with one or more of the Licensed Marks must continue to be of sufficiently high quality as to provide protection of the Licensed Marks and the goodwill they symbolize, and ABC further acknowledges that the maintenance of the high quality standards associated with such products is of the essence of this Agreement.

8.2 QUALITY STANDARDS. ABC and its Authorized Dealers, Affiliated Companies and Subsidiaries shall use the Licensed Marks only on and in connection with ABC Business Products that meet or exceed in all respects the Quality Standards.

8.3 QUALITY CONTROL REVIEWS. At XYZ's request, ABC agrees to furnish or make available to XYZ for inspection sample ABC Business Products marked with one or more of the Licensed Marks. XYZ may also independently conduct customer satisfaction surveys to determine if ABC and its Subsidiaries, Affiliated Companies and Authorized Dealers are meeting the Quality Standards. ABC shall cooperate with XYZ fully in the distribution of such surveys. In the event of a challenge by XYZ, XYZ shall, at the request of ABC, provide ABC with copies of customer surveys used by XYZ to determine if ABC is meeting the Quality Standards. If ABC is notified or determines that it or any of its Subsidiaries, Affiliated Companies or Authorized Dealers is not complying with any Quality Standards, it shall notify XYZ and the provisions of Article IX and Section 4.3 shall apply to such noncompliance.

8.4 PRODUCT DISCONTINUATION. If, at any time during or after the term of this Agreement, ABC discontinues the sale of a ABC Business Product that has been marked with one or more of the Licensed Marks, ABC shall substantially comply with the discontinuation procedure used by XYZ for such or similar products immediately prior to Separation Date.

ARTICLE IX

QUALITY STANDARD ENFORCEMENT

9.1   INITIAL CURE PERIOD. If XYZ becomes aware that ABC or any Subsidiary, Affiliated Company or Authorized Dealer sublicensee is not complying with any Quality Standards, XYZ shall notify ABC in writing, setting forth in reasonable detail a written description of the noncompliance and any requested action for curing such noncompliance. ABC shall then have thirty (30) days after receipt of such notice ("Initial Cure Period") to correct such noncompliance or submit to XYZ a written plan to correct such noncompliance which written plan is reasonably acceptable to XYZ.

9.2   SECOND CURE PERIOD. If noncompliance with the Quality Standards continues beyond the Initial Cure Period, ABC and XYZ shall each promptly appoint a representative to negotiate in good faith actions that may be necessary to correct such noncompliance. The parties shall have thirty (30) days following the expiration of the Initial Cure Period to agree on corrective actions, and ABC shall have thirty (30) days from the date of an agreement of corrective actions to implement such corrective actions and cure or cause the cure of such noncompliance ("Second Cure Period").

9.3   FINAL CURE PERIOD. If the noncompliance with the Quality Standards remains uncured after the expiration of the Second Cure Period, then at XYZ's election, ABC, or the noncomplying Subsidiary, Affiliated Company or Authorized Dealer, whichever is applicable, promptly shall cease offering the noncomplying ABC Business Products under the Licensed Marks until XYZ determines that ABC, or the noncomplying Subsidiary, Affiliated Company or Authorized Dealer, whichever is applicable, has demonstrated its ability and commitment to comply with the Quality Standards. Nothing in this Article IX shall be deemed to limit ABC's obligations under Section 4.3 above or to preclude XYZ from exercising any rights or remedies under Section 4.3 above.

ARTICLE X

PROTECTION OF LICENSED MARKS

10.1   OWNERSHIP AND RIGHTS. ABC agrees not to challenge the ownership or validity of the Licensed Marks. ABC shall not disparage, dilute or adversely affect the validity of the Licensed Marks. ABC's use of the Licensed Marks shall inure exclusively to the benefit of XYZ, and ABC shall not acquire or assert any rights therein. ABC recognizes the value of the goodwill associated with the Licensed Marks, and that the Licensed Marks may have acquired secondary meaning in the minds of the public.

10.2   PROTECTION OF MARKS. ABC shall assist XYZ, at XYZ's request and expense, in the procurement and maintenance of XYZ's intellectual property rights in the Licensed Marks. ABC will not grant or attempt to grant a security interest in the Licensed Marks, or to record any such security interest in the United States Patent and Trademark Office or elsewhere, against any trademark application or registration belonging to XYZ. ABC agrees to, and to cause its Subsidiaries and Affiliated Companies to, execute all documents reasonably requested by XYZ to effect further registration of, maintenance and renewal of the Licensed Marks, recordation of the license relationship between XYZ and ABC, and recordation of ABC as a registered user. XYZ makes no warranty or representation that trademark registrations have been or will be applied for, secured or maintained in the Licensed Marks throughout, or anywhere within, the world. ABC shall cause to appear on all ABC Business Products, and all Collateral Materials, such legends, markings and notices as may be required by applicable law or reasonably requested by XYZ.

10.3   SIMILAR MARKS. ABC agrees not to use or register in any country any Mark that infringes XYZ's rights in the Licensed Marks, or any element thereof. If any application for registration is, or has been, filed in any country by ABC which relates to any Mark that infringes XYZ's rights in the Licensed Marks, ABC shall immediately abandon any such application or registration or assign it to XYZ. ABC shall not challenge XYZ's ownership of or the validity of the Licensed Marks or any application for registration thereof throughout the world. ABC shall not use or register in any country any copyright, domain name, telephone number or any other intellectual property right, whether recognized currently or in the future, or other designation which would affect the ownership or rights of XYZ in and to the Licensed Marks, or otherwise to take any action which would adversely affect any of such ownership rights, or assist anyone else in doing so. ABC shall cause its Subsidiaries, Affiliated Companies and Authorized Dealers to comply with the provisions of this Section 10.3.

10.4   INFRINGEMENT PROCEEDINGS. In the event that the ABC Director of Intellectual Property or ABC Trademark Counsel learns of any infringement or threatened infringement of the Licensed Marks, or any unfair competition, passing-off or dilution with respect to the Licensed Marks, ABC shall notify XYZ or its authorized representative giving particulars thereof, and ABC shall provide necessary information and assistance to XYZ or its authorized representatives at XYZ's expense in the event that XYZ decides that proceedings should be commenced. Notwithstanding the foregoing, ABC is not obligated to monitor or police use of the Licensed Marks by Third Parties other than as specifically set forth in Section 4.3. XYZ shall have exclusive control of any litigation, opposition, cancellation or related legal proceedings. The decision whether to bring, maintain or settle any such proceedings shall be at the exclusive option and expense of XYZ, and all recoveries shall belong exclusively to XYZ. ABC shall not and shall have no right to initiate any such litigation, opposition, cancellation or related legal proceedings in its own name, but, at XYZ's request, agrees to be joined as a party in any action taken by XYZ to enforce its rights in the Licensed Marks. XYZ shall incur no liability to ABC or any other Person under any legal theory by reason of XYZ's failure or refusal to prosecute or by XYZ's refusal to permit ABC to prosecute, any alleged infringement by Third Parties, nor by reason of any settlement to which XYZ may agree.

ARTICLE XI

TERMINATION

11.1   VOLUNTARY TERMINATION. By written notice to XYZ, ABC may voluntarily terminate all or a specified portion of the licenses and rights granted to it hereunder by XYZ. Such notice shall specify the effective date of such termination and shall clearly specify any affected Licensed Marks, ABC Business Products or services.

11.2   SURVIVAL. Any voluntary termination of licenses and rights of ABC under Section 11.1 shall not affect ABC's licenses and rights with respect to any ABC Business Products made or furnished prior to such termination.

11.3   OTHER TERMINATION. XYZ acknowledges and agrees that its rights to terminate the licenses granted to ABC hereunder are solely as set forth in Section 4.3 and Articles VII and IX.

ARTICLE XII

DISPUTE RESOLUTION

12.1   NEGOTIATION. The parties shall make a good faith attempt to resolve any dispute or claim arising out of or related to this Agreement through negotiation. Within thirty (30) days after notice of a dispute or claim is given by either party to the other party, the parties' first tier negotiating teams (as determined by each party's Director of Intellectual Property or his or her delegate) shall meet and make a good faith attempt to resolve such dispute or claim and shall continue to negotiate in good faith in an effort to resolve the dispute or claim or renegotiate the applicable section or provision without the necessity of any formal proceedings. If the first tier negotiating teams are unable to agree within thirty (30) days of their first meeting, then the parties' second tier negotiating teams (as determined by each party's Director of Intellectual Property or his or her delegate) shall meet within thirty (30) days after the end of the first thirty (30) day negotiating period to attempt to resolve the matter. During the course of negotiations under this Section 12.1, all reasonable requests made by one party to the other for information, including requests for copies of relevant documents, will be honored. The specific format for such negotiations will be left to the discretion of the designated negotiating teams but may include the preparation of agreed upon statements of fact or written statements of position furnished to the other party.

12.2   NONBINDING MEDIATION. In the event that any dispute or claim arising out of or related to this Agreement is not settled by the parties within fifteen (15) days after the first meeting of the second tier negotiating teams under Section 12.1, the parties will attempt in good faith to resolve such dispute or claim by nonbinding mediation in accordance with the American Arbitration Association Commercial Mediation Rules. The mediation shall be held within thirty (30) days of the end of such fifteen (15) day negotiation period of the second tier negotiating teams. Except as provided below in Section 12.3, no litigation for the resolution of such dispute may be commenced until the parties try in good faith to settle the dispute by such mediation in accordance with such rules, and either party has concluded in good faith that amicable resolution through continued mediation of the matter does not appear likely. The costs of mediation shall be shared equally by the parties to the mediation. Any settlement reached by mediation shall be recorded in writing, signed by the parties, and shall be binding on them.

12.3   PROCEEDINGS. Nothing herein, however, shall prohibit either party from initiating litigation or other judicial or administrative proceedings if such party would be substantially harmed by a failure to act during the time that such good faith efforts are being made to resolve the dispute or claim through negotiation or mediation. In the event that litigation is commenced under this Section 12.3, the parties agree to continue to attempt to resolve any dispute or claim according to the terms of Sections 12.1 and 12.2 during the course of such litigation proceedings under this Section 12.3.

ARTICLE XIII

LIMITATION OF LIABILITY

IN NO EVENT SHALL EITHER PARTY OR ITS SUBSIDIARIES OR AFFILIATED COMPANIES BE LIABLE TO THE OTHER PARTY OR ITS SUBSIDIARIES OR AFFILIATED COMPANIES FOR ANY DAMAGES, INCLUDING WITHOUT LIMITATION SPECIAL, CONSEQUENTIAL, INDIRECT, INCIDENTAL OR PUNITIVE DAMAGES OR LOST PROFITS OR ANY OTHER DAMAGES,

HOWEVER CAUSED AND ON ANY THEORY OF LIABILITY (INCLUDING NEGLIGENCE) ARISING IN ANY WAY OUT OF THIS AGREEMENT, WHETHER OR NOT SUCH PARTY HAS BEEN ADVISED OF THE POSSIBILITY OF SUCH DAMAGES; PROVIDED, HOWEVER, THAT THE FOREGOING LIMITATIONS SHALL NOT LIMIT EACH PARTY'S OBLIGATIONS EXPRESSLY ASSUMED IN EXHIBIT K OF THE SEPARATION AGREEMENT; PROVIDED FURTHER THAT THE EXCLUSION OF PUNITIVE DAMAGES SHALL APPLY IN ANY EVENT.

ARTICLE XIV

MISCELLANEOUS PROVISIONS

14.1   DISCLAIMER. EACH PARTY ACKNOWLEDGES AND AGREES THAT ALL LICENSED MARKS AND ANY OTHER INFORMATION OR MATERIALS LICENSED OR PROVIDED HEREUNDER ARE LICENSED OR PROVIDED ON AN "AS IS" BASIS AND THAT NEITHER PARTY NOR ANY OF ITS SUBSIDIARIES OR AFFILIATED COMPANIES MAKES ANY REPRESENTATIONS OR EXTENDS ANY WARRANTIES WHATSOEVER, EXPRESS, IMPLIED OR STATUTORY, WITH RESPECT THERETO INCLUDING WITHOUT LIMITATION ANY IMPLIED WARRANTIES OF TITLE, ENFORCEABILITY OR NON-INFRINGEMENT. Without limiting the generality of the foregoing, neither XYZ nor any of its Subsidiaries or Affiliated Companies makes any warranty or representation as to the validity of any Mark licensed by it to ABC or any warranty or representation that any use of any Mark with respect to any product or service will be free from infringement of any rights of any Third Party.

14.2   NO IMPLIED LICENSES. Nothing contained in this Agreement shall be construed as conferring any rights by implication, estoppel or otherwise, under any intellectual property right, other than the rights expressly granted in this Agreement with respect to the Licensed Marks. Neither party is required hereunder to furnish or disclose to the other any information (including copies of registrations of the Marks), except as specifically provided herein.

14.3   INFRINGEMENT SUITS. Except as set forth in Section 4.3, (i) neither party shall have any obligation hereunder to institute any action or suit against Third Parties for infringement of any of the Licensed Marks or to defend any action or suit brought by a Third Party which challenges or concerns the validity of any of the Licensed Marks and (ii) ABC shall not have any right to institute any action or suit against Third Parties for infringement of any of the Licensed Marks.

14.4   NO OTHER OBLIGATIONS. NEITHER PARTY ASSUMES ANY RESPONSIBILITIES OR OBLIGATIONS WHATSOEVER, OTHER THAN THE RESPONSIBILITIES AND OBLIGATIONS EXPRESSLY SET FORTH IN THIS AGREEMENT OR A SEPARATE WRITTEN AGREEMENT BETWEEN THE PARTIES. Without limiting the generality of the foregoing, neither party, nor any of its Subsidiaries or Affiliated Companies, is obligated to (i) file any application for registration of any Mark, or to secure any rights in any Marks, (ii) to maintain any Mark registration, or (iii) provide any assistance, except for the obligations expressly assumed in this Agreement.

14.5   ENTIRE AGREEMENT. This Agreement, the Separation Agreement and the other Ancillary Agreements (as defined in the Separation Agreement) constitute the entire agreement between the parties with respect to the subject matter hereof and shall supersede all prior written and oral and all contemporaneous oral agreements and understandings with respect to the subject matter hereof. To the extent there is a conflict between this Agreement and the General Assignment and Assumption Agreement between the parties, the terms of this Agreement shall govern.

14.6   GOVERNING LAW. This Agreement shall be governed by and construed and enforced in accordance with the laws of the State of ____ as to all matters regardless of the laws that might otherwise govern under principles of conflicts of laws applicable thereto.

14.7   DESCRIPTIVE HEADINGS. The descriptive headings herein are inserted for convenience of reference only and are not intended to be part of or to affect the meaning or interpretation of this Agreement.

14.8   NOTICES. All notices and other communications hereunder shall be in writing and shall be deemed to have been duly given when delivered in person, by telecopy with answer back, by express or overnight mail delivered by a nationally recognized air courier (delivery charges prepaid), by registered or certified mail (postage prepaid, return receipt requested) or by e-mail with receipt confirmed by return e-mail to the respective parties as follows:

if to XYZ:

XYZ Corporation

_____

_____

Attention: _____

Telecopy: _____

if to ABC, Inc.:

_____

_____

Attention: _____

Telecopy: _____

or to such other address as the party to whom notice is given may have previously furnished to the other in writing in the manner set forth above. Any notice or communication delivered in person shall be deemed effective on delivery. Any notice or communication sent by e-mail, telecopy or by air courier shall be deemed effective on the first Business Day following the day on which such notice or communication was sent. Any notice or communication sent by registered or certified mail shall be deemed effective on the third Business Day following the day on which such notice or communication was mailed. As used in this Section 14.8, "Business Day" means day other than a Saturday, a Sunday or a day on which banking institutions located in the State of _____ are authorized or obligated by law or executive order to close.

14.9   NONASSIGNABILITY. Neither party may, directly or indirectly, in whole or in part, whether by operation of law or otherwise, assign or transfer this Agreement, without the other party's prior written consent, and any attempted assignment, transfer or delegation without such prior written consent shall be voidable at the sole option of such other party. Notwithstanding the foregoing, each party (or its permitted successive assignees or transferees hereunder) may assign or transfer this Agreement as a whole without consent to a Person that succeeds to all or substantially all of the business or assets of such party. Without limiting the foregoing, this Agreement will be binding upon and inure to the benefit of the parties and their permitted successors and assigns.

14.10   SEVERABILITY. If any term or other provision of this Agreement is determined by a nonappealable decision of a court, administrative agency or arbitrator to be invalid, illegal or incapable of being enforced by any rule of law or public policy, all other conditions and provisions of this Agreement shall nevertheless remain in full force and effect so long as the economic or legal substance of the transactions contemplated hereby is not affected in any manner materially adverse to either party. Upon such determination that any term or other provision is invalid, illegal or incapable of being enforced, the parties hereto shall negotiate in good faith to modify this Agreement so as to effect the original intent of the parties as closely as possible in an acceptable manner to the end that the transactions contemplated hereby are fulfilled to the fullest extent possible.

14.11   FAILURE   OR   INDULGENCE   NOT   WAIVER;   REMEDIES CUMULATIVE. No failure or delay on the part of either party hereto in the exercise of any right hereunder shall impair such right or be construed to be a waiver of, or acquiescence in, any breach of any representation, warranty or agreement herein, nor shall any single or partial exercise of any such right preclude other or further exercise thereof or of any other right. All rights and remedies existing under this Agreement are cumulative to, and not exclusive of, any rights or remedies otherwise available.

14.12   AMENDMENT. No change or amendment will be made to this Agreement except by an instrument in writing signed on behalf of each of the parties to such agreement.

14.13   COUNTERPARTS. This Agreement may be executed in two or more counterparts, all of which, taken together, shall be considered to be one and the same instrument.

WHEREFORE, the parties have signed this Trademark Ownership and License Agreement effective as of the date first set forth above.

XYZ Corporation   ABC, Inc.

By: _____   By: _____

Name: _____   Name: _____

Title: _____   Title: _____

Resources

The Empire Builders and Blueprint Series

W elcome to the Resource section of the Empire Builders Series: Masterclasses in Business and Law. Here, we provide a carefully curated collection of practical tools and materials designed to complement the strategies and insights discussed throughout the series. This section is your gateway to deeper understanding and application, offering everything from sample agreements and checklists to detailed case studies and guidelines. Whether you're forging a new business, protecting intellectual property, or planning for expansion, these resources are intended to empower you with the necessary tools to effectively implement and navigate the complex landscape of business and law. Embrace these resources as your companion in building and sustaining a robust empire.

Empire Builders Series:
Masterclasses in Business and Law

In the dynamic world of business, where innovation intersects with opportunity, success often hinges not only on creativity but also on a deep understanding of the legal and operational landscapes. The Empire Builders Series is meticulously designed to arm aspiring entrepreneurs, seasoned business owners, creative professionals, and legal experts with the comprehensive knowledge and strategies needed to navigate these complexities and build lasting empires.

Each book in the series serves as a foundational pillar, offering expert guidance and actionable insights in specific areas of business and law; tailored to foster growth, innovation, and success in today's competitive marketplace:

1. **Brick by Brick**: This guide acts as your blueprint for building a business from the ground up. It offers essential strategies, legal insights, and operational tactics crucial for establishing a solid foundation for any business venture.

2. **Mark Your Territory**: Dive deep into the world of trademarks with this essential guide, designed to help you protect and effectively leverage your brand in today's competitive market.

3. **From Idea to Empire**: Transform your entrepreneurial dreams into reality with this exhaustive guide to business planning. Learn how to craft a compelling business plan that not only attracts investors but also sets the stage for a successful enterprise.

4. **Beyond the Pen**: Safeguard your creative works and master the intricacies of copyright law with this expert guide, tailored specifically for writers, artists, musicians, and digital content creators.

5. **Legal Ink**: Demystify the complex legal landscape of publishing with practical advice on negotiating contracts and protecting intellectual property, essential for authors and publishers.

The Empire Builders Series stands as a testament to the power of knowledge and the importance of mastering the strategic and legal aspects of business management. Each book is designed not merely to inform but to inspire action and lead to success. Embark on this journey to build your empire, one masterclass at a time.

Brick by Brick:
The Entrepreneur's Guide to Constructing a Company

The first book in the Empire Builders Series: Masterclass in Business and Law is "Brick by Brick: The Entrepreneur's Guide to Constructing a Company."

Summary: "Brick by Brick" is an indispensable resource for entrepreneurs who are poised to transform their innovative business ideas into successful enterprises. This comprehensive guide meticulously outlines the complexities of business formation, providing detailed, step-by-step instructions and vital insights into the legal, operational, and strategic aspects of starting and running a thriving company.

Part 1: Laying the Foundation – Focuses on selecting the appropriate business entity, delving into the legal implications of each option and the economic considerations vital for establishing a solid foundation for your business.

Part 2: Operational Mechanics – Discusses the operational aspects of setting up partnerships and LLCs, navigating corporate governance, maintaining corporate records, and managing capital and shareholder relationships effectively.

Part 3: Advanced Strategic Planning – Offers insights into managing structural changes, handling stock and ownership issues, expanding operations across state lines, and deploying tax strategies to ensure compliance and optimize financial performance.

Part 4: Implementation Tools and Resources – Provides practical tools such as sample agreements, startup task checklists, and comprehensive guidelines for drafting business plans and the incorporation process, enabling entrepreneurs to effectively implement their business strategies.

"Brick by Brick" not only serves as a guide but acts as a complete blueprint for building a robust business capable of thriving in today's competitive market. It arms aspiring entrepreneurs with the necessary knowledge and tools to navigate the complexities of business formation. From drafting your first business plan to preparing for incorporation, this book delivers invaluable insights and practical advice to establish a strong foundation and sustain growth.

Mark Your Territory:
Navigating Trademarks in the Modern Marketplace

The second book in the Empire Builders Series: Masterclass in Business and Law is "Mark Your Territory: Navigating Trademarks in the Modern Marketplace."

Summary: "Mark Your Territory" provides an indispensable resource for anyone involved in the branding and legal aspects of their business, offering a comprehensive guide to understanding, acquiring, and effectively managing trademarks. This book is crucial for ensuring that trademarks, which are vital assets to any business, are properly protected and leveraged.

Part 1: Fundamentals of Trademarks – Introduces the basics of trademarks, including their legal framework, the process of trademark selection and registration, and their importance in identifying business sources and ensuring product quality.

Part 2: Strategic Trademark Management – Focuses on the ongoing management of trademarks, detailing strategies for maintaining rights, monitoring for infringements, addressing challenges in digital marketing, and managing global trademark portfolios.

Part 3: Advanced Topics in Trademarks – Delves into more complex issues such as preventing trademark dilution, managing renewals, understanding the specific needs of service marks in advertising, and navigating the intricacies of trademark licensing and emerging legal trends.

Part 4: Practical Tools and Resources – Provides practical aids like sample trademark filings, management checklists, and insightful case studies, equipping readers with tangible tools and real-world examples to apply the concepts discussed effectively.

Designed for entrepreneurs, business owners, and legal professionals, "Mark Your Territory" equips readers with actionable strategies and essential tools for effective trademark management. It ensures that readers can maintain their brand's uniqueness and legal protections, thus securing a competitive edge in the marketplace.

From Idea to Empire:
Mastering the Art of Business Planning

The third book in the Empire Builders Series: Masterclass in Business and Law is "From Idea to Empire: Mastering the Art of Business Planning."

Summary: "From Idea to Empire" offers an indispensable roadmap for entrepreneurs eager to transform their innovative ideas into successful businesses. This comprehensive guide equips readers with a strategic blueprint for drafting robust business plans that attract investors and serve as a roadmap for navigating the transition from startup to thriving enterprise.

Part 1: Conceptualizing Your Business – This section lays the groundwork by assisting readers in defining their business vision, understanding market needs, analyzing competitors, and setting clear business objectives. It also guides readers in selecting an effective business model that aligns with their long-term goals.

Part 2: Strategic Planning – Delve into creating detailed marketing strategies, operational plans, and financial projections. This part covers risk management and technological integration, ensuring the business plan is both innovative and executable.

Part 3: Articulating Your Plan – Focuses on the actual drafting of the business plan, including how to write an engaging executive summary, develop compelling proposals, and master communication and negotiation tactics with potential investors and partners.

Part 4: Execution and Review – Outlines the necessary steps to launch the business successfully, monitor its performance, and make adjustments based on real-world feedback and market dynamics. This section also explores strategies for sustainable growth and long-term viability.

"From Idea to Empire" is more than a mere planning manual; it's a strategic guide that provides budding entrepreneurs with the necessary knowledge, tools, and confidence to build a business capable of facing today's market complexities. With practical advice, real-world examples, and essential resources, this book is a vital tool for anyone ready to evolve their business concept from idea to a profitable empire.

From Idea to Empire: Abridged Edition

The third book in the Empire Builders Series: Masterclass in Business and Law is "From Idea to Empire: Abridged Edition."

Summary: "From Idea to Empire: Abridged Edition" delivers the essential roadmap for turning business ideas into successful enterprises—streamlined for readers seeking concise and actionable insights. While the original edition provides an expansive resource with success stories and detailed case studies, this abridged version focuses solely on the strategic elements of business planning, offering the tools needed to conceptualize, design, and execute a winning business strategy.

By eliminating supplementary stories and focusing on the practical frameworks, this edition is perfect for readers eager to dive straight into the mechanics of business planning without distraction. It provides the knowledge required to develop robust business models, articulate compelling proposals, and successfully launch and grow a business in today's dynamic marketplace.

Part 1: Conceptualizing Your Business – Laying the Foundation – In this section, readers learn how to define their business idea, identify market needs, analyze competitors, and set clear objectives. It introduces essential business models and helps entrepreneurs align their vision with long-term goals.

Part 2: Strategic Planning – Mapping the Path to Success – Here, readers will discover how to design effective marketing strategies, operational plans, and financial projections. Topics like risk management and technological integration are covered to ensure every business plan is both realistic and innovative.

Part 3: Articulating Your Plan – Communicating with Precision and Impact – This section emphasizes the importance of clarity in communication. Readers will learn how to craft compelling executive summaries, develop strong proposals, and master negotiation strategies for working with investors and partners.

Part 4: Execution and Review – Launching and Scaling with Purpose – The final section covers essential steps for launching a business successfully, monitoring performance, and making real-time adjustments. It also addresses strategies for sustainable growth, long-term resilience, and market adaptation.

About This Edition:
The Abridged Edition is crafted for readers who prefer a focused, no-frills approach to business planning. By presenting the core methodologies from the original book in a concise format, this version allows entrepreneurs to absorb key concepts quickly and efficiently. Whether you're a first-time entrepreneur or a seasoned business owner, this streamlined guide provides the essential tools needed to transform an idea into a thriving business.

Why This Edition Matters:
"From Idea to Empire: Abridged Edition" underscores that great business planning doesn't require lengthy explanations—it requires clear strategies and actionable frameworks. This edition emphasizes the importance of focus, discipline, and adaptability in building a successful business.

Designed to complement busy entrepreneurs, it delivers the same powerful strategies as the original book but in a more accessible format. Readers can quickly refer to specific sections, apply the knowledge, and move forward with confidence in their business endeavors.

"From Idea to Empire: Abridged Edition" is the perfect companion for entrepreneurs who need to move swiftly from concept to execution. With straightforward advice and practical insights, this edition equips readers to create robust business plans and take decisive action toward building their own empire.

Beyond the Pen:
Copyright Strategies for Modern Creators
The fourth book in the Empire Builders Series: Masterclass in Business and Law is "Beyond the Pen: Copyright Strategies for Modern Creators."

Summary: "Beyond the Pen" serves as a crucial guide for artists, writers, musicians, and digital creators who seek to effectively navigate the complexities of copyright law and protect their creative assets. This comprehensive resource provides a deep dive into the mechanisms, legal frameworks, and strategic practices necessary to safeguard intellectual property in today's rapidly evolving digital landscape.

Part 1: Understanding Copyright Law – This section lays the groundwork by covering the essentials of copyright, including how to register works, the extent of legal protection available, and the nuances of international copyright laws. It equips creators with the crucial knowledge needed to assert and defend their rights.

Part 2: Navigating Use and Fair Use – Focuses on the vital concept of fair use, offering real-world scenarios and detailed guidance on how to handle copyright infringements and resolve disputes effectively without compromising creative freedom.

Part 3: Licensing and Monetization – Explores strategic approaches to structuring and managing licensing agreements, understanding diverse revenue models, and handling collaborations, ensuring creators can monetize their works effectively while maintaining control over their usage.

Part 4: Copyright in the Digital Age – Addresses the challenges and opportunities presented by new technologies, digital rights management, and online content sharing platforms. This part also examines the impact of social media on copyright and anticipates future trends that could influence creators' rights.

"Beyond the Pen" is more than just a legal manual; it is a strategic resource that empowers creators to protect, manage, and prosper with their intellectual property in today's interconnected market. Packed with practical examples, expert advice, and actionable strategies, this book is an indispensable tool for anyone looking to navigate the legal challenges and seize the opportunities in the modern creative landscape.

Legal Ink:
Navigating the Legalese of Publishing

The fifth book in the Empire Builders Series: Masterclass in Business and Law is "Legal Ink: Navigating the Legalese of Publishing."

Summary: "Legal Ink" offers an indispensable guide for authors seeking to navigate the complex world of publishing contracts. This comprehensive book demystifies legal jargon and provides a clear roadmap to understanding and managing the intricacies of publishing agreements effectively.

Part 1: The Grant of Rights – This section explains the various types of publishing rights, offering guidance on how to negotiate and manage these rights effectively to safeguard the author's interests.

Part 2: Your Obligations – Details the commitments authors must uphold under publishing contracts. It emphasizes the implications of these obligations for an author's literary career and advises on managing multiple contractual commitments.

Part 3: Getting Your Book to Market – Covers the practical aspects of the publishing process from the final manuscript preparation to marketing and distribution. This part ensures authors understand the steps involved and their roles in bringing their book to market.

Part 4: Follow the Money – Breaks down the financial components of publishing contracts, including advances, royalties, and accounting clauses. It offers crucial advice on how to negotiate for fair compensation.

Part 5: Parting Ways – Discusses strategies for effectively managing the conclusion of a publishing agreement, including rights reversion and contract termination, providing tactics for authors to regain control of their work.

"Legal Ink" acts as more than just a guide—it's a strategic tool for any author looking to deeply understand and master the legal framework of publishing contracts. With this book, writers are equipped to make informed decisions, negotiate better terms, and ensure their rights are protected throughout their publishing journey. It is an essential resource for anyone looking to confidently handle the legalities of publishing and secure the success of their work in the competitive marketplace.

The Empire Blueprint Series:
Case Studies for Business Success

Welcome to the Case Studies section of The Empire Blueprint Series: Case Studies for Business Success. This collection serves as an essential companion to the theoretical knowledge presented in the earlier volumes. Here, we delve into real-world applications and successful business practices through detailed case studies, showcasing how various entrepreneurs and businesses have navigated challenges, seized opportunities, and achieved success in their respective fields.

In this series, you will encounter a variety of scenarios that illustrate the practical implementation of business strategies and legal frameworks. Each case study not only highlights successes but also discusses the obstacles faced and lessons learned along the way. Whether you're a budding entrepreneur, a seasoned executive, or a legal professional, these insights will provide you with invaluable perspectives and tools to enhance your own business endeavors.

Each book in the series includes:

1. **70 Case Studies in Vision, Strategy, and Personal Branding**: This volume explores the journeys of entrepreneurs who have effectively crafted their visions and built strong personal brands. It highlights strategies for aligning personal values with business goals and creating a lasting impact in the marketplace.

2. **70 Case Studies in Leadership, Innovation, and Resilience**: This volume examines leaders who have driven innovation and fostered resilience within their organizations. The case studies showcase their approaches to overcoming challenges and inspire others to cultivate a culture of adaptability and forward-thinking.

3. **74 Case Studies in Growth, Digital Presence, and Legacy Building**: This volume delves into the strategies employed by businesses that have successfully navigated digital transformation and growth. It emphasizes the importance of establishing a strong online presence and building a legacy that resonates with future generations.

Each case study in The Empire Blueprint Series: Case Studies for Business Success is crafted to offer actionable insights and inspiration for readers. By examining these real-world examples, you will gain a deeper understanding of the strategies that drive business success and how to apply these lessons to your own ventures.

70 Case Studies in Vision, Strategy, and Personal Branding: The Foundations of Success, Volume 1

The first book in The Empire Blueprint Series: Case Studies for Business Success is "70 Case Studies in Vision, Strategy, and Personal Branding: The Foundations of Success," Volume 1

Dive deeper into the essential elements of business success with Volume 1: 70 Case Studies in Vision, Strategy, and Personal Branding. This volume not only presents a wealth of real-world examples but also serves as a practical toolkit for aspiring entrepreneurs and seasoned professionals alike. Here, you will find a curated collection of resources designed to complement the case studies and enhance your understanding of effective business practices.

From strategic planning templates and personal branding frameworks to time management guides and storytelling techniques, these resources empower you to implement the insights gleaned from the case studies. Explore practical tools for optimizing your online presence, launching impactful marketing campaigns, and engaging audiences across various platforms.

With a focus on innovation and adaptability, this resource section is your go-to companion for navigating the complexities of today's business landscape. Whether you're looking to craft an inspiring vision, develop effective strategies, or build a standout personal brand, the materials provided will equip you with the actionable insights needed to achieve meaningful success. Embrace the tools and inspiration within these pages, and take your entrepreneurial journey to new heights.

70 Case Studies in Leadership, Innovation, and Resilience: building a Thriving Enterprise, Volume 2

The second book in The Empire Blueprint Series: Case Studies for Business Success is "70 Case Studies in Leadership, Innovation, and Resilience: Building a Thriving Enterprise," Volume 2

Enhance your understanding of effective leadership with Volume 2: 70 Case Studies in Leadership, Innovation, and Resilience: Building a Thriving Enterprise. This resource section is designed to complement the rich insights presented throughout the volume, providing you with practical tools and frameworks to elevate your leadership journey.

Within this section, you'll find a variety of resources that address the core themes of this book—leadership, innovation, and resilience. From templates for developing effective communication strategies to guides on fostering a collaborative corporate culture, these materials are crafted to support your growth as a leader. Explore negotiation techniques, emotional intelligence assessments, and frameworks for ethical leadership that will help you build trust and loyalty within your teams.

The resources also include practical tips for embracing digital transformation and integrating innovative technologies into your business practices. Learn how to leverage these tools to drive growth, enhance customer engagement, and maintain a competitive edge in today's dynamic market.

With a focus on creating lasting value and building a legacy, this section equips you with actionable insights and strategies to navigate challenges with confidence. Whether you are an entrepreneur launching a new venture or an executive steering an established enterprise, these resources will empower you to lead with purpose and resilience.

Dive into these valuable tools and insights, and discover how to turn challenges into opportunities, fostering an environment where innovation and sustainable growth thrive.

74 Case Studies in Growth, Digital Presence, and Legacy Building: Strategies for Long-Term Success, Volume 3

The third book in The Empire Blueprint Series: Case Studies for Business Success is "74 Case Studies in Growth, Digital Presence, and Legacy Building: Strategies for Long-Term Success," Volume 3

Unlock the secrets to sustainable success with Volume 3: 74 Case Studies in Growth, Digital Presence, and Legacy Building: Strategies for Long-Term Success. This resource section is designed to enhance your understanding and application of the powerful insights shared throughout the volume, providing you with practical tools and strategies for thriving in today's competitive landscape.

In this section, you'll find a wealth of resources that align with the key themes of this book—growth, digital engagement, and legacy building. From templates for strategic goal-setting and growth frameworks to guides on optimizing digital marketing efforts, these materials will help you implement the actionable insights gained from the case studies.

Explore best practices for storytelling and community engagement in the digital realm, along with practical tips for leveraging social media to amplify your brand's presence. Discover frameworks for navigating the complexities of innovation and operational efficiency, ensuring your business not only grows but flourishes sustainably.

The resource section also emphasizes the importance of legacy building, offering tools for effective succession planning and community involvement. Learn how to align your everyday decisions with your long-term vision, ensuring that your enterprise leaves a lasting impact for future generations.

Whether you are an entrepreneur embarking on a new venture, an executive scaling operations, or a professional seeking to elevate your digital presence, these resources will empower you to lead with purpose and confidence. Dive into the practical tools and insights provided here, and equip yourself to navigate challenges, innovate boldly, and create a meaningful legacy.

In conclusion, the Resource section of the Empire Builders Series and Empire Blueprint Series serves as valuable extensions of the learning journey you've embarked upon. By utilizing these carefully chosen tools and materials, you are better equipped to apply the principles and strategies discussed in the series to real-world scenarios. Each resource has been tailored to enhance your understanding and effectiveness in the realms of business and law, ensuring you have the practical support necessary to navigate challenges and seize opportunities. We hope these resources prove instrumental in helping you build and sustain your business empire, transforming knowledge into actionable success.

L. A. Moeszinger also known as simply "L" is the face behind the AuthorsDoor Leadership Program: AuthorsDoor Series: *Publisher & Her World*, AuthorsDoor Advanced Series: *Publisher & Her World*, and AuthorsDoor Masterclass Series: *Publisher & Her World*. The program comprises, books, courses, and workbooks. The courses expand upon the books. The workbooks go into further detail, outlining step-by-step instructions. Courses are *free*; books and workbooks are available for purchase on Amazon and other retailer sites. She has been launching the careers of self-publishers since 2009, and she also writes the AuthorsRedDoor.com blog on writing, publishing, and marketing. L is also the co-founder of The Ridge Publishing Group and its imprints.

She is an American author, publisher, and creator who resides in Coeur d'Alene, Idaho, with her husband and two dogs. She writes under the pseudonyms: Ann Patterson and Ann Carrington for her business law pieces; L. A. Moeszinger for her writing, publishing, and marketing pieces; Lori Ann Moeszinger for her biblical books and personal pieces; and a handful of others for her Manhattan Diaries series. She believes strongly in faith, blessings, and working her butt off . . . and she thinks one of the best things about being an author-publisher—unlike the lawyer she used to be—is that she can let her passion out.

Original Package Design
© 2024 AuthorsDoor Leadership Program
Cover Design: Eric Moeszinger
Author Photo © 2023 Edwin Wolfe

Parent Website: https://www.RidgePublishingGroup.com and

    blog site https://www.PublisherAndHerWorld.com

Publisher Website: https://www.GuardiansofBiblicalTruth.com and

    blog site https://www.Jesus-Says.com

Author website: https://www.LAMoeszinger.com and New Youniversity sites:

    https://www.NewYouniversity.com, https://www.ManhattanChronicles.com

Bridge Website: https://www.AuthorsDoor.com and

    blog site https://www.AuthorsRedDoor.com

Entertainment website: https://www.EthanFoxBooks.com and

    blog site https://www.KidsStagram.com

Want More?

The ideas in this book are expanded upon throughout the AuthorsDoor Leadership Program of books, courses, and workbooks. Follow our Facebook page. Join our Facebook private group. Watch our YouTube channels: AuthorsDoor Group, Authors Red Door #Shorts, and Publisher and Her World at Ridge Publishing Group. Listen to our Podcast channel: Publisher's Circle; or email me: *Hello@AuthorsDoor.com*

AuthorsDoor Hubs

Get insights from the articles we write on our *website* (AuthorsDoor.com). You'll find more publications to help authors sell better, pitch better, recruit better, build better, create better, and connect better. You are also invited to visit our *blog* and find out what we're talking about now. Sign up for our *AuthorsDoor Leadership Program Newsletter* and join the conversations going on there with our private community (Publisher's Circle); visit: *www.AuthorsRedDoor.com*

Publisher & Her World Blogs

Enter a world where the sometimes shocking and often hilarious climb to the top as an author-publisher is exposed by a true insider. Faced with on-going trials and tribulations of the world of self-publishing, L. A. Moeszinger is witty and sometimes brutally candid in her postings. If you enjoy getting the inside scoop on the makings and thoughts behind self-publishing, this is the blog for you! *www.PublisherAndHerWorld.com*

This
book was art
directed by John Jared.
The art for both the cover and the
interior was created using pastels on toned
print making paper. The text was set in 10 point Times
New Roman, a typeface based on the sixteenth-century type designs
of Claude Garamond, redrawn by Robert Slimback in 1989.
The book was printed at Amazon and IngramSpark.
The Managing Editor was Jack Clark. The
Production was supervised by
Jason Reed and Ed
Warren.